MANAGED CARE AND MODERNIZATION
A PRACTITIONER'S GUIDE

David Cochrane, with Sherry Aliotta,
David Colin-Thome, Margaret Conroy,
Robert Larsen and Rita Lewis

Open University Press
Buckingham • Philadelphia

Open University Press
Celtic Court
22 Ballmoor
Buckingham
MK18 1XW

email: enquiries@openup.co.uk
world wide web: www.openup.co.uk

and
325 Chestnut Street
Philadelphia, PA 19106, USA

First Published 2001

A catalogue record of this book is available from the British Library

ISBN   0 335 20586 0 (pb)   0 335 20587 9 (hb)

Library of Congress Cataloging-in-Publication Data
Cochrane, David, 1954–
    Managed care and modernization : a practitioner's guide / David Cochrane, with Sherry Aliotta . . . [*et al.*].
        p. ; cm.
    Includes bibliographical references and index.
    ISBN 0-335-20587-9 – ISBN 0-335-20586-0 (pbk.)
    1. Managed care plans (Medical care)–Great Britain. 2. Health care reform–Great Britain. 3. National Health Service (Great Britain). I. Aliotta, Sherry. II. Title.
    [DNLM: 1. National Health Service (Great Britain). 2. Managed Care Programs–Great Britain. 3. Managed Care Programs–United States. 4. Delivery of Health Care, Integrated–Great Britain. 5. Delivery of Health Care, Integrated–United States. 6. Health Care Reform–Great Britain. 7. Health Care Reform–United States. 8. Quality Assurance, Health Care–Great Britain. 9. Quality Assurance, Health Care–United States. 10. State Medicine–Great Britain. 11. State Medicine–United States. W 130 FA1 C663m 2001]
    RA412.5.G7 C63 2001
    362.1'04258'0941–dc21

                                                                    00-065221

Typeset by Graphicraft Limited, Hong Kong
Printed in Great Britain by St Edmundsbury Press Limited,
Bury St Edmunds, Suffolk

To Duncan, in memory of a true friend

CONTENTS

NOTES ON CONTRIBUTORS

Sherry Aliotta RN, BSN, CCM   Sherry L. Aliotta is president and CEO of S.A. Squared, Inc. in Farmington Hills, Michigan, USA. She has worked in senior care management positions in the United States, and has been active in the field of case management for over 15 years. She has worked as a case manager in home health, indemnity insurance, worker's compensation, geriatrics, and managed care. In 1996, she was named 'Distinguished Case Manager of the Year' by the Case Management Society of America. She speaks throughout the United States on case management, and has authored numerous articles and book chapters.

David Cochrane   David is co-founder and director of Conrane Consulting. After a career as a senior NHS planner he moved into consultancy with Ernst Young and Price Waterhouse. He completed a PhD in social policy at LSE before becoming an independent consultant in 1991 and combining forces with Margaret Conroy three years later. His project work has taken him into his interest in the US managed care. This has developed through the experience of senior American consultancy colleagues and national opinion formers in the UK as an honorary fellow in health management at the University of Manchester. His related work has included developing evidence-based disease management programmes, implementing UK case management projects, and utilization-based strategy. He has published on workforce development, strategy and the history of psychiatry.

David Colin-Thome OBE, MBBS, FRCGP, MFPHM, MHSM   David has been a GP since 1971 and he is senior partner at Castlefields Health Centre in Runcorn. This practice has been leading-edge nationally, was a first-wave fundholder and total purchasing pilot. Having gone part-time in 1994, David is also national clinical director for primary care (England) and primary care adviser to the London and North West Regions and to Dorset Health Authority and Community Trust. He is a part-time fellow of the Health Services Management Unit at Manchester University, on the editorial advisory board of two journals, the *Journal of Management in Medicine* and *Employing Medical and Dental Staff*. David has also been on the Steering Group of the Future Healthcare Workforce Project since its inception. He publishes regularly on primary care reform and development. David has also been on the Steering Group of the Future Healthcare Workforce Project since its inception. He is a devoted parent, grandfather and Everton supporter. He writes here in a personal capacity.

Margaret Conroy   Margaret is co-founder and director of Conrane Consulting. Following a senior career in human resources in both the NHS and the Department of Health she has remained at a leading-edge of thinking and development in workforce modernization. She implemented the first patient-focused hospital project at Kingston Hospital. This led to her directing the national Future Healthcare Workforce Project during the last five years whose influential reports have challenged conventional professional demarcations. The project has since moved to the centre of national policy on defining staff roles for the NHS and is now in its third phase. Margaret has also led the agenda on introducing more systematic, needs-based workforce planning in British Healthcare.

Robert R. Larsen MD   After spending six years building and running a village hospital in India, Robert Larsen practised General Surgery in Colorado for 15 years. He then became medical director of FHP Healthcare, a large HMO in California. More recently he has worked as a vice president for McGraw Hill Publishing Company and is the CEO of MD Execs, Inc, a company that provides temporary medical director services and international healthcare consulting services. He is also editor-in-chief of *Managed Solutions*, an Internet-based journal on managed healthcare, and writes a weekly managed care News and Views column.

Rita Lewis   Rita has been active in consumer representation and patient advocacy for over 20 years. She was chaired the Association of Community Health Councils for England and Wales from 1990 to 1992. She served on the Mental Health Act Commission originally as a lay member during the 1980s and subsequently as a consultant. She now serves as a consumer member of the United Kingdom Central Council for Nurses, Midwives and Health Visitors, and the General Osteopathic Council. She is also a member of the Advisory Group on Medical and Dental Education, Training and Staffing and was appointed as a non-executive director of Epsom and St. Helier NHS Trust in April 1999. Rita has published on consumer representation and is a regular contributor to conferences in this field.

LIST OF ABBREVIATIONS

AAPCC	Average Adjusted per Capita Cost
ACT	assertive community treatment
AHPR	Agency of Healthcare Policy and Research
AMA	American Medical Association
BMA	British Medical Association
CHC	Community Health Council
CHI	Commission for Health Improvement
CMHT	community mental health team
COPD	Chronic Obstructive Pulmonary Disease
CPI	Consumer Price Index
DALY	disablement adjusted life year
DHA	district health authorities
DME	durable medical equipment
DOH	Department of Health
DSU	day surgery unit
ECG	electrocardiogram
ECT	electroconvulsive therapy
EE	expressed emotion
ENT	ear, nose and throat
FFS	fee-for-service
FHP	Family Health Plan
GDP	gross domestic product
GHA	Group Health Association
GNP	gross national product
GP	general practitioner
HCFA	Health Care Financing Administration
HEDIS	Health Plan Employers' Information and Data Set
HIMP	Health Improvement Programme
HIP	Health Insurance Plan of New York

HMO	Health Maintenance Organization
HRT	hormone replacement therapy
IPA	Independent Practice Association
IHD	ischaemic heart disease
LOS	length of stay
LSE	London School of Economics
MCOs	Managed Care Organizations
NCQA	National Committee for Quality Assurance
NHS	National Health Service
NHSE	NHS Executive
NICE	National Institute for Clinical Excellence
NSF	National Service Framework (for Mental Health)
OECD	Organization for Economic Cooperation and Development
PCG	Primary Care Group
PCP	Primary Care Physicians
PCT	Primary Care Trust
PMS	Personal Medical Services
PPO	Preferred Provider Organization
RCN	Royal College of Nursing
RCT	Randomized Controlled Trial
RVS	Relative Value Studies
SHMO	Social Health Maintenance Organization
SIGN	Scottish Inter-Collegiate Guideline Network
TPP	Total Purchasing Pilot
UK	United Kingdom
US	United States
UM	utilization management
URTI	upper respiratory tract infection
WHO	World Health Organization

INTRODUCTION

In 1997, the Labour government in the United Kingdom (UK) embarked on an ambitious programme of National Health Service (NHS) modernization. There was substantial structural change proposed by the 1997 White Paper, *The NHS: Modern, Dependable,*[1] the dozen or so major policy documents which have followed and not least the historic NHS National Plan for the service's second millennium. In the past, governments have often been accused of using structural change as a smokescreen to mask inadequate investment in the NHS. Historically the UK has undoubtedly had its healthcare on the cheap relative to OECD comparator nations while the NHS has shouldered more than its fair share of reorganizations. At last, however, we appear to have a government (and now seemingly an all-party consensus) determined to reverse chronic under-investment in the NHS. Whereas the United States (US) has been reining in healthcare expenditure growth from 12 per cent annually a few years ago to only 3 per cent at the end of the Clinton administration, the NHS is to get 30 per cent growth in real terms over only four years.

As we argue in this book, both the Labour modernization agenda and those Tory reforms which it retained owe much to the experience of US managed care organizations (MCOs). Historically this is only fitting since the founders of the Health Maintenance Organizations in California, the home of modern managed care, were inspired, in part at least, by three key elements of the NHS – the pooling of financial risk against a fixed budget, the removal of financial barriers to access and a delivery system based in primary care acting as gatekeeper to secondary care.

In the mid-1990s, however, US managed care systems had developed to a point where they had much to offer back in return. The British authors in this book first became interested in this experience as members of a 1994 study tour with Manchester University to FHP Healthcare in Southern California, then the second largest HMO in the US and subsequently incorporated into PacifiCare. The interest thus generated motivated the Department of Health (DOH) to commission a British-led evaluation of managed care and also attracted the attention of other UK-based health-care analysts. Initial reaction ranged from hostility in some quarters to encouragement, as in the case of Ray Robinson and Andrea Steiner's 1998 book *Managed Healthcare*[2] which was the product of the DOH commission.

Other leading commentators went further and argued that the NHS already has the major elements of a managed care system in place. We would dispute this view at present. To support the case, we develop an optimal model of managed care in Chapter 1 of this book. This also traces the more recent history of managed care organizations (MCOs) and the pressures and dynamics in the US economy, government and society which have promoted managed care to the predominant model in a pluralistic healthcare market. We also review the findings in the evaluative literature on managed care against the core objectives on the NHS. Managed care owes both its domestic and increasingly international success to the quality of the professional work of people such as Dr Robert Larsen who was Medical Director of FHP during the 1990s. Now a leading US commentator and writer on managed care, he gives an expert practitioner's perspective in Chapter 2 on the history, current challenges and future direction for MCOs in the US. The agenda he generates has many parallels with the NHS, including the need to standardize quality based on outcome data in order to inform clinical management, and more sophisticated systems for cost control and contracting to incentivize both quality and efficiency.

However, the primary aim of this book is to give practical guidance on applying managed care techniques to further the NHS modernization agenda which we as authors support. Chapter 3 sets out the components of this policy and identifies those areas for service and policy development which managed care can facilitate and which therefore constitute the focal point of this book. It also offers some analysis and comment on the strengths and weaknesses of the NHS Plan. We begin in Chapter 4 at the start of everyone's healthcare journey, in primary care. A one-time leader of the GP fundholding movement and former Labour Party Parliamentary Candidate, Dr David Colin-Thome writes from his experience as a general practitioner (GP) and Regional Director of Primary Care in London, and from his wider international experience. He sets a challenging agenda for primary care as provider and manager of healthcare processes. Arguing that the new primary care *is managed care* he sees major opportunities for the new Primary Care Trusts to employ prevention, early intervention, quality assurance through evidence-based medicine, and clinical governance and utilization management to improve the investment decisions in primary care commissioning.

Improving clinical quality begins with the evidence base. Chapter 5 therefore focuses on how to apply evidence-based medicine in chronic disease management programmes, to develop care pathways and guidelines across a continuum of primary, intermediate and secondary care then how to use these documents to plan and contract for integrated models of service delivery. Evidence-based medicine is a core component of utilization management (UM) – perhaps the single most effective of all managed care techniques. Also known as demand management, some of these techniques are already familiar in the UK. With a focus on primary and ambulatory care in Chapter 6 and on in-patient care in Chapter 7, these and a wide range of other UM techniques are located in a systematic healthcare management approach which spans all service sectors and interventions including prevention and appropriate self-care. Given the supply problems, inequitable access issues and quality deficiencies facing the NHS, there is a huge UM agenda to parallel the managed care experience of the last ten years and radically re-engineer healthcare provision in the UK.

The ageing population poses the NHS one of its biggest challenges. The over-65s make up 70 per cent of emergency admissions to hospital, crowding out elective programmes and generating the annual winter beds crisis in the NHS which has become almost as traditional as Christmas itself. Case management is a relatively new managed care initiative which offers enormous potential benefit to the service. Targeting the high-utilizing, 'at-risk' 5–10 per cent of the older population, case management has shown impressive results in improving health status, reducing service usage and improving client satisfaction. Sherry Aliotta, a pioneer of the US programme as an HMO manager and consultant, describes the service and documents its history and the challenges of measuring outcomes in Chapter 8. She then reviews published outcome studies including some early UK experience at Castelfields Health Centre where Dr Colin-Thome is the Senior Partner.

When we first became interested in the experience of managed care organizations to further the NHS reform agenda we faced criticism that we were omitting mental health services. Chapter 9 therefore seeks to redress this. On reflection, and based on both the National Service Framework and the evidence base, we conclude that mental health services are highly appropriate to systems of managed care. Indeed, this chapter serves as a model of how these techniques can be integrated around the needs of one of the most challenging client groups – people with schizophrenia.

There are three further major agendas to consider. First, managed care has led internationally on performance management in healthcare, whether on quality, with the founding of the National Committee on Quality Assurance, or on cost control. This has undoubtedly influenced the major policy drive given in the modernization agenda to the National Performance Assessment Framework. The core management technique here is benchmarking. Hence in Chapter 10 we set out a practical but sophisticated approach to using benchmarks in healthcare management to re-engineer care processes and promote cost-effectiveness.

A core objective of managed care is to deliver services by the most appropriate, competent staff. Supply problems for key professional staff threaten to undermine the momentum of NHS modernization. However, the current inflexibility and narrowness of professional boundaries and demarcations compound the problem and constitute impediments to re-engineering care processes. Perhaps more than anyone over the last five years, Margaret Conroy has led the national debate on modernizing the workforce through the Future Healthcare Workforce Project. In Chapter 11 she describes how staffing is being redesigned at both national and local service provider levels and integrated into a workforce planning process which is truly needs-led and patient-focused.

Last but not least there is the case for consumer empowerment in British healthcare. This is the one area where the modernization proposals appear a little conservative. In contrast, for American retirees at least, the social insurance mechanism that is the Medicare programme combined with the competition between managed care organizations for their custom, and the right to change plans on a monthly basis, places the consumer firmly in the driving seat. Add to this the member services departments of the better HMOs whose *raison d'être* is to ensure each enrollee gets the best out of the services on offer and we have a best practice model for consumer empowerment. Hence perhaps the most disappointing section of the NHS Plan is Chapter 3 which reviews alternative funding mechanisms for the NHS and dismisses social insurance – the predominant European model – without regard to consumer empowerment as an assessment criterion for a modern healthcare system.

To be fair to New Labour, Rita Lewis in the final chapter of this book finds much merit in the new proposals on patient advocacy. She is nonetheless impelled to explore the scope for greater consumer participation and empowerment in the NHS. Her conclusions that British healthcare consumers remain limited in choice and influence compared to our American and European counterparts sets a challenging and radical agenda for a future phase of healthcare reform and modernization.

The emphatic re-election of New Labour in June 2001 has given added impetus to our agenda. Provided the economy and tax revenues remain buoyant, UK spending on health care will move to a European Union average. However the alarmingly low turnout at the polls should give ministers pause for thought on how better to engage more people more actively in the political process – particularly over spending decisions in our vital public services.

David Cochrane

NOTES AND REFERENCES

1 Department of Health (1997) *The NHS: Modern, Dependable,* Cmnd 3807. London: Department of Health.
2 R. Robinson and A. Steiner (1998) *Managed Healthcare.* Buckingham: Open University Press.

Part one

CONTEXTS

MANAGED CARE AT THE CROSSROADS

David Cochrane

Before embarking on the main course of the book, we need to provide some relevant background on the experience of managed care in the United States. To begin with, the current 'financial crisis' facing managed care is reviewed. We then review terminology and set some definitional boundaries on our delineation of managed care organizations. Proceeding to the evolution of managed care in the US, we explore those issues which have fuelled its rapid development over the last three decades of the century to become the predominant American healthcare system. These have mirrored some of the determinants of British health policy such as the requirement of any advanced industrial nation for a healthy workforce, pressure from labour unions, and the need to manage public expenditure. Factors peculiar to the US have included the macro-economic imperatives of containing healthcare expenditure, the power of consumerism in American culture and the battle for public opinion fought on the quality front. We then review the performance of managed care against its major US competitor system, fee-for-service indemnity insurance, before setting out an optimum model for a managed care organization which will facilitate our major goal of assisting the modernization agenda of the NHS.

The turn of the twenty-first century marked something of a watershed year for managed care in the United States. From its promotional position in the early 1990s as an ideal solution to the complex challenges of American health reform,[1] it now finds itself on the defensive on virtually all crucial fronts. Since becoming a major market player, managed care is consistently attacked by critics over the quality of its service provision and limits placed on consumer choice. This was inevitable in a country where the major competitive models are preferred provider delivery systems with highly-paid doctors on a fee-for-service basis funded by the powerful indemnity insurance industry. Healthcare is one of the largest commercial industries in the US and the aggressive forces of competition are primarily concerned to protect market share. In this context managed care has confronted three powerful vested interests – the enormous earnings potential of specialist doctors, the profit margins of the major insurers and the financial viability of the acute hospital sector where surplus capacity is endemic.

In its defence, managed care had been able to claim with confidence that it could outperform the rest of the American healthcare industry on the major challenge in a country spending 14 per cent of its GDP on healthcare – cost control. Indeed, the model has been credited with dramatically reducing annual growth in national healthcare expenditure in the US from the heady heights of 10 and 12 per cent in the 1980s down to 3.6 per cent in 1998.[2] It is therefore not difficult to understand why the American healthcare industry was jolted in the spring of 1999 when the State of California took over the physician groups of MedPartners Provider Network, covering 1 million members, because of concerns over its lack of solvency. This was a pre-emptive strike to avoid repeating the trauma of the bankruptcy of FPA Medical Management of San Diego, which had occurred a year earlier with the consequent disruption of the healthcare provision for its 400,000 enrollees and their families. The deteriorating cash flow position of many of the largest health maintenance organizations (HMOs) began to send waves of panic through Wall Street, and the stock values of managed care organizations fell. Some healthcare investment analysts then began to draw resonant comparisons to an industry standing on the deck of the Titanic.

Calming the waters, the head of the US federal government's Health Care Financing Administration (HCFA) employed the more measured language of a 'market adjustment'. HCFA funds the US government's Medicare programme which guarantees healthcare provision to senior US citizens with a ten-year cumulative employment record and has been a driving force behind the expansion in the number of elderly Americans enrolled into managed care. According to the *Los Angeles Times* of 29 March 1999, managed care had been a victim of its own success in acquiring market share while responding to pressure to reduce costs without compromise to quality. As a consequence, some physician groups had simply squeezed themselves out of financial viability. Those Wall Street investors who had grown accustomed to 25 per cent annual growth in earnings were simply pulling the plug, leaving it to others content with more modest returns of 5 per cent and 10 per cent per year to salvage the vessel. Fighting back from a position of market domination, most of the larger managed care organizations announced price increases for 1999 of 5–7 per cent, rises likely to be repeated for each of the following four years.

On balance then, although managed care is currently a little beleaguered in the US, it is far from being in decline. Moreover, it is a model of healthcare funding and delivery that has begun to attract serious attention from British health policy analysts in the context of the challenges facing the NHS over the first decade of the new millennium.[3] The aim of this work to date has been largely to investigate whether managed care offers the potential to take the NHS strategic agenda forward. The conclusions have been that there are indeed techniques and selected elements of the American experience which offer that potential. More pertinent still, the Labour government is driving the NHS through an ambitious 'modernization' agenda which is replete with ideas drawn from managed care (as we will show in Chapter 2).

Managed care borrowed three key elements of the NHS – pooling of risk against a fixed budget, removing financial barriers to access for enrolees and service delivery based in primary care. It is only fair, therefore, that the NHS gets something back in return. The key to deciding which techniques are relevant to the modernization agenda, however, lies in developing a clear understanding of managed care and its achievements in addressing similar issues to those faced in the UK. We can then move to how to apply the more helpful aspects of the managed care experience in specific areas of healthcare delivery and management in the NHS drawing on some worked examples drawn from the National Health Service itself.

WHAT IS MANAGED CARE?

Managed care, a little like the philosopher's elephant, is easier to describe than to define. In *Making Managed Healthcare Work* Boland strikes a note of caution at the outset to anyone with expectations that any set of ideas can solve every seemingly intractable health policy problem: 'Managed care is not a panacea for rising healthcare costs, over-utilisation, cost-shifting, excess capacity and all the other ills which plague the (US) healthcare industry.'[4]

A distinction must be drawn between managed care and a managed care organization (MCO) like a Health Maintenance Organization (HMO) or Preferred Provider Organization (PPO) or the dozen or so other models in Kongstvedt's typology.[5] These organizations employ some or all of managed care techniques to deliver predetermined and agreed healthcare benefits packages to 'members' or 'enrolees'. These packages are known as 'plans'. It is really these techniques which define managed care along Wagner's continuum from indemnity insurance schemes which may require pre-certification for elective surgery or case management of high-cost conditions through to an HMO like Kaiser Permanente which owns and manages its own service delivery networks.[6]

These techniques have been designed to realize objectives that are common to any advanced healthcare delivery system which is 'to maximise value to healthcare purchasers by channelling volume to high quality providers'. However, two key characteristics of the American context have provided a framework for the pursuit of these aims. The first is the healthcare cost 'explosion' over the last two decades. The forces behind this are neatly summarized by Boland and Abramowitz[7] and will be familiar to a UK audience, although their impact in the US has been rather more extreme.

- healthcare inflation outstripping the general rate;
- an ageing population and associated high use of healthcare resources due to severe chronic disease;
- rising consumer expectations;
- focus in service delivery on acute care or sickness response rather than prevention;
- inefficient management of healthcare resources;
- care that is ineffective or simply unnecessary;
- excess capacity of acute hospitals with average occupancy in the US down to only 64 per cent by 1989 indicating 15 per cent excess capacity;
- unwillingness on the part of politicians and health benefit managers to address excess capacity which has undermined the financial position of hospital companies, with some smaller providers going 'belly-up';
- growth of high-priced technology;
- increasing litigation by users, defensive medical practice and malpractice insurance rates.

The second factor is the strength of the American healthcare consumer. There is a powerful ethic of choice in the US which is readily exercised in an insurance-based system where the money simply follows the user. Managed care has therefore evolved within an imperative to maintain customer satisfaction as a central management objective.

There are two major groups of customers in American healthcare – employers and individuals. The market further segments into four main categories:

- *Commercial* or people of working age funded through the health benefits offered by large employers under mandatory statute.
- *Individuals funded by Medicare* or the national programme funded by the Federal government for people aged over 65 with ten years' cumulative employment record.
- *Individuals funded by Medicaid* (known as Medical in the State of California) or programmes provided by each individual state for people with insufficient means who meet the qualification criteria. These include elderly people with no work record, families with children, and groups with special needs such as those with severe and chronic mental ill-health or a catastrophic physical illness such as AIDS.
- *Individuals who self-fund* – a small part of the business made up of those who paid their own insurance premiums direct.

Employers review their contracts on an annual basis. Medicare- and Medicaid-funded individuals can change plans on a monthly basis. The need to monitor and sustain customer satisfaction is thus a commercial necessity for managed care organizations.

In summary, then, the performance objectives of any Chief Executive Officer of an MCO would be:

- cost control and financial viability;
- customer satisfaction;
- quality management.

Profitability would be added in those MCOs which are profit-making although many, including some of the biggest, are not-for-profit organizations.

There are a number of core managed care processes which are discussed in a little more detail later in the chapter and throughout the book. These include pre-paid premiums covering most healthcare services; integrated delivery systems; utilization management; primary care-based purchasing and service delivery; quality management; alignment of incentives; capitation-based payment systems; and member services. Managed care organizations use these techniques to differing degrees along a continuum of increasing management of costs and quality. There are several types of MCOs using these techniques. However, we will focus on the two most common forms – Health Maintenance Organizations and Preferred Provider Organizations or PPOs.

Health Maintenance Organizations (HMOs)

HMOs broke ranks with mainstream American healthcare in the 1960s by bringing together the functions of insurer and provider of services into one organization. A little like the NHS itself, they finance and deliver comprehensive health services to an enrolled or funded population.[8] Services are largely free at the point of use with some nominal co-pays for doctor visits, pharmacy, etc. – depending on the scope of the plan. HMOs have also led the field in the US in health prevention or maintenance, and devolution of care from specialists to primary care doctors acting in a gatekeeper role. Wagner differentiates five types of HMO: staff, group practice, network, Independent Practice Association (IPA) and direct contact.[9]

- In the *staff model* or *closed panel*, the HMO owns all its facilities and employs all its staff including medical staff. This was one of the earliest of the modern models.
- The *group model HMO* contracts with group practices of multi-specialty doctors. Group practices share facilities such as an extended primary care centre or hospital. These groups can be 'captive' if they contract with a single HMO or 'independent' if they have a range of purchasers.
- In the *network model* the HMO contracts with a range of group practices of doctors usually through capitation or the provision of a fixed

premium to fund physician services to a defined population. These groups may be multi-specialty or 'primary care groups' (often including specialists in general medicine, paediatrics and obstetrics). In each case the group is responsible for compensating any subcontracting physicians and in so doing shares the financial risk of contracts to hospitals and other providers who complete the network of service delivery. A number of network HMOs began life as staff models but found it easier to influence cost and quality without the direct management line to service delivery.

- In the *IPA model* associations of independent practitioners contract to an HMO through the mechanism of a distinct legal entity which acts as their agent. IPA doctors continue to see their own patients and maintain their own offices and medical records. IPAs can be hospital- and community-based. They are often developed and nurtured by HMOs as a means of extending the network of services beyond those doctors prepared to work in tighter organizational and management structures.
- In the *direct contract model*, the HMO will contract direct with independent physicians without the IPA intermediary.

Preferred Provider Organizations (PPOs)

PPOs are models of MCOs which have developed to address the choice issue while maintaining cost control mechanisms. A PPO provides a channel through which participating providers contract with employer health plans or insurance schemes. As within HMOs, participating providers will be governed by utilization management or other managed care procedures. The major difference lies in terms of choice and access. Enrollees in a PPO can go outside the central plan's prescribed provider network provided they pay additional insurance and/or co-pay when they use the services. Moreover, some PPOs will go to some lengths to ensure they have contracts with the more publicly reputed providers, such as teaching hospitals.

The choice of provider extends to circumventing the primary care gatekeeper role and going direct to preferred specialist doctors on the traditional American model. However, failure to comply with the utilization parameters which increases the cost of care beyond the contract prices would result in financial penalty to the provider. In this way the PPO can provide a mechanism for sustaining cost control while widening choice for individuals with the means to access it. Many traditional HMOs have also diversified their product range to include PPO schemes in response to market demand, particularly from the commercial sector. PPOs used to be available only to more senior members of a workforce who could afford the additional contributory premiums charged. However, over 90 per cent of employer-paid plans now offer a PPO to all employees.

ORIGINS AND DEVELOPMENT OF MANAGED CARE IN US

Perhaps the major defining characteristic of managed care in the US is the provision of healthcare against a single annual fixed premium paid in advance. Although some form of prepaid healthcare existed in the US before the First World War, modern forms of managed care had their origins in the western United States in the major public works of the 1930s which dragged America out of the Great Depression. The Kaiser Construction Company had the contract for building an aquaduct in the California desert to carry water from the Colorado River to the city of Los Angeles and further north to build the Grand Coulee Dam in Washington State. In 1937, in response to trade union pressure, the company founded Kaiser Foundation Health Plans to finance healthcare for its employees and their families, before extending the scheme to its shipyard workers constructing the American Wartime Navy. Also in 1937, Group Health Association was founded in Washington DC at the behest of the Home Owner's Loan Corporation in response to the number of mortgage defaults due to the cost of medical treatment.[10] Other employee health plans, including Kaiser Permanente, as well as healthcare cooperatives, were established during the 1940s, and the first individual practitioners' associations or IPAs appeared in California in the 1950s. Robert Larsen documents this period in more depth in Chapter 3.

Strange bedfellows – federal government cost control and Californian social experimentation

The 1960s was the decade of social radicalism and the first period of rapid growth for managed care. The movement was led by the State of California which had always been at the forefront of social experimentation in the United States, and internationally. By 1970 there were over 30 health maintenance organizations and the model attracted the attention of the Nixon administration as a means of controlling its rising Medicare budget.

In 1973, the HMO Act was passed. This statute overrode legislation in some states which restricted the growth of HMOs. It also provided grants to found or expand these organizations. The Act also addressed early concerns about restriction of consumer choice by obliging employers to offer their employees a choice of managed care or an indemnity plan – a requirement later lifted by subsequent amendment. HMOs could now apply for federal qualification provided they met certain standards in terms of the comprehensiveness of the benefits package offered, range of provider networks, quality assurance systems, financial stability and member grievance systems. Federal qualification was a market advantage giving access to the commercial market and to the grants on offer from the government.[11] A further sophistication was the requirement for 'community rating' or the weighting of the premium level within a limited range – usually no more than 10 per cent – around the average price to reflect the health status of an employer's workforce proxied by age, sex and industry type.

Medical politics and cost control – shifting from specialist-led to primary care-led service delivery

It was about this time that California-based HMOs took another radical step forward. Fee-for-service (FFS) funded by insurance had fostered medicine to be specialist-led. The expectation of Americans was to see a consultant for whatever medical problem they might have. Even a relatively minor skin inflammation would mean a visit to a senior dermatologist. Up until that time, primary care doctors, also called general practitioners in the United States, constituted a somewhat stigmatized minority. However, in the early 1970s a group of medical directors from a number of health plans in California visited the UK. On that study tour they borrowed the idea that a quality healthcare delivery system could indeed be based in primary care.[12] There was enormous potential for cost mitigation in adapting this model to the US.

So began the growth of panelling members to Primary Care Physicians or PCPs at ratios of around 1600 to 1 full-time equivalent. PCPs – the title still preferred over the term GP in the US – would deliver much of the medical care direct and act as a gatekeeper to specialist services. By the mid-1990s, within managed care at least, the balance of PCPs to specialists within the healthcare network had swung to 2 to 1, with two-thirds of all medical consultations taking place between the PCP and the member and only one-third with specialists.[13]

Spiralling US healthcare expenditure and macro-economic management

By 1976, 6 million Americans were enrolled in managed care. This figure more than tripled during each of the next two decades until by 1995 there were 56 million enrollees in MCOs. By 1999 this figure had risen to 175 million Americans in some form of managed care. The driving force behind this trend has been the need to control healthcare costs in the US as part of macro-economic management. In the mid-1980s, the US was top of the Organization for Economic Cooperation and Development (OECD) league table on gross domestic product (GDP) committed to healthcare, but towards the bottom on average life expectancy, infant mortality rates and satisfaction ratings among consumers.[14] Ten years later expenditure had swelled to 14 per cent of GDP compared to an OECD average of nearer 8 per cent. Forty per cent of this cost was met direct by the American taxpayer. This growth rate was simply no longer economically or politically sustainable as the Clinton administration and the Republican Congress fought to rein in the US budget deficit and, not least, claim the credit for achieving it. In 1995, Medicare and Medicaid/Medical alone accounted for 16 per cent of the $203 billion deficit.[15] The Balanced

Budget Act of 1997 included one measure to address this. It ended a prior requirement for states to obtain a special waiver from HCFA in order to oblige their Medicare beneficiaries to transfer to managed care.

For the larger employers, healthcare had become the third largest cost item next to salaries and raw materials and was undermining the competitiveness of American products in both domestic and foreign markets.[16] So corporate America took to managed care to contain its costs. In 1993, the managed care market share for the commercial under-65 population had grown to just over 50 per cent. By 1999 between 85 and 92 per cent of people enrolled in health plans paid for by their employers were in some form of MCOs.

In contrast, Medicare proved to be a more volatile market. The advantage for the federal government is clear. The annual premium it pays to an HMO for each Medicare beneficiary is based on 93 per cent (recently reduced from 95 per cent) of the cost in the fee-for-service sector of a minimum package of benefits. (The actual net premium is subject to regional variations reflecting local healthcare cost.) Hence the Health Care Financing Administration saves 7 per cent per head for seniors (over-65's) enrolled in managed care organizations versus fee-for-service indemnity schemes. Despite this significantly lower revenue base, some of the larger HCFA-accredited, for-profit HMOs were making more money from the Medicare programmes than the commercial members. They have also been able to provide benefits beyond the minimum HCFA package and thus include pharmacy. Not only has this proved a market advantage with seniors, it also helps ensure compliance with treatment programmes versus other plans where elderly people have to meet their own drugs costs. The quality and cost advantages to the HMO is that compliance helps keeps seniors healthier and out of hospital.

Even with the additional benefits on offer, market penetration among Medicare-funded Americans has proved more resistant. Even in Southern California only 42 per cent of Medicare beneficiaries are enrolled in MCOs and in some states in the south – Mississippi for example – penetration is zero.[17] Beneficiaries have a wide choice of healthcare plan and are entitled to change plans on a monthly basis and take their funding with them. The impact of negative publicity for managed care has so far kept a cap on the penetration in the Medicare market. For example, Bernard and Shulkin reviewed 277 articles on managed care from the national press. Published in 1998, their study concluded that two-thirds of the articles portrayed so unfavourable a message that the reader was less likely to join or might even decide to leave an MCO.[18]

The 1990s – market growth, regulation on quality and utilization management

The next series of major developments therefore proved something of a double-edged sword for managed care. Employers, federal and state governments have joined forces to regulate and monitor managed care organizations on quality. The concern with quality in the managed care sector, not reflected in the fee-for-service sector to anything like the same degree, grew out of the following:

- The managed care industry needed to address the criticism from competitors that it compromised quality and choice to save money.
- This pervasive popular view of managed care was shared by the employees of corporate America who found themselves being increasingly enrolled into MCOs and fed back their perceptions to employers that they were opting for second best.
- The federal government was under pressure from lobbying on the part of the indemnity insurance and fee-for-service sector who were losing a lot of business and cited grounds of quality in order to try and reverse this trend.
- The medical lobbies, led by the American Medical Association, exerted both direct pressure on Washington and indirectly on the politicians through their patients. Debate about whether this anxiety arose out of genuine concern for the clinical quality of services or alarm at the impact on the earnings potential of American specialist doctors would be the subject of a book in itself.

In 1991 the National Committee for Quality Assurance (NCQA) was established as an independent body and began accrediting HMOs on a voluntary basis. Twelve years earlier, NCQA had been founded within the managed care sector in response to the war on quality waged by its major critics. Also at that time, the large employers who contracted with MCOs collaborated to develop a performance monitoring framework and required reporting on Version 1 of the Health Plan Employers' Information and Data Set (HEDIS). HEDIS was adopted and developed by NCQA who in 1993 began to use HEDIS Version 2 as an accreditation tool. Presented as a 'standardised, objective information about the quality of MCOs',[19] HEDIS has developed as much as a pragmatic approach to measuring the measurable as it did as an analytical approach to defining objective quality measures and standards.[20]

Although in theory NCQA accreditation is voluntary for HMOs bidding for commercial contracts, it is a distinct market advantage since it is required or requested by corporations such as American Airlines, Boeing, AT & T, Chrysler, Citybank, IBM, Pepsi-Cola and Xerox. It has become a mandatory requirement by HCFA for any MCO wishing to contract for Medicare business and increasingly so, state by state, for Medicaid. Maintaining and reporting the database is a substantial undertaking in itself. During an accreditation survey, health plans are reviewed against more than 60 standards resulting in the assignment of one of four accreditation levels – Excellent, Accredited, Provisional or Denied. Only about 10 per cent of health plans score 'Excellent'. Accreditation can thus be a stressful experience for any HMO. Once accredited, plans are required to submit regular reports according to HEDIS audit criteria. In 1999 *HEDIS 2000* is a six-volume manual. There are more than 50 measures which must be regularly reported.

As a result of their strenuous efforts to comply with NCQA and HEDIS, managed care organizations can console themselves with independently audited hard data which supports their contention that they provide services which rival the fee-for-service system on quality (see below). In the competitive market of American healthcare, this is powerful information. However, it has not come cheaply. Much of the data has to be captured manually from group practices of physicians. It is a resource-intensive enterprise with the cost to an average health plan of reporting to HEDIS at around $2 million a year.

UTILIZATION MANAGEMENT – THE KEY TO SUCCESS

MCOs have enjoyed success in sustaining efficiency through the employment of utilization management. Utilization management or demand management is the key healthcare management system employed by managed care organizations to control service use and thus cost within parameters of quality. Utilization management has been defined by Kongstvedt as 'the activities of a healthcare system which control resource use by reducing *the need* for more intensive services'.[21] It is a system of approaches employed to manage demand in any healthcare system which cannot ration – such as the NHS emergency hospital service. The aims are both to prevent healthcare service need and to ensure that when it is delivered it is at the least intense level in resource terms. Specific techniques include *admission diversion* through hospital at home or home sitting services; simply not admitting patients for diagnostic procedures; switching surgical procedures to a day basis; and early discharge initiatives such as hospital hotels, use of step-down or improved integration of social care.

Admission diversion is only one side of the coin, however. In the US managed care sector, these initiatives were largely in place by the early 1990s when analysts of hospital utilization began to express concerns that admission rates among the elderly were spiralling out of control and length of stay was beginning to flatten out. Sustaining trends of reducing hospital utilization since that time have been widely attributed to *admission prevention* strategies – notably *to case management* and *chronic disease management*.

Case management was originally designed as a total quality management approach to individuals, mostly people aged over 65, with poor health status. The programme developed in the early 1990s following federal government concerns that expenditure on its Medicare programme, which funds healthcare provision for retired people, would be unsustainable as the population age structure changed over the next ten to fifteen years.

Analysis of resource use at that time by HCFA and the American Hospital Administration showed under 10 per cent of 30 million Medicare beneficiaries accounting for nearly 70 per cent of expenditure. Case management targets this small group of high service users and employs secondary prevention to improve health status and prevent acute exacerbations of chronic and/or 'catastrophic' conditions and thus some admissions to hospital. It is an 'assertive outreach' service based in primary care. Case managers – usually senior nurses – assess and plan packages of care and ensure resources within the healthcare system are deployed to meet the needs of each individual. Specific areas of work include ensuring medical problems are sorted out; educating the client about the disease process including awareness of early warning signs and how and when to access the healthcare system; reviewing current medications; and facilitating compliance with treatment programmes. Sherry Aliotta describes and assesses this service in Chapter 8.

The aim of disease management is to take a more proactive approach to managing a disease in order to improve the likelihood of favourably altering its natural history.[22] It is a comprehensive and integrated approach. The outcome should include improving the quality of care and thus quality of life for the individual and reducing the cost of management of each individual – in particular by reducing their need for hospital-based care. Disease management works across three levels of prevention: primary, secondary and tertiary. It is described more fully in Chapter 5.

EVALUATIONS OF MANAGED CARE

To what extent has managed care met its own objectives? Detailed evaluations of the experience have been carried out recently on both sides of the Atlantic, including Robinson and Steiner's book commissioned by the Department of Health. These exercises are 'meta-analyses' of the American evaluative literature which compares managed care with its primary competitive model in the US, the fee-for-service indemnity system. Although thorough, they are inevitably limited in terms of any assessment of applicability of managed care techniques to the needs of the National Health Service. They also focus largely on the corporate objectives of managed care organizations – cost control, quality and utilization management and consumer satisfaction. The NHS has still more fundamental objectives such as equity and comprehensive cover regardless of means which are still only one side of a philosophical divide in the US. British anxiety about drawing on US experience tends to focus on the absence of these aims in mainstream US health policy. However, in addition to reviewing managed care against the American success parameters, it is possible to answer the following questions which legitimately arise in the UK:

- Does managed care control costs by limiting or denying access to services?
- Do managed care organizations screen out groups in the population who have high healthcare needs and thus demand – such as high-risk groups for healthcare provision, socially deprived groups and elderly people with established chronic conditions?

Cost containment

Robinson and Steiner found some accounting difficulties in making direct comparison between managed care and the fee-for-service sector and their conclusions were largely inconclusive.[23] However, as we have seen, the US federal government is persuaded of the case. Moreover, the increasing penetration of MCOs within the US healthcare market has been associated and credited with dramatic reductions in annual healthcare cost inflation from 12 per cent to 3.6 per cent during the 1990s. The containing impact of managed care growth on national healthcare costs is known as 'spillover savings'. In 1997 the American Association of Health Plans commissioned its own study from the Lewin Group which estimated that over the five-year period from 1991 to 1996 spillover savings amounted to up to $28 billion. There are also clear price differentials. HCFA saves 7 per cent per head for Medicare beneficiaries who choose to enrol in an HMO. In the commercial sector the savings are proportionately higher. In 1996 the annual premium for an employee and his or her family in managed care was just over $3000. This is 15 per cent lower than fee-for-service, often for a more comprehensive benefits package with fewer co-payments; 94 per cent of HMOs included pharmacy as a commercial benefit, for example. Managed care premiums have also been increasing at significantly slower rates than those in fee-for-service.[24]

The NHS was then spending the equivalent of about $1000 per head and it is tempting to make direct comparisons. Unfortunately, the substantially higher cost base in the US makes such exercises problematic and of little relevance. Not least, staff costs are substantially higher in the US. Nursing salaries which constitute the single largest component of cost in the NHS can be two or three times higher in the US for equivalent jobs.

Service utilization

Robinson and Steiner were more definite in this area. Managed care was associated with fewer hospital admissions and shorter lengths of stay. Also physicians in MCOs were more likely to opt for less costly treatment alternatives given equal efficacy between them. For example, Milliman and Robertson compile the most authoritative databases of healthcare service utilization in the United States.[25] This is subdivided into 'commercial', or the under-65 population, and Medicare. The data is case-mix specific and shows all American delivery systems categorized according to the extent to which they use techniques of utilization management. There are three classifications in turn a little pejoratively labelled 'loosely managed' (largely fee-for-service), 'moderately managed' and 'well managed' (comprehensive HMO networks) systems. The 1997 data using these categories shows substantial differences in acute hospital utilization for all conditions and procedures. Length of stay should not be compared direct to the UK since the figures are for the acute stage only. Step-down and rehabilitation utilization is shown separately in the US data.

	Admission rate (per 1000)	Length of stay (days)
Commercial		
Loosely	77	4.1
Moderately	63	3.57
Well	49	2.72
Medicare		
Loosely	284	6.99
Moderately	217	6.79
Well	149	4.68

Source: Milliman and Robertson (1997)[26]

Use of hospital stay is kept within quality parameters, however, as defenders of managed care are at pains to point out. Length of stay by condition or procedure falls within the range recommended by the American medical colleges.[27]

If there is one area where managed care actually promotes higher service utilization it is in the field of health promotion. Health maintenance organizations, as their name suggests, have always prided themselves on their emphasis on primary and secondary prevention not simply as a quality issue but also as a sound business investment. Prevention should reduce utilization at the more costly levels of service delivery – notably hospital admission. Leaving aside any discussion as to the efficacy of these programmes for now, MCOs consistently out-perform fee-for-service in preventive healthcare such as screening, well person check-ups, smoking cessation, immunization programmes or exercise and dietary advice and support services. Robinson and Steiner found the evidence 'most persuasive' in this area.[28]

Quality

Quality has been one of two dimensions of performance on which managed care has been consistently attacked by its competitors. This is not justified. As we have seen, the industry founded what is now the country's leading independent accreditation agency on quality in healthcare – NCQA. It has also been common for the larger HMOs to commission independent quality reviews for organizations such as the RAND Corporation to address this marketing Achilles Heel.[29] Miller and Luft have undertaken two systematic reviews of 31 research studies on quality in MCOs which span 17 years to early 1997.[30] Some of these have been commissioned by HCFA to focus on the Medicare or over-65 population. The reviews concluded that quality of care in MCOs was either on a par with or better than the fee-for-service sector. Robinson and Steiner divided the 23 studies they reviewed into the typology formulated by Donabedian in the early 1980s – structure, process and outcome. They concluded that fee-for-service and managed care performed largely equally well within each parameter, with some significant evidence of higher process quality for MCOs.[31]

Consumer satisfaction and choice

If expressed dissatisfaction rates are any measure, Americans have always been more critical of their healthcare system than the British. In 1988, a meagre 10 per cent of Americans felt that their healthcare system worked 'pretty well'[32] and only 40 to 45 per cent declared themselves very satisfied with the care they received.[33] As we have seen, managed care has a bad image in the US, fuelled by a largely hostile press. Similarly, the research reviewed by Robinson and Steiner revealed customer satisfaction as the one performance measure on which managed care consistently underscored against fee-for-service.[34] In contrast, the data from two major surveys of satisfaction rates in MCOs and fee-for-service reported by the American Association of Health Plans in 1998 shows satisfaction rates of around 90 per cent for both systems.[35]

It seems much depends on the terminology used in the questions. NCQA requires regular monitoring of consumer satisfaction so its data is more complete. It is also more stringent in its reporting since satisfaction rates with accredited MCOs are reported only where consumers are 'completely' or 'very' satisfied. Even at 56 per cent nationally (across a range of regional variations from 53 per cent to 63 per cent) the figures for NCQA-accredited MCOs are relatively high for the US and provides evidence that these organizations are performing reasonably well in this area.

Asked whether a choice of doctor or hospital is important to them on a rating of zero to ten, Americans consistently scored nine.[36] Since much of the evaluation of comparative quality shows MCOs performing well, critics of managed care have turned to choice as the major line of attack. It is true that few if any HMOs can compete with an extensive fee-for-service indemnity plan in this area. However, choice is a relative concept and the debate in the US tends to be more about the range and extent of choice of provider. Ninety-two per cent of HMOs now offer workers covered by their employers some form of PPO for FFS – although often a co-pay is required. However, even within the network, HMOs routinely offer enrollees a choice of primary care physician and hospital which is quite extensive. For example, IEHP, an HMO in Southern California, specializes in health plans for people funded by the State Medical programme (California's version of Medicaid). Its members are offered a choice of up to 500 primary care physicians working in group practices, and 23 hospitals. PCPs recommend the specialist to the patient but again a choice of several will be offered. Members may change PCP up to twice a year if dissatisfied. The member is also provided with advice on making the selection by the Member Services Department based in the HMO headquarters who are also responsible for monitoring satisfaction and resolving grievances.[37]

Access

Do managed care organizations deny care? First, it has become the norm in the United States, even in indemnity plans, for the referring doctors to require prior authorization of some – usually the very expensive elective – forms of treatment. A medical decision is rarely overturned, however. According to the American Association of Health Plans, denial rates, defined as a health plan refusing to fund a treatment recommended by the doctors, are around 1 per cent in medical and surgical acute care.[38] NCQA report satisfaction rates of 85 per cent with access – defined as MCO members who have not had problems accessing the care they or their doctors believed to be necessary.[39] Moreover, waiting lists are an unknown quantity in the better MCOs. In the State of California, for example, it is a state requirement that patients should wait no more than two weeks for an initial consultation, and surgery – if required – would be routinely scheduled within two to four weeks after that. Even people on Medical would invoke the plan's grievance procedures if they were made to wait three months for elective hospital treatment.

What then of healthcare-related services such as social care? In the United States social care is funded either through individuals' own resources or supported by the state Medicaid programmes. Provision can be patchy from state to state depending on the local political tradition. The integration of health and social care networks is the responsibility of case managers who are either nurses or social workers employed by MCOs (see Chapter 8). Medicaid will fund packages of community-based services such as home helps or short- and long-term placements in nursing home care. Social care is means-tested and co-pays of around $10 per week may be charged for community-based services. There are also programmes in some states to pay carers at the national minimum wage level of $5.75 (1999 figures). Sixty-five per cent of nursing home costs in the US are now met by Medicaid.

Recently there have been calls for more consistency in social care provision through the unification of publicly funded health and social care budgets. HCFA's response to date has been to establish four pilot programmes called Social Health Maintenance Organizations (SHMOs). The SHMOs are funded through Medicare at a higher rate than is payable to conventional HMOs. One of these operates from Long Beach and also draws on the State Medical Programme. Its case managers have the authority to provide packages of social care to maintain a client in the community at a cost of up to 95 per cent of the cost of nursing home care – which is about $36,000 per annum. Over the next few years, it is envisaged that the federal government will increase contracts with managed care organizations to provide health and social care particularly for elderly people and other high-cost client groups on Medicaid, such as those with chronic mental health needs. Whether this will extend the SHMO model or simply build on the existing provider networks remains to be seen, although case management will continue to grow as the planner and coordinator of needs and resources.

Managed care and high-risk populations

Finally, are managed care enrollees representative of the American population at large in terms of health status? First, during the 1990s the number of Medicaid beneficiaries in managed care increased from under 10 per cent to over 50 per cent. This trend seems likely to be sustained into the next century now that states have the authority to require Medicaid beneficiaries to enrol in managed care. Second, when an HMO contracts with an employer to provide health plans to the workforce, it is simply not allowed to screen any individuals, so accepts whatever risks there may be. So with its mix of Medicaid and over 90 per cent of employees from all types of industry, managed care covers a cross-section of American society under 65. These figures support studies quoted by the American Association of Health Plans that have found no difference in the health status of MCO enrollees and the general population, although HMOs cover more low-income families and more minority groups than fee-for-service.[40] As far as the over-65s are concerned, Medicare is a national comprehensive programme covering all cultures and income levels (when the beneficiary was working). HMOs with Medicare contracts are simply not allowed under HCFA regulations to refuse any individual applying to enrol, regardless of pre-existing conditions. They have to take all comers.

That leaves the reducing number of Americans with no health insurance cover at all, which has been estimated to be as low as 5 per cent of the population. There are two major groups: those single persons (often students) from poorer backgrounds who do not meet the Medicaid eligibility criteria because they have no special chronic ill-health needs or are childless, and those younger people who do not regard themselves as in need of health insurance and deprioritize it as an expenditure item. These people can access neither managed care nor the fee-for-service sector and are reliant on America's hard-pressed public hospitals. Their plight is a structural weakness in the US healthcare system.

AN OPTIMUM MODEL

So managed care performs well compared to fee-for-service on most significant criteria. However, as with any healthcare delivery system, such as the NHS for example, there are variations in quality, range and access to services and resource management between managed care organizations. In any comparative healthcare management analysis, we should not seek to emulate the worst aspects of any system but examine the applicability of the best. To do the argument of this book full justice, therefore, it is necessary to develop a paradigm for managed care which reflects the best practice in the United States. This can be found in some of the managed care organizations which have developed in Southern California, although it is readily acknowledged that high-quality managed care systems can be found in other parts of the country.

Why California? The state has the highest GDP per capita of any in the US. Not only do its healthcare consumers therefore have maximum purchasing power, they also have as wide a choice as any in the US healthcare market. Its white middle-class population, at least, is among the most demanding even of American consumers. Yet market penetration for managed care is highest in this state. Therefore, to the extent that consumer preference is an important measure of quality in American healthcare delivery, the models found in Southern California are unsurpassed elsewhere in the managed care sector.

Not least, the state has a strong claim as the home of the modern fully integrated HMO, and has the widest choice of plans and thus the most intense competition between managed care organizations. Therefore, to explore the application of managed care techniques to the United Kingdom's healthcare development agenda over the next ten years, we need to develop a model based on best practice in Southern California. This would have the following components:

- A single annual payment guarantees a comprehensive healthcare delivery system.
- The central payer organization – the HMO – sub-contracts service purchasing to primary care-based associations of 'GPs' and other community-based healthcare professionals.
- Primary care delivers most of the care and hospital costs are under 40 per cent of the total expenditure.
- There is an integrated quality management process based on clinical effectiveness and consumer satisfaction.
- Clinical effectiveness is assumed by employing evidence-based clinical guidelines.

- Prevention and health maintenance are integrated service objectives.
- Care delivery systems are integrated with each provider's role designed on criteria of clinical appropriateness, resource effectiveness and patient focus.
- Utilization management techniques are widely employed.
- To guarantee quality and appropriate levels of service utilization, the HMO has a performance monitoring system for its contracted providers.
- The central payer organization has an autonomous member services department which provides information on choice of providers and use of the healthcare network, monitors satisfaction, seeks to redress grievances and complaints and, critically, feeds back information into the management process.
- Finally, strategic and operational objectives and financial incentives are aligned throughout the system.

These then are the major elements of a high-quality, comprehensive managed care system. Each of these sub-systems of healthcare management will be revisited in detail in the course of this book to show why they are central to the development needs of the British National Health Service which flow from the Labour government's modernization agenda.

NOTES AND REFERENCES

1 FHP Healthcare (1993) *Managed Care: Today's Proven System, Tomorrow's Healthcare Solution*, Evidence to the First Lady's Commission on Healthcare Reform.
2 *Los Angeles Times*, 28 March 1999, p. C1.
3 R. Robinson and A. Steiner (1998) *Managed Healthcare*. Buckingham: Open University Press.
4 P. Boland (1993) *Making Managed Healthcare Work*, p. xvii. Gaithersburg, MD: Aspen.
5 P.R. Kongstvedt and D.W. Plocher (1997) Integrated health care delivery systems, in P.R. Kongstvedt, *Essentials of Managed Health Care*, pp. 49–69. Gaithersberg: Aspen.
6 E.R. Wagner (1997) Types of managed care organisation, in P.R. Kongstvedt, op. cit., p. 38.
7 P. Boland and K.S. Abramowitz (1993) Changing trends in healthcare delivery, in P. Boland, op. cit., pp. 3–8.
8 Wagner, op. cit.
9 Ibid.
10 P.D. Fox (1997) An overview of managed care, in P.R. Kongstvedt, op. cit., pp. 4–5.
11 Ibid, pp. 6–7.
12 Personal communication from Dr Charles Gumbiner, Founder and then President of FHP Healthcare, Fountain Valley, CA.
13 P.R. Kongstvedt (1997) Primary care in closed panel plans, in Kongstvedt, op. cit., p. 81.

14 H. Taylor and J.I. Morrison (1993) Attitudes towards managed healthcare, in P. Boland, op. cit., pp. 54–5.
15 P.D. Fox (1996) An overview of managed care, in P. Kongstvedt, *The Managed Care Handbook*, p. 19. Gaithersburg, MD: Aspen.
16 P. Boland (1993) Market overview and delivery systems, in P. Boland, op. cit., pp. 4–5.
17 *American Association of Health Plans Website*, http://www.aahp.org
18 D.B. Bernard and D.J. Shulkin (1998) The media vs managed health care: are we seeing a full count press?, *Archives of Internal Medicine*, 158 (19): 2109–11.
19 NCQA (1999) *National Committee for Quality Assurance: An overview*, NCQA website, http://www.ncqa.org/
20 P.D. Fox, op. cit.
21 D.W. Plocher (1996) Disease management, in Kongstvedt, op. cit.
22 Kongstvedt, op. cit.
23 Robinson and Steiner, op. cit., p. 74.
24 The Lewin Group (1997) *Managed Care Savings for Employers and Households*; KPMG (1996) Foster Higgins, National Survey of Employer-Sponsored Health Plans (Source: AAHP website, http://www.aahp.org).
25 Milliman and Robertson (1997) *Health Management Guidelines*, Vol. 1 (November). Irvine, CA: Milliman and Robertson.
26 Ibid.
27 AAHP website, http://www.aahp.org, *Managed Care Facts*, p. 12, January 1998.
28 Robinson and Steiner, op. cit., p. 79.
29 Personal communication from Dr Charles Gumbiner, FHP, op. cit.
30 R.H. Miller and H.S. Luft (1997) *Health Affairs*, September/October; *Journal of the American Medical Association* (1994), May.
31 Robinson and Steiner, op. cit., pp. 79–97.
32 Taylor and Morrison, op. cit., p. 55.
33 Ibid, p. 56.
34 Robinson and Steiner, op. cit., pp. 97–101.
35 AAHP website, op. cit.
36 Taylor and Morrison, op. cit., p. 58.
37 Interview with the Medical Director of IEHP, April 1999.
38 AAHP website, http://www.aahp.org, *Dispelling Managed Care Myths*, p. 2, 1999.
39 NCQA website, http://www.ncqu.org/ *The State of Managed Care Quality Report*, p. 14, 1998.
40 American Association of Health Plans (1998) *Demographic Characteristics of HMO Enrollees*, June (AAHP website, op. cit.).

2

MANAGED CARE: AN AMERICAN PRACTITIONER'S PERSPECTIVE

Robert Larsen

THE DEVELOPMENT OF MANAGED CARE – THE EARLY YEARS, 1920s TO 1930s

Prior to the 1930s American healthcare was a simple free enterprise system based upon the buying and selling of services. If you felt ill, you went to the doctor. Usually at the end of the visit the physician, based partly upon the patient's ability to pay, set a fee. For example, if the patient was poor, there might be no charge. Sometimes the patient had no idea what the fee would be until the bill arrived. Patients trusted their doctors to be fair, and doctors trusted their patients to pay. Fees increased at roughly the same rate as inflation.

This system worked satisfactorily for affluent people. Most people considered fees as fair and affordable. For example, a visit to a doctor ranged from $1–5 and an appendectomy cost $25–50. Not so the poor, who simply avoided going to the doctor, or buying the medicine. As a result, there was unnecessary morbidity and mortality and preventive medicine was seldom given consideration in this system. Medicine was reactive. Immunizations and screening tests were rare, except through public school systems. Yet for most people this simple system was all there was.

Following the stock market crash of 1929 and the ensuing depression that went on through the 1930s economics forced some changes in this healthcare system. People were finding it was difficult to pay medical bills and still put food on the table. Doctors started to feel the pinch. Average income for physicians in California fell from $6700 in 1929 to $3600 in 1933.[1] As early as 1910 the Western Clinic in Tacoma, Washington offered prepaid outpatient care by the group,[2] but this wasn't a true HMO. In 1929 Baylor Hospital (Texas) established healthcare for 1500 teachers. This was the beginning of the health insurance company Blue Cross.[3] In 1939 the California Medical Society established Blue Shield to reimburse for physician services. In 1929 two Los Angeles physicians, Donald Ross and H. Clifford Loos, devised a system of healthcare that would be prepaid by the employer. They sold this concept to the Los Angeles County Department of Water and Power. In this system, the county agency would pay a fixed sum to the Ross–Loos Clinic for each employee including the family members. The clinic would then provide the physician services without charging the patient. In 1937 a cooperative, the Group Health Association (GHA), was started in Washington DC to reduce the number of mortgage defaults resulting from medical expenses. This was opposed by the American Medical Association which was later indicted on charges of violating the anti-trust legislation for this attempt to suppress the GHA.[4] At that time Southern California was growing rapidly and it was difficult to find good employees. The county wanted to provide the perks necessary to keep their good workers. This prepaid system was an exception to the traditional way of receiving healthcare, but it also fore-shadowed what was to come decades later.

INTO THE 1940s – KAISER AND THE ERA OF INDEMNITY PROLIFERATION

Organized labour was a strong movement in Southern California in the years immediately preceding the Second World War. Pearl Harbor and the ensuing involvement of America in the war required ships, tanks and steel products on a large scale. Henry Kaiser, a steel manufacturer, needed good labourers, because he had more contracts than he could fill. The labour union came to him and demanded extra perks for working in the Kaiser mills, including healthcare. So Kaiser established a healthcare system for the workers and their families working on the Grand Coulee Dam in 1933. Later he established a similar plan for shipbuilders in San Francisco. Soon he found he was providing healthcare to large numbers of people and had a number of employed doctors working in Kaiser clinics.

In 1942 he formed the Kaiser Permanente Health system. He separated the health plan into two non-profit organizations. The doctors, hospitals and clinics comprised Kaiser Permanente, which would contract with Kaiser Healthplan to provide the healthcare. This was modelled on the Ross–Loos clinic as a prepaid healthcare system. The fixed fee would be negotiated each year with the parent organization. The Kaiser Permanente system could also contract with other companies or labour unions to provide healthcare to their employees and members. In 1945 he opened this system to the general public. These pioneering projects were isolated, and although they were the foundation of the managed care movement to come, they covered very few people in the 1940s.

Following the end of the Second World War, America again experi-enced an economic change. The war had stimulated the economy and brought the country out of the depression of the 1930s. Men returned from the service where they were accustomed to free military healthcare only to find they had to pay out of their pockets for care. The Veterans' Affairs department developed extensive hospital systems to care for many of these veterans. As workers returned to their jobs, and there seemed to be more money available, inflation rose like a spectre to cause new alarms. Healthcare costs, like the general inflation, rose, and the simple free enterprise system of healthcare was creating more hardship than it did in the 1920s and 1930s.

Health insurance companies sprang up like weeds, selling a product that would help ease the burden of healthcare. For a defined monthly premium they would reimburse the policy holder a percentage (usually 80 per cent) of their medical bills. Drugs were not a part of these indemnity products, but were paid out of pocket when the patient could afford it. Blue Cross and Blue Shield became a major health insurer in this period. Several life insurance companies like Prudential and Connecticut General (CIGNA) began to write healthcare insurance as well. So the 1940s became the era of indemnity health insurance proliferation.

During this decade there were also several new experiments into prepaid healthcare. Labour unions became stronger, making more demands of employers. In response to these demands of labour, new prepaid health plans began to spring up. In 1947, a cooperative for healthcare was formed called the Group Health Cooperative of Puget Sound in Seattle. In New York City the Health Insurance Plan of New York (HIP) was formed, and in California Robert Gumbiner converted his group practice into a prepaid health plan, the Family Health Plan (FHP) to provide healthcare to the employees of the Long Beach school system. These two systems differed in that in FHP physicians were employees of the health plan, while in HIP physicians were in independent group practices.

POSTWAR INTEREST – THE GOLDEN AGE OF HEALTHCARE PROFITABILITY

The 1950s are remembered as the golden age of medicine. There was general prosperity in the country. The consumer price index (CPI) rose at an annual rate of 2.8 per cent while physicians' incomes increased at 5.9 per cent.[5] The federal government was pouring money into hospital construction through a programme known as the Hill–Burton funds. As a result of the Second World War, the government was also pouring sums into research and training. The government wanted to be sure that there would be no future doctor shortage. 'Medical Schools couldn't spend the money fast enough', claimed Warren Bostick, who later became the president of the California Medical Association.[6]

The 1950s were also the years of growing indemnity insurance.[7] By early 1950 over 50 per cent of the people in the US had some kind of health insurance. By spreading the risk of getting ill, it was possible for insurance companies to provide this insurance at an affordable premium. Often this insurance only covered costs incurred in the hospital setting. As a result hospitals were filled with patients having diagnostic tests. For example, barium X-rays were done as an in-patient procedure so that they would be covered by the insurance.

Hospital beds were at a premium. In order to encourage the construction of more hospitals and medical schools, the government extended the Hill–Burton programme. Hospitals were making money at a frightening rate, and if they decided to expand to make more money, they needn't dip into reserves, for there was the Hill–Burton money just for the asking.

Insurance companies began to notice a wide variation in charges made by physicians for a given procedure. There seemed to be no definition of services. The California Medical Association published the Relative Value Studies (RVS) in 1956. This attempted to define all healthcare procedures and assign a relative, non-monetary value to each. For example, an appendectomy was priced at 10 times the value of an office visit. This required a conversion factor to assign a monetary value to each procedure, but this wasn't formalized until 1963 when the 'reasonable and customary' concept was applied to physician fees.[8]

1960s – HEALTHCARE AS A RIGHT

Healthcare inflation continued, and now had reached an annual double-digit percentage of increase. Employers were regretting the healthcare benefit granted in the 1940s, because the cost was cutting into net profits at an alarming rate. There were pleas for the federal government to intervene. There was talk of a National Health Insurance arrangement, but this couldn't get passed in Congress. Instead, in 1965 Congress responded by passing the Health Insurance for the Aged Act. This established a system for the government to pay for health insurance for those receiving Social Security benefits, and to assist the states in providing healthcare for the indigent. These two systems were called Medicare and Medicaid respectively.[9]

In 1966, President Lyndon Johnson announced his 'Great Society' plan. Part of this plan claimed that healthcare was a right, not a privilege. This led to the infusion of huge sums of federal money into the healthcare industry. Not just medical schools, but graduate medical education was funded by government funds. This encouraged the 'specialization' of physicians. Residency programme positions for specialists increased dramatically.

1970s – HEALTHCARE INFLATION AND THE GROWTH OF MANAGED CARE

Until now, there were only a few isolated prepaid health plans in the country. Most of them were staff models, where physicians were employees of the health plan, or group models like Kaiser, with physicians organized into a group practice and contracting exclusively with one health plan. Healthcare costs were now approaching 12 or 13 per cent of the gross national product (GNP), and employers and the government were becoming worried about the future cost of healthcare.

The Nixon administration established a task force to examine healthcare costs and make recommendations for the future. Two people, Dr Paul Ellwood, a Minnesota physician, and an economist from Stanford, Alain Enthoven, were key players in developing the new policy. In fact in May 1970, Dr Ellwood coined the term Health Maintenance Organization (HMO) for the first time.[10] He envisioned a system of healthcare that would combine insurance and healthcare – that would encourage competition on both price and quality in the market.

Because not all insurance companies could put together a staff model or group model quickly, physicians began to join together in associations called Independent Practice Associations (IPAs), and for some insurers these were relied upon to provide the healthcare. By utilizing IPAs even large national indemnity insurance companies began to offer an HMO option to employers as well as their traditional indemnity insurance plan.

Soon almost every metropolitan community had an HMO. Critical mass was a community of over 1 million people, because only 5–8 per cent of the population would select this form of healthcare. However, the medical community saw the HMOs as a major threat to their comfortable, costly system of providing medical care. State medical societies and the AMA vehemently opposed all this new development. The California Medical Association refused to let HMO doctors join. Universities refused to let HMO physicians on the clinical faculty. HMO physicians were considered too inadequate to make a living in the traditional healthcare fee-for-service system, and physicians publicly ridiculed their HMO colleagues. In spite of this, employers were turning more and more to the lower cost of insurance from the HMOs.

1980s – FURTHER PRESSURE FOR GROWTH AND THE FIRST HMO PUBLIC FUNDING

In states like California, over 25 per cent of employees were receiving healthcare from an HMO. However, by 1980 healthcare cost was now up to nearly 14 per cent of the GNP, and the inflation rate was frightening. The costs were as frightening to the government as to employers, because the government was paying nearly 25 per cent of the nation's healthcare bill through the Medicare, Medicaid and the War Veterans' Administration programmes along with insurance for the federal employees. In 1983 Robert Gumbiner, founder of FHP, felt that HMOs could provide Medicare coverage at much lower cost with added benefits. He pioneered the first HMO-based Medicare risk pilot project in Southern California.

He built clinics designed only for senior care. He added pharmacy, dental, spectacles, and other benefits in a prepaid programme that received only 95 per cent of what Medicare was costing the government in the fee-for-service system. He showed that not only was this feasible, but that FHP could make a generous profit as well.

Dr Gumbiner expanded this programme into the Medicaid programme as well, and soon nearly half of the FHP programme was either Medicare or Medicaid patients. By the mid-1980s the official Medicare/Medicaid risk programmes for HMOs were in place. The government calculated the cost of healthcare for elderly people for any given county and used a percentage of this to determine the reimbursement rate. This was called the Average Adjusted per Capita Cost of healthcare (AAPCC).

Most HMOs were slow to launch Medicare risk programmes. It was common knowledge in the industry that healthcare for elderly people was very costly, and there was a high risk of losing money from a Medicare HMO product. In the late 1980s there were scandals involving HMOs that were taking the prepaid reimbursement but lacked sufficient delivery systems to provide the care. The Medicare HMO programme looked doomed for the entire nation, but after investigation it was found that most HMOs were operating these programmes in good faith.

1990s – QUALITY AND MARKET DOMINANCE

HMOs had proved that they could control the cost of healthcare. Healthcare inflation was at the lowest rate in decades. Now was the time to show that they could also improve the quality of life for their members. Improved 'outcomes' were the next great challenge. Hence the 1990s was to become the new decade of quality. Courses in quality and consumer satisfaction and service were taught to all HMO employees. Repeatedly, managed care claimed that quality would differentiate HMOs in this decade and expectations were high that managed care could escape the reputation of being only interested in price. If an HMO could show that its members were healthier, happier and receiving the best care, it would become the leader.

However, instead of quality, expansion and competition took precedence. HMOs were growing rapidly. By 1990 40 per cent of the healthcare in California was provided by HMOs. Essentially every state had at least one HMO. Managed care had become the primary system for healthcare across the country. HMO physicians were no longer shunned; in fact many state medical societies had started an HMO plan. The cost difference between HMOs and indemnity insurance was dramatic. Not only did indemnity insurance cost more, but the employee had to pay large amounts out of pocket to meet co-pays and deductible requirements. Essentially every employer offered an HMO plan to the employees.

Geographic expansion became essential for the HMOs. Growth was the driving force and this required moving into new markets. Every HMO seemed to be striving to become a national system of delivering care. Mergers and acquisitions were daily events. It was felt that eventually the industry would be dominated by only a handful of large nationwide health plans.

At the same time, it became recognized that to attain this growth and expansion capital was required. In order to gain access to ready capital, health plans that had traditionally been not-for-profit organizations converted to for-profit plans. Unfortunately, often there are psychological changes that develop in an organization when it converts from not-for-profit to for-profit. First, a greater bottom line profit is expected. Stockholders are not content with a net profit of 4 or 5 per cent. Profits need to increase by 10–20 per cent over the previous year. This cannot happen without a large membership base. Second, there are a host of incentives in for-profit conversion that can change the attitudes of management. Growing the price of the stock is important because of the stock options gained by top executives. Mergers and acquisitions bring a windfall into these same pockets. Each of these activities seems to generate an attitude of short-term acquisitiveness.

By the end of the 1990s more than 60 per cent of Americans were getting their healthcare from a managed care organization. A handful of HMOs accounted for the bulk of this membership. Mergers were no longer just the big fish gobbling up the little fish. Big fish were buying big fish. FHP, after acquiring a couple of smaller HMOs, was bought by PacifiCare. Aetna bought US Healthcare, and then Prudential. Humana acquired several smaller organizations. United Healthcare of Minnesota purchased Metrohealth which had been formed by the merger of the Metropolitan and Travelers organizations. Kaiser continued to grow, not by acquisition but by price competition.

Bigger was not necessarily better. The dollars for these acquisitions, combined with the need to appease stockholders and top management renumeration packages, had to come from somewhere. Profit margins began to narrow, and by 1997 most HMOs were no longer profitable, but were reporting losses.[11] As losses mounted, many HMOs simply closed their doors, or were taken over by the states in which they operated, until the members could be shifted to another struggling organization.

At the same time as these financial problems arose, consumer and provider dissatisfaction was widely prevalent. The news media and politicians had a field day publishing the stories of patients who had been denied appropriate care. Physicians watched their incomes stagnate or even decline, and were outspoken about the shortcomings of the health plans. Many physicians moved into political office in both the state and national legislature, to promote reform.

By the end of this decade new laws and court rulings have made it nearly impossible for a health plan to operate efficiently. Multimillion-dollar judgments against the large HMOs are a daily occurrence. The result has been the resurgence of healthcare inflation into double-digit numbers. *The very problem that had spawned the managed care movement was haunting employers once again.* No longer did managed care control the cost of healthcare. Employers were no longer able to control the cost of a healthcare benefit for their employees. The new millennium came with most of the healthcare players hoping for a new system for the coming decade.

It is clear therefore that the cost of healthcare was the key driving force for the managed care movement in the US. Consumers, employers and the government payers sought cheaper healthcare. Extrapolating the inflationary trends prior to the movement towards managed care frightened all the players. General Motors claimed that 10 per cent of the cost of a new automobile went to provide healthcare for the assembly line workers. The government predicted an early demise of the Medicare programme because of impending bankruptcy.

There were a few optimists who also felt this was an opportunity to improve the quality of care. Some HMOs in the early 1990s advertised on the appeal of better quality healthcare. The National Committee for Quality Assurance (NCQA) was born and soon moved into the process of accrediting health plans for quality. But in spite of all this, controlling cost was clearly the driving force.

CURRENT MANAGEMENT AGENDAS – CONTROLLING COSTS

Changing physician behaviour

Fifty to eighty per cent of healthcare costs are controlled by physicians.[12] The early HMOs were very similar to indemnity insurers. There was a prepaid premium to provide care for a defined population. There were few interventions or attempts at controlling utilization. These HMOs were staff models (owning their own services) or group models, and cost control was maintained by paying only for the benefits purchased and by attempts to control the practice patterns of the physicians. Waste was to be eliminated. Inappropriate care was not paid for. Unnecessary services were excluded. Dr Gumbiner, founder of FHP, often said, 'We will provide all the healthcare that is needed – and no more.'

Providing 'health maintenance' could also attain savings. Physicians and patients were not accustomed to getting regular screening tests. As pointed out in the previous chapter, fee-for-service medicine meant in practice the diagnosis and treatment of acute medical problems. Detecting disease before symptoms occurred was uncommon, but became an important transformation in the way of thinking for health professionals.

It was easier to influence the behaviour of physicians in a staff or group model. The doctors were employees of the insurer, and if they practised in a fashion that was counter to the goals of the organization, they were let go. So in the early days working for an HMO required someone who was open to change, and was willing to consider the cost of the diagnosis and treatment. The first effort was to make the physicians aware of the costs of their therapies. Prior to managed care, physicians never thought about the cost of the medicine or treatment they were using. Now physicians were expected to know the relative cost of one drug compared to an alternative drug.

Physician practice variation results in waste and increased cost of healthcare. In 1982 John Wennberg demonstrated highly different rates of certain surgical procedures in one community compared to another[13] These changes were the result of different training and economic pressures. They indicate that in some settings more healthcare is being delivered than is appropriate.

Changing physician behaviour is not an easy task. Physicians are 'knowledge workers' and are programmed to think that they have most of the answers. Non-physician managers or lay managers have little influence over physicians. Their lack of medical knowledge allows them to be readily ignored by the physician. Peer pressure or education from a respected colleague can have some influence on changing physician behaviour. Thus came the birth of the medical director. This person had to have above average medical knowledge, and high leadership qualities to be successful. He or she had to be able to determine what was appropriate, necessary, or required and then educate the physician. Although the physicians often saw the medical director as a member of management (the enemy), the medical director proved to be an effective step towards changing physician behaviour. The successful medical director was not just someone who could say 'no', but was an educator who knew what he or she was talking about and was able to influence others.

Schroeder[14] looked at several mechanisms for changing physician behaviour. Education alone was generally unsuccessful. Feedback that compares a physician's practice patterns with peers gave mixed results. Removing barriers and administrative hassles was better, but difficult to implement. Financial incentives were the most successful. In fact, probably the best strategy is to use all of these techniques and not rely on any one.

A subtle way of affecting physician practice habits is by providing data that compares one's practice with one's peers. Measuring utilization of services and reporting the results to a physician can make a significant difference. If a physician gets an electrocardiogram on every patient over 40 with each office visit, patients may think he is very thorough. If this physician sees that he is getting more than twice as many electrocardiograms as his colleagues average for a similar practice, it may dawn on him that some of these tests are not necessary.

Evidence of clinical effectiveness can assist. More recently there have been clinical guidelines developed from best practices for certain conditions. The MedStat Group conducted a claims-based analysis of physician use of guidelines and found that physicians are not practising according to best practice data available to them. Only 29 per cent of diabetics received annual eye examinations. Only 40 per cent of patients with CHF received an echocardiogram within three months of their initial diagnosis. Only 25 per cent of patients with asthma received inhaled anti-inflammatory drugs. Although these numbers are not good, they are a significant improvement from five years earlier when the guidelines were not readily available.[15] Managers have a difficult time understanding why these measures to mould physician behaviour are not 100 per cent successful. They do make a difference, and will reduce healthcare costs by 15 to 40 per cent but, because of the mindset of the physician, they are far from universally effective.

Limiting clinically unnecessary treatment

'All the healthcare necessary, and no more.' This implies that some of the healthcare people were accustomed to receiving was unnecessary or inappropriate. Therefore which benefits would be provided had to be defined and communicated to the purchaser. Cosmetic surgery was relatively easy. This is nice and may provide some psychological support, but it is seldom 'necessary'. But what about breast reconstruction after a mastectomy, or a cleft lip? Most physicians would consider these cosmetic procedures to be necessary. So even the most straightforward benefits could require interpretation and some flexibility. Soon health plans had a giant notebook, called the *Benefit Interpretation Manual*, so that utilization, claims and medical personnel could be consistent in interpreting any given benefit. Purchasers exercised discretion over which benefits they would buy for their employees. One might elect to avoid in-patient mental health benefits, while another excluded AIDS treatment. Services such as vasectomies or fertilization procedures were commonly excluded, because these had no effect on the employee's capacity to work for the employer.

In addition in managed care it was an early requirement that only those services provided by the plan's physicians were covered. This meant that employees now had to give up their family doctor and move to a physician in the health plan. In the staff or group model this was a limited list of available physicians. The American consumer was unused to consulting a primary care physician. No longer could the patient go directly to the ophthalmologist for eye problems, or the dermatologist for skin problems. Access to certain services was also limited by requiring authorization prior to obtaining these services. This will be discussed in the section on utilization but, by inserting a gatekeeper, utilization of these services was reduced, and dollars saved.

Some employees with health plan coverage were willing to pay more to use any physician they wanted, rather than be limited to the employed or contracted physicians. This evolved into a product called Point of

Service plan. In this plan the patient had a choice of the managed care product or an indemnity-like product. If they elected to go outside the plan's providers either a higher co-pay was required, or there was reimbursement of only 60 to 80 per cent of the billed services. For a period this was a popular product, but did little to control the cost of healthcare.

Coordination of benefits is a further important cost saving process. Many people have more than one health coverage. A second coverage may be car accident coverage, workers' compensation, or through a spouse's employer. Twenty or thirty years ago, a patient could make money by going to the hospital if he or she had multiple coverage. Today that is not possible. In every claim one plan is primary. Determining which plan is primary and which is secondary, and coordinating the payment of claims between these, is the key to coordinating benefits.

New technology plays a major role in healthcare inflation. Physicians are attracted to prescribing or recommending these new technologies. In training, physicians are taught that the best doctors are those who know all the latest drugs or therapies, and use them. At the same time TV and the Internet is informing patients about these therapies in a way never seen before. Patients come to their doctor's office with demands for something they've heard or read about, with little consideration for its appropriateness in their situation. Some new technologies are experimental. Experimental medicine is not a covered benefit, and represents one more way in which costs are controlled by limiting benefits. Several ways of managing these costs have been developed.

One option is to outsource technology assessment by using reliable vendors. These vendors use expert specialists to evaluate new technologies and make recommendations for the appropriate use of these technologies. This is a service that costs many thousand dollars per year, but is credible.

If technology assessment is kept 'in house' then each health plan should have a Technology Assessment Committee that evaluates the new costly technology and develops a guideline for its appropriate usage. This guideline needs the buy-in from the physicians who are most likely to use it. The guideline then assists the utilization personnel and medical director as well as the physicians. Some organizations outsource this committee and use a technology assessment service. These services have the advantage of review by many qualified experts before a usage opinion is provided.

Patients are often not satisfied with this and still demand the new technology. In order to prevent litigation against the health plan, a system of external review is commonplace today. Often the external reviewer is a professor from the academic community, and he or she will give an opinion as to whether or not this technology is appropriate for a specific patient.

Since most health plans cover medications, there needs to be a system to control this cost. This is called the formulary. It is another example of limiting access to a benefit. Drugs are covered if they are on the plan's list of covered drugs. If a patient wants a drug not on the list, it has to be paid for out of his or her own pocket. If a patient needs a drug not on the formulary list, a review of that specific patient's medical record is necessary before it can be approved. The formulary also generates savings for the health plan. If the health plan approves only one or two drugs in a class, the manufacturers will compete by offering special rates to get their drug on the formulary. Sometimes contracts are written that allow a percentage of the drug cost to be reimbursed to the health plan quarterly in the form of a kick-back. This can amount to millions of dollars of savings.

The effectiveness of controlling cost by limiting access or benefits is high. Consumers accept these measures as part of the price of cheaper healthcare. Physicians do not like these measures, for they feel it places the health plan between them and their patients, but gradually even physicians are adapting to these measures.

Utilization management

Although it can be argued that utilization management is another method of limiting access to service, it is separate because it became a science in itself. This was a system imposed upon physicians, and seldom regarded as physician-friendly. Most health plans tried to develop utilization guidelines that reflected good medical practice, and some even tried to get physician buy-in or approval of these guidelines.

The simplest and earliest of the utilization management systems was prior authorization or pre-certification. Certain high-cost or frequently over-utilized services required approval by the HMO's medical affairs department before they were provided. The list of these services was often very long. It started with hospital admissions. All hospital admissions (except for emergencies) had to be pre-approved. Other expensive procedures, such as CT scan, MRI, and expensive new technologies and drugs, were soon added to the list. The setting for the care to be provided is important. Surgery done in an outpatient setting may cost a small fraction of what it costs in a tertiary hospital.

It is also important to be sure the lowest qualified level of provider is being used. Can the service be given by a nurse or a physician extender? Does it require a specialist or a primary care physician? Obviously these considerations and the guidelines for determining them must be communicated to the physicians and hospitals, usually at the time of contracting, so that the patient would not be misled.

The second utilization tool developed was the management of the length of stay of patients in hospital (LOS). In the fee-for-service system, hospitals provided interventional therapies and diagnostic procedures eight hours per day, five days per week. The rest of the time was merely maintenance and nursing. A physician could order a diagnostic test one morning and it would not be done until the next day, after the doctor had made his rounds. The doctor would review the results on the third day, and then decide if additional tests were required. It was not uncommon in the early days of managed care for patients to use over 500 annual bed-days per 1000 for non-senior (under 65) members and three or four times this amount for senior (over 65) patients. Utilization nurses were placed in the hospital and visited on every patient each day. They were responsible for ensuring that tests and procedures were performed and reported to the physician on the same day as ordered. They were also responsible for patient discharge, once the patient was stable, or could be cared for at home. If the patient could not be cared for at home, but could be cared for in a less expensive nursing facility, or with the aid of home health, arrangements were expedited by the hospital utilization nurse, to get the patient out of the hospital. Since an acute hospital bed-day cost an average of over $500, this could amount to significant savings.

The third and latest addition to utilization management was the institution of case management. There are some patients, usually with chronic conditions, that end up being high utilizers of medical services – for instance, those with problems such as AIDS, asthma, or chronic obstructive pulmonary disease, or transplantation candidates. Because of the managed care limitations to access, these patients often failed to get timely care, and would end up going to the Emergency Room for care, or require frequent hospital admissions. The case manager could cut through all the obstacles and get immediate appointments with specialists, or diagnostic tests, without going through prior authorization and utilization. Case management proved to be a significant boost to the quality of care as well as a cost saving. In these conditions, timeliness could make a major impact on health status and lifestyle for the patient.[16]

The effectiveness of these utilization management tools is great. Of all the cost-controlling measures, utilization management has had the biggest impact in reducing the cost of healthcare.

Contracts and risk pooling

The health plan uses a variety of providers to give healthcare to the members. These include hospitals, physicians, physician extenders, skilled nursing facilities, surgery centres, home health agencies, durable medical equipment (DME), physical therapy and diagnostic centres. These providers need a contract with the health plan, so that each understands its specific role and the mechanisms for reimbursement. Because the health plan can guarantee a certain amount of business, the health plan can leverage this volume to obtain discounts from normal reimbursement rates.

Today most health plans in the US have carried this one step further with incentives or capitation where providers are paid to serve a given *population* rather than provide an agreed volume of *activity*. The health plan shares in the risk of the cost of healthcare by establishing certain targets. Part of the reimbursement money is set aside into a pool that can serve as an incentive for providers who attain the targets, but is withheld from those who do not. These targets can be any component of the healthcare delivery – such as bed days, pharmacy costs, or specialist physician costs.

When the providers have experience at successfully controlling the cost of healthcare, they may assume the full risk through capitation. In this model, the hospital or physicians are given a fixed amount per member per month for providing necessary healthcare. If the care costs more, they lose, but if they control costs, they pocket the balance. The science for setting capitation rates is flawed and frequently the providers find they cannot be successful with the funds provided. This has given capitation a bad name among many providers.

The effectiveness of controlling costs by contracts, and especially by capitation, is high. The health plan has a fixed monthly prepayment for healthcare. If they can control or fix the costs for this service (capitation) the chance for success is much greater. At a minimum, negotiating a reduced reimbursement rate prior to the provision of the healthcare allows for the ability to project costs.

CLAIMS ADJUDICATION

The systems outlined above are complex. Having the prior authorization guidelines, contracts, fee schedules, etc. in place is not enough. Before the bills are paid, it is necessary to be sure that the rules are being followed and that the service was appropriate. Did the patient receive the service that was previously authorized? Claims adjudication is also the system that identifies fraud and abuse. Most claims are simple and can be paid promptly, but as many as 10 per cent need careful scrutiny before paying. Complex software has been written to screen claims and identify those that require evaluation or additional information.

The insurer will not pay all claims. The insurer may be secondary, and the primary insurer is responsible. Maybe the service was provided without required pre-certification. Maybe the service was inappropriate or unnecessary. Maybe the service was not a covered benefit, or was experimental. Any denied claims cause distress, and it is better if the member or provider knows that a claim will be denied before the service is given, but few people read their contracts.

The effectiveness of this process is high, but not as high as with capitation. If there is capitation, the numbers of claims are reduced or are for information only, because the payment was made up front. A claim still needs to be submitted so that the health plan will know what service has been provided.

IMPROVING QUALITY

Earlier in this chapter we said there were two reasons for managed care – controlling cost and improving quality of healthcare. It is normal for people to worry about cost the most, so it is a greater driving force. As costs are reduced as much as possible, quality then becomes more important. When premium rates are similar for various health plans, quality becomes the point of differentiation.

The cornerstone for improving quality is measurement. It is important to know what care is being provided and how it stacks up with predefined benchmarks. Measurements require data. Data requires systems that can capture information reliably. This information needs to be compared to a standard or benchmark. Benchmarks require longitudinal measurements over time as well as population. Until recently this has not been possible. Data collection in medicine is only very recent, and measuring outcomes is a new process.

Measuring process

Because the longitudinal data was not available to measure outcomes, the early quality measurements looked at the processes of providing care. Credentialling of providers is an excellent example. Before a physician or hospital is accepted into the health plan network of providers, the qualifications and track record are analysed. This is called credentialling. Confirmation of the medical school and residency training is the first step. Reports from the specialty board that has certified the physician are requested. In the US there is the National Practitioner Data Bank that records any restrictions on the licence or privileges of each physician. The malpractice claims history is also included.

Other processes that were measured were components of good healthcare. How long is the waiting time to get a routine appointment? How many expectant mothers had a prenatal visit in the first trimester? What percentage of diabetic patients have had a test for Haemoglobin A1-C? Measuring these processes does not assure quality, but is a weak indicator of the quality of care being provided. The National Committee on Quality Assurance (NCQA) developed a set of measurements of this type. This was called Health Plan Employers' Information and Data Set (HEDIS). This set of measures was then used to determine if a managed care organization was qualified for certification in quality. HEDIS has been revised and expanded annually for the past five years, but remains one of the best process measurements for quality. NCQA is trying to move progressively into outcomes measurements for the future.

Measuring outcomes

What happens to the patient is the *sine qua non* of healthcare quality. Does the patient live or die? Are there complications? How long is the patient off work? Is the patient able to take care of himself or herself following therapy? Is hospitalization required to manage the health problem? Is the health status of the patient improving or getting worse?

One outcome measured by NCQA is patient satisfaction. Granted, the patient may not be the most qualified judge of healthcare quality, but whether or not patients are satisfied with the care they are receiving is a measure of the quality of the health plan.

Outcome studies are also key to the development of process guidelines. If longitudinal outcomes are measured for large populations, the best practices can be established with enough reliability to reduce the variation of physician practice patterns. This has both quality and cost implications. For example, if treating Otitis Media with no antibiotic has the same outcome as that of using antibiotics, then elimination of antibiotics from the practice patterns of physicians saves money and eliminates the complications of using antibiotics.

Because more attention has been given to reducing the cost of healthcare than to improving the quality, quality measures are still in their infancy. Improved data systems will be a giant step to improved quality. Patient education through the Internet will describe best practices and force physician compliance. Using measurements such as life expectancy and hospitalization rates, there are indications that managed care has improved the quality of life of Americans.

HEALTHCARE 2000 – MANAGED CARE IN THE NEW MILLENNIUM

The only certain prediction in healthcare is that there will be change. The facts are that healthcare inflation has reached double-digit numbers. Providers and patients are not satisfied. Quality is talked about, but amazingly little is done about it, because it is seen as a costly move at a time with little profit available for its pursuit. Politicians see healthcare as a great campaign issue.

So what will healthcare look like in the new millennium? First, employers cannot continue to pay more for this benefit for employees. They will move to granting a fixed amount for this benefit, and let employees decide where and how to spend it. This puts more power into the hands of the employee, but will also mean more out-of-pocket expense for the consumer. Many HMOs will continue to survive as insurers, but their role will lessen, for they will be seen only as middlemen in the system, especially when direct contracts with providers prove to be cheaper. Many will not survive. Stockholders are not interested in companies that do not make a profit. The result will be more direct contracting between employees and providers, cutting out the middleman (insurers). The Medical Savings Account system that has failed in the 1990s may again become a more attractive option to many employees. The management of healthcare will be left to the consumer and the physician. These two are not skilled in management and the result will be increased healthcare inflation.

How will employees make informed decisions about where to spend their healthcare dollars? The increased availability of data will aid them in this decision. The performance ratings of insurers, as well as individual providers, will be readily available on the Internet. The history of individual clinicians and hospitals will become freely accessible. Ideally outcomes will be the key piece of information. Do the patients of one doctor or group of doctors live healthier lives and get their immunizations and screening tests regularly when compared to another? Patient satisfaction data is often meaningless because it is an emotional response, and will play a smaller role. Hopefully the doctor–patient relationship will again emerge as the key to quality healthcare.

When patients are paying the bill, there may be less demand for the hi-tech procedures or the use of high-cost drugs compared to generics. Employees are no longer going to be able to make demands for these products and procedures for the cost will come from their limited benefit or from their pockets. The physician's role changes from gatekeeper to counsellor. He or she will be able to make recommendations but the ultimate decision will be that of the consumer. Patients may not always make the wisest choice, but this will be the price to pay for the privilege of controlling one's healthcare.

How will this new system impact on the cost and quality of healthcare? If this system reduces the amount of the healthcare dollar going to stockholders and top executives, there will be a modest decrease in cost. If patients reduce their demand for high-tech procedures and costly pharmaceuticals, this will add to this cost reduction. On the other hand, if, in contracting with physicians and hospitals, they pay a higher fee than the HMOs had been able to negotiate, this will more than offset the cost savings. Employers will be delighted to have a fixed cost to their healthcare benefit. The same system may become attractive to Medicare, Medicaid and the Veteran Association's systems as well. Moreover, in the 1930s and 1940s, patients often failed to buy the prescribed medicines because of the cost. This pattern may emerge again. With more of the expense coming out of pocket, patients may take more responsibility for leading a healthy lifestyle in order to save money, but this has not been part of historical experience.

Without good data on outcomes, quality improvements will be challenging. If the data is available for physicians to know which therapies produce the best results, variability in practice may improve, which certainly would improve quality. If patients are able to select their healthcare delivery systems based upon supporting evidence of relative quality, providers will be required to provide quality care.

The collection of good data for outcomes measurements is costly. HMOs have found that information systems require more dollars each year. Provider groups have not been making the necessary investments. It will probably require government subsidization or tax relief to implement these data systems.

In summary, we started with a problem with healthcare inflation. This drove us to a new system of providing healthcare, called managed care. It was successful in reducing healthcare inflation but reduced subscriber freedom and options in the process. As a result new legislation and court rulings came about to try to force managed care to be all things for all people. The result was that HMOs were no longer able to manage the healthcare delivery systems or control healthcare inflation. Having gone full circle, it appears that a new paradigm will be necessary. Patients cannot have both cheap and all-encompassing healthcare. They will have to make the choices. Once they find that healthcare is costly, they will appeal to the government for relief. This may prompt a new impetus to universal health coverage.

NOTES AND REFERENCES

1 P. Starr (1984) *The Social Transformation of American Medicine*, p. 270. New York: Basic Books.
2 T.R. Mayer and G.G. Mayer (1985) HMOs: origins and development, *New England Journal of Medicine*, 312: 590–4.
3 Ibid.
4 Starr, op. cit., p. 305.
5 Starr, op. cit., p. 354.
6 Editorial (1992) California medicine, Part III, *The California Physician*, February: 30–5.
7 P. Kongstvedt (1996) *The Managed Health Care Handbook*, 3rd ed. Gaithersburg, MD: Aspen.
8 Editorial, op. cit.
9 L.O. Prager (1998) Evolution or Extinction: Doctors often not practicing what clinical guidelines preach, *Modern Healthcare*, 19 October.
10 An interview with Paul Ellwood Jr, MD Managed Care, November 1997.
11 Starr, op. cit., p. 12.
12 J. Eisenberg and S. Williams (1981) Cost containment and changing physicians' practice behavior, JAMA 246 (19): 2195–1.
13 J. Wennberg and A. Gittelsohn (1982) Variations in medical care among small areas, *Scientific American*, 254 (4): 120–34.
14 S. Schroeder (1987) Strategies for reducing medical costs by changing physicians' behavior, *International Journal of Technical Assessment in Health Care*, 3: 39–50.
15 *American Medical News*, 13 September 1999.
16 C.M. Mullahy (1998) *The Case Manager's Handbook*. Gaithersburg, MD: Aspen.

3

THE NHS MODERNIZATION AGENDA

David Cochrane

LABOUR AND AMERICAN MEDICINE

The aim of this chapter is to set out the New Labour health service modernization agenda and identify those elements which managed care experience and techniques can promote. In this context, it is somewhat ironic that Labour Party health policy since the Second World War has a recurrent theme of antagonism to most of the experience of the US healthcare system. Generations of Labour Party advisers mostly based at the London School of Economics (LSE) – from Richard Titmuss in the 1950s through Brian Abel-Smith in the 1960s and 1970s – created an intellectual tradition through the Fabian Society of antagonism to 'marketplace medicine' as inefficient, inequitable and divisive.

This tradition was challenged in the 1990s by another left-of-centre academic, also from the LSE, who had studied the work of the large staff model HMO Kaiser Permanente and found much to commend to his Fabian colleagues.[1] The influence of Howard Glennerster and a younger generation of LSE health policy experts chimed well with the political affinity between New Labour and the Clinton administration. The outcome was the New Labour government's new policy which (as we will argue) resonates with the influence of US managed care. Subsequently, Labour Secretaries of State for Health have held summit meetings with their American counterparts to explore common agendas.

But even Abel-Smith and Titmuss would probably feel relatively relaxed knowing that the fundamental objectives of the NHS are not challenged. Launched on a slogan of 'universalise' the best, the service had set off in 1948 in search of a four-sided Holy Grail:

- comprehensive services;
- consistent high quality;

- equity defined as resource allocation on criteria of need;
- largely free at the time of use or, at least, imposing no financial barriers to access.

From the moment it survived the first right-wing challenge in the 1950s, the NHS acquired a fifth aim of making effective use of its resources. Then in the 1970s and 1980s, in the wake of the growth of consumerism, it acquired a sixth, which is to be responsive to the views and experiences of service users. To complete the picture, we should draw out a seventh implicit objective which the NHS had gradually acquired, of promoting physical and mental health rather than simply responding to sickness. This first surfaced into formal policy in the preventive healthcare initiatives launched in the 1970s.

THE THATCHER REFORMS – LABOUR'S WORST FEARS CONFIRMED?

These objectives seemed to come under serious threat during the 1980s when right-wing policies had become mainstream in a dominant Conservative government. The *Guardian* newspaper obtained a leaked copy of a policy discussion document from within 10 Downing Street which reviewed options for ending the principle of universalism in British health policy and moving towards privatization. Public reaction was largely hostile, and the government felt obliged to distance itself from these ideas. However, the document created a climate of suspicion which was to surround the publication of the Thatcher government's health reforms in January 1988. Produced by a more centrist Tory Secretary of State, a widely considered and often self-proclaimed supporter of the NHS, the White Paper *Working for Patients*[2] and the supportive Working Papers which followed included several features borrowed from American managed care. Kenneth Clarke's political skill lay in placating the right wing by introducing market mechanisms into the NHS while preserving its overall integrity. However, suspicion about the government's longer term intentions remained and coloured responses to the reforms. Borrowing managed care ideas was seen as the first step towards the marketplace medicine which Labour had always opposed.

First, following consultation with Professor Alan Enthoven of Stanford University in California, a well-known proponent of managed care in the United States, the functions of providing and paying for healthcare under the NHS – both of which lay with district health authorities (DHAs) – were separated. Second, there would be a contractual arrangement between purchasers and providers. The role of the DHA would change radically from managing and delivering secondary care to assessing healthcare need and ensuring that appropriate services were purchased to meet that need – rather like the primary role of the health maintenance organization.

Secondary providers would become semi-independent 'self-governing' Trusts no longer managerially accountable to the DHA but directly to a new Management Executive within the Department of Health. Self-governing Trusts were to mirror private companies in three ways. They were to have boards of executive and non-executive directors – the latter being drawn from the business world. The initial proposals were that they would also be required to make an operating surplus. Third, through the mechanism of capital charging they were to pay for their capital assets through an annual revenue payment based on disposal value. Coming from a government committed to privatization of public enterprise, the proposals for NHS Trusts were bound to fuel suspicion. Accordingly they were attacked in the press by Robin Cook, the then Labour frontbench spokesman on health, as the first stage in a covert strategy to privatize British hospitals.

Also shadowing the private sector, there would be an 'internal market' in the NHS through which Trusts would compete for their businesses from new health authorities acting as purchasers and agree 'contracts'. Intended as a mechanism for introducing more precision into provider funding, contracting posed a number of immediate challenges to the NHS which was unused to precisely costing individual service programmes such as orthopaedics or general medicine. The process began with crude 'block contracts' which were simply service programmes for which an annual amount of money would be allocated against an indicative level of activity usually based on the recent trends. Contracting also gave rise to a flurry of management activity to develop baseline data for these processes. The procedures put in place were credited with a massive increase in process work and so-called 'transaction costs'.

One of the most radical departures contained in what became widely known as 'the reforms' was the GP fundholding scheme, an idea widely attributed to the economist Alan Maynard and inspired by primary care purchasing groups then developing in the US managed care sector. Up until the introduction of this policy the provision of secondary and primary care had been managerially and professionally separate. British doctors were in two distinct tribes – general practitioners (GPs) delivering primary care, and hospital doctors. The only point of professional interface was the local working relationships between GPs and consultants on referrals for elective hospital care. Moreover, whereas consultants were salaried employees – albeit many part-time – GPs had maintained their independent contractor status as a condition for participating in the NHS in the first place. They were paid on a capitation basis supplemented by a range of incentives and other supplementary payments which had been negotiated over the years under a system known as the 'red book'. GPs were also removed from mainstream NHS management. The Department of Health knew how much it spent on primary care and monitored GP numbers and staffing but otherwise had very little information on the clinical activity of GPs and no direct mechanisms for influencing it.

GP fundholding was a voluntary scheme for large practices with list sizes of around 10,000. They would be given directly devolved budgets initially to purchase a limited range of acute elective care. These budgets would be top-sliced from the allocations to DHAs on a formula basis. As an inducement to participation, fundholders were offered grants for management costs and computing, and to incentivize efficient use of hospital services they were allowed to retain any surpluses provided they were invested in services for patients. Although this measure was supposed to avoid any question of personal gain for fundholders, those in the first wave, at least, managed to retain substantial funds, much of which they invested in practice premises which, of course, usually belonged to the partners practising there.

The fundholding scheme began to turn the tide of Labour opinion in favour of GP purchasing and US managed care. First, it was evaluated by Howard Glennerster whose findings appeared just before the 1992 general election and were largely favourable. In the subsequent book, he also favourably reviewed the managed care model in Kaiser Permanente, the large staff model health maintenance organization in the US.[3] These findings strengthened the position of a number of prominent fundholders who were also Labour Party members or supporters.

Having won the 1992 election, the Conservatives took the findings of this evaluation as a green light to extend fundholding in scope and coverage. In 1994 the government announced its intention to promote a 'primary care-led' NHS with two developments.[4] The range of services to be purchased directly by GPs was extended through 'community fundholding' to include community nursing services and mental health. Second, there were two forms of fundholding which mirrored primary care purchasing groups in the US managed care sector. An initial four pilot 'total fundholding' projects were established with the scope to purchase all secondary services with the exception of the most expensive – usually tertiary – services. This was extended to 53 by 1996 with a second wave of 34 planned for the following year. Set up for three years, they were formally sub-committees of the health authority which retained responsibility for their resource use. Their population bases varied from individual group practices with list sizes of around 10,000 to groups of practices covering over 80,000 people. Total first-wave coverage at 1.75 million remained relatively marginal within the NHS as a whole.

At the same time, individual fundholders grouped into 'multi-funds' rather like Independent Practitioners' Associations in the US. One of the largest in Birmingham covered nearly half the city. These multi-funds had two advantages:

- They were able to share administration and transaction costs, often appointing Chief Executives and support staff.
- Although they paid full costs as prices to hospitals, the real costs to the provider Trusts of this elective business were usually at the margins

of less than 50 per cent. So as organizations with large purchasing budgets, multi-funds had considerable negotiating strength.

By changing referral patterns, fundholders could switch revenue between NHS providers and even use the private sector. This was not simply a threat to the power of acute Trusts in the NHS; it also divided primary care. Many non-fundholding GPs believed that this negotiating power generated a two-tier service, with NHS Trusts giving patients in fundholding practices priority of access. Fundholders for their part argued that they were improving responsiveness of secondary care to primary care for all GPs, and were in turn supported when the Audit Commission investigated this issue and found little evidence of a two-tier service. However, opponents of fundholding within the medical profession also contended that holding cash-limited budgets for patient care interfered with the relationship between doctor and patient. Concerns about the financial implications could influence a GP's choice of treatment option. This was something of a spurious argument given that GPs had always played a gatekeeper role and modified their referral patterns in relation to resource availability. As more service supply became available, so GPs would lower their referral thresholds and refer more patients from their pool of unmet need. This was one factor driving the persistently rising demand in the NHS as more supply came on stream.

On the positive side, fundholding brought primary care into mainstream NHS planning and management activity for the first time. It certainly shifted the balance of power and influence within medicine towards GPs and away from the hitherto much more powerful hospital doctors. GP fundholders had some incentive to scrutinize hospital utilization and contain patient care with the practice. There is evidence from some Total Purchasing Pilots of reduced hospital referrals and admissions. Claims that they reduced overall costs and improved patient care remain controversial. Indeed, the management and transaction costs may have been higher.[5]

By the time the Conservatives lost the 1997 election, about 60 per cent of GPs had joined the scheme. Many others remained implacably opposed. To engage them in the contracting process nonetheless, some district health authorities encouraged them to form commissioning consortia. GP commissioners did not hold the budgets but worked in collaboration with the health authority on purchasing committees. This model was particularly associated with Nottingham Health Authority in the Trent Region.

Overall, though, the Tory Party NHS reforms suffered from built-in fragmentation and inefficiencies in service delivery, funding and administration. Although charged with assessing health need and commissioning care, health authorities had substantial elements of secondary care expenditure removed from their control and vested with fundholding. Moreover, they could not directly influence service delivery in primary care itself, where most healthcare activity took place. For their part, NHS Trusts were obliged to work with a multitude of small organizations often making differing demands for marginal amounts of business. Transaction costs or the management time and effort required were high. Moreover, the internal market existed in name only. Health authorities remained staunchly loyal to local Trusts. Private sector providers complained that they were never allowed to compete freely with NHS Trusts – particularly in London where some private hospitals were offering elective surgical procedures at lower cost than some of the NHS hospitals. Finally, annual NHS contracts militated against strategic planning over three to five years – the timescale for new capital developments or professional staff training.

To their credit, however, the reforms injected a new sense of dynamism and introduced long overdue business and financial acumen into the NHS. They also shifted the balance of power between managers and the professions in the Service. Moreover, by separating commissioning and providing and establishing primary care purchasing the Tory reforms provided a framework for refinement and development for the next government.

NEW LABOUR – MODERNIZATION AND MANAGED CARE

New Labour swept into power with a number of clear commitments. These were designed to restore the objectives and integrity of the NHS rather than dismantle all the Tory reforms. Whatever the objective truth about fundholding, perceptions and beliefs are powerful forces in politics. The Labour Party was committed to a primary care-led NHS but also to abolishing fundholding as inefficient and divisive. Labour was also committed to abolishing the internal market and replacing it with a more collaborative approach which facilitated more coherent strategic planning in health authorities and Trusts. Previously hostile to Trusts, it changed its position and decided to retain the purchaser/provider distinction. The aim would be to provide a modern NHS true to its founding principles which was 'once more the envy of the world'.[6]

The NHS was to find out with great speed what these broad aims were to mean in practice when the White Paper *The NHS: Modern, Dependable* appeared in December 1997, barely eight months into government. A resonant image of a 1948 public information leaflet announcing the service's original launch set the tone for the document's restatement of NHS objectives, with new variations in emphasis, set out in six principles:

- *Universality*: A national service giving fair access to consistently high quality services.
- *Collaboration and patient focus*: Working in *partnership* across organizational boundaries with the patient at the centre of the process.
- *Efficiency*: Maximizing each pound spent on patient care through rigorous performance management.

- *Localness*: Local doctors and nurses in the driving seat on service delivery, seemingly to herald a shift from managerialism.
- *Quality* would drive all decisions and guarantee excellence to patients.
- *Public confidence* would be restored by accountability, openness and responsiveness to consumers.

INTEGRATED CARE AND PLANNING

The approach to the Tory reforms was to 'keep what works and discard what failed'. The proposals were replete with concepts and terminology from managed care. First, the internal market ceded to a concept called 'integrated care' which is never really defined in the White Paper but has since been widely interpreted as integrated planning, resource deployment and care delivery. Integrated care is to be coordinated through a new health authority strategic planning mechanism called the Health Improvement Programme (HIMP). Prior to the 1991 reforms, health authorities had produced five-yearly strategic plans which largely informed capital investment in the secondary sector. This process had lapsed and been replaced by one-year business plans and ad hoc business cases for individual capital schemes, both vested with Trusts. Health Improvement Programmes revived and extended strategic planning in the NHS. They are designed to inform service investment decisions not simply on capital but also staffing and information technology. However, they extend the old model by beginning with an assessment of healthcare need, and incorporating primary care and local authority health-related services. Also new, the service plans in the HIMP are meant to be clinically informed, evidence-based, and patient-focused.

The HIMP is a central component of a strengthened health authority function within a more centralist and directive model of government healthcare policy making. First, the DHA role in the planning process in NHS Trusts has been significantly strengthened. DHAs are to decide on the range and location of healthcare services for residents. They were given reserve powers to ensure that capital and consultant staffing investment decisions are consistent with the HIMP. Some prominent DHAs are now extending this to all staff groups. DHAs also acquired a strengthened performance management function to determine local standards and targets in quality and efficiency 'in the light of national priorities and guidance', and ensure delivery.[7] DHAs also lost that area of activity which had preoccupied them managerially for the previous eight years or so, namely commissioning. In contrast, functions such as planning and performance monitoring had been deprioritized, leaving DHAs with a major organizational development agenda to reacquire these skills.

Moreover, any doubts that a new era of health planning had dawned in the UK were swept aside in July 2000 with the publication of the first NHS National Plan – which is reviewed below.[8]

PRIMARY CARE PURCHASING

The commissioning function devolves to Primary Care Groups (PCGs) – again a term borrowed from managed care. The White Paper is a ten-year programme. In the White Paper, a series of stages of development was envisaged for PCGs beginning with the 'Trent' GP commissioning model through to Stage 4 where they become Primary Care Trusts (PCTs) with full budgetary management for commissioning and incorporating the management of local community services. The government has been encouraging more rapid movement from PCG to PCT, with the first wavers established in April 2000. PCTs bring together a number of organizational components from the plurality of GP purchasing organizations set up by the previous government.

- They are locality-based on populations of around 100,000.
- They hold the budget for all secondary care services like Total Purchasing Pilots (TPPs).
- Pursuing the principle of integrated delivery, as Trusts they manage all community nursing such as health visiting and district nursing. This had been a proposal from fundholders looking for more influence over service delivery from these staff groups. However, PCGs have community nurses appointed to Boards. It has also followed that PCTs should acquire the management of the national network of community hospitals previously managed within community Trusts, so that an average Trust is likely to have a budget of around £100 million.
- PCGs and PCTs are also responsible for local needs assessment and service planning.
- Unlike other GP purchasing organizations whose GP membership was largely self-selecting, PCGs are organized geographically incorporating fundholders and non-fundholders alike.
- Finally, and a refinement introduced by the 2000 National Plan, Trusts will able to apply for Level 5 status which will empower them to commission health-related social care services particularly in mental health and care of the elderly.

This is a major organizational development agenda. PCGs with large complements of non-fundholders are requiring a longer lead-in time to move to Trust status. There is also a continued heated debate as to whether GPs would eventually become employees of PCTs, and some may well opt for this by expanding the principles of Personal Medical Services (PMS) pilots. These organizations bring the various funding streams of primary and community health care services into a unified budgetary system. In some pilots, all members of the primary care team, medical and nursing, work on similar contractual arrangements with some GPs opting for salaried status. They have thus abandoned the traditional model of independent contractors with remuneration determined by the national 'red book'. The government has (for the time being at least) accepted that those who wish to retain their independent practitioner status may do so, although PMS is to be encouraged for more wide-scale adaptation as a model within the NHS. Hence as providers of secondary and community care and purchasers of secondary care, PCTs parallel the Independent Practitioner Associations in managed care, albeit within a public accountability framework.

For an organization which has experienced so much structural change in the last ten years, it is difficult for anyone in the NHS to see any set of proposals as static. PCTs are being created on a large-area basis and will assume 75 per cent of NHS expenditure in their commissioning budgets. Along with the enlarged health authorities, they may eventually report to regional government through new decentralized authorities.

QUALITY AND CLINICAL GOVERNANCE

Consistent high quality has been an implicit but elusive objective in the NHS since 1948. Equality of access on clinical need has always been a central objective. Nevertheless, the service has been characterized by inequalities of access, levels of service utilization, quality of care delivery and health outcomes as measured by results of treatment and indicators of health status by age, sex, ethnicity and socio-economic group. Moreover, although management activity devoted to quality assurance is well established at local level in the NHS, it has tended to exist as a secondary sphere of activity alongside financial control and driving more volume of activity through the system. Therefore, the most radical and groundbreaking element of New Labour's modernization programme is the commitment given to nationally consistent quality which seeks to end inequalities in access, delivery and outcomes of healthcare interventions. For the first time, the NHS has a national quality strategy, set out in the document *A First-Class Service*, to integrate quality management as a prime objective neatly summed up in the Secretary of State's phrase that 'quality and efficiency are both sides of the same coin'.[9]

The strategy divides into three logical components:

- setting quality standards;
- mechanisms for assuring implementation;
- structures and processes for monitoring and audit.

The national structures and processes put into place to implement it are again rather like those in the United States that have developed to monitor and audit quality in the managed care sector.

Setting quality standards

Two mechanisms will set standards. First, a new body, the National Institute for Clinical Excellence (NICE), has been established as a Special

Health Authority reporting directly to the Secretary of State. Its role is to appraise 30 to 50 new and existing clinical interventions against the evidence base. In so doing it acts as a clearing house for the various tools of evidence-based medicine, such as clinical guidelines, prescribing formularies, audit methodologies and lifelong learning for clinical staff to keep up-to-date with new practice. For new interventions the Department of Health undertakes 'horizon scanning' to identify new clinical treatments and procedures, including costly items such as new medications, and submit them to NICE a year before they are due for launch. Commercial companies marketing new drugs or equipment to the NHS will also be required to submit them alongside their supporting evidence. NICE will commission multi-professional appraisal groups to review the submissions on grounds of clinical and cost-effectiveness.

NICE has already begun to issue guidance for launch and scope of use in the NHS, in some cases suggesting that further research is required after launch, or withholding approval pending further research and evidence. Guidance on uptake will ensure that interventions with good evidence of effectiveness will be actively promoted, and those found to be effective only in particular circumstances are employed selectively. This guidance is not intended to be binding on a health authority or on PCG commissioning services; however, it will be difficult for these organizations, faced with so many competing demands, to sanction expenditure on expensive new treatments which NICE does not support. Given the large grey areas in evidence-based medicine, there may have to be more latitude if NICE finds evidence is insufficient to give a clear judgement.

For existing interventions, NICE identifies 'unjustified variations in use and uncertainty about clinical and cost-effectiveness'.[10] Since NICE was launched there has been some public controversy over its role in relation to expensive new drug treatments for which the evidence is less than clear but which are nonetheless promoted by special patient interest groups. However, its authority to prescribe on currently available services could well prove the most contentious in practice. Large elements of service delivered in the NHS have evolved in response to problems or crises which arose several years ago, or as a result of professional staff who provide them moving into new spheres of activity usually without any objective assessment of the supportive evidence base, cost-effectiveness or competencies required.

To date it has fallen to the Audit Commission and National Audit Office to assess the cost-effectiveness of existing services. Although always clinically informed, the recommendations of the Audit Commission can be readily dismissed by hostile clinical staff on the grounds that as an organization it is finance-driven. Appraisal on grounds of clinical and cost-effectiveness through an agency such as NICE is a subtle but powerful shift of emphasis. Its findings will be more difficult to dismiss, with the risk that it could run headlong into particular interests within the

NHS should it conclude that interventions they provide are of doubtful clinical value or could be provided more effectively and/or more cheaply in other ways. Advisedly, therefore, NICE does not have powers to monitor implementation, taking it out of the direct line of any fire and mitigating any temptation to temper its recommendations in the face of local political concerns or short-term operational constraints.

NICE is not alone in its task. At a broader service level, the government is producing a series of National Service Frameworks (NSFs). These were developed by expert reference groups drawing on the views of stakeholders such as professionals, service managers, users, carers and partner agencies such as social services and voluntary organizations. The programme for the first two years incorporates quite specific disease management fields such as ischaemic heart disease and diabetes, and quite broad client groups such as mental health and older people.

The content of NSFs set out in the quality strategy includes:

- the evidence-base covering needs assessment; current performance, including significant gaps and pressures; and evidence of clinical and cost-effectiveness;
- national standards and timescales for delivery;
- key interventions recommended and associated costs;
- a performance management framework based on benchmarking techniques.

The first NSFs – cancer, ischaemic heart disease (IHD) and mental health – demonstrate a priority to set national standards and timescales, key interventions and some performance measures. These range from reducing general population risk factors such as smoking and lack of exercise, requirements for services in primary and secondary care to manage established disease and standards for delivery, right through to specific clinical investigative and treatment procedures (such as drug therapies for symptom relief) where the NSFs overlap with the work of NICE and require coordination in timing and content. Other recommendations are aimed at ensuring that there are good clinical administrative procedures in place such as readily available, retrievable and comprehensive patients' notes, a patient register, and accessible clinical audit data no more than 12 months old. Patient management within and between each level of service will be based on agreed local protocols and guidelines, although a lead-in time of over two years is allowed for this work. The National Service Framework for mental health also requires particular services such as assertive outreach teams to be put into place.

Mechanisms for delivery

There are three delivery mechanisms for the quality strategy. First, since quality is a primary objective of healthcare planning and delivery, the mechanism for achieving it needs to be integral to the management process itself. *Clinical governance* is aimed at providing a framework through which the NHS can become accountable for quality and can create an environment in which 'excellence in clinical care will flourish'.[11]

For the first time, statutory accountability for quality is vested with chief executives of NHS Trusts, in the same way as financial control. Each Trust has a formal structure, such as a clinical governance committee and lead clinician, and reporting mechanisms including an annual clinical governance report. This is tasked to ensure full participation by all doctors, compliance with standards set by NICE and the NSFs, the routine application of evidence-based practice and monitoring mechanisms. This also incorporates systems for identifying and rectifying poor performance at an early stage through critical incidence reporting, monitoring complaints and support to staff raising concerns about the conduct and performance of colleagues.

The second mechanism is designed to ensure public confidence that clinicians are keeping pace with advances in treatment. Lifelong learning through continuous professional development to ensure that the knowledge and skills of clinicians keeps pace with advances in their fields is integrated with the changing direction of service delivery, and not least with the development needs of themselves as individuals. Third, the professions are expected to continue to regulate themselves. However, self-regulation is now subject to greater public scrutiny and public accountability for standards set nationally.

Monitoring

There are three monitoring mechanisms, two external to the service and one internal. First, the Commission for Health Improvement (CHI), a new statutory body 'at arm's length from the government' but accountable directly to the Secretary of State, has powers of scrutiny and inspection. Its core functions include:

- at national level providing leadership on the principles of clinical governance and conducting service reviews to monitor implementation of NSFs;
- at local level to visit NHS Trusts every three to four years and scrutinize their clinical governance arrangements and progress in implementing standards set by NICE and the NSFs;
- similarly auditing the work of health authorities and PCGs to promote and encourage clinical governance principles in Trusts or elsewhere in primary care;
- investigating specific problems perhaps identified by the Regional Office or a Primary Care Group where NHS Trusts are failing to deliver on aspects of the Health Improvement Programme;
- eventually to assume responsibility for the conduct of special inquiries into serious incidents in the NHS.

There is thus a direct sanction on Trusts. However, CHI intends to generate a climate of change by producing reports for the Trust shared with health authorities and PCGs and summarized for the public. Implementation of recommendations will be followed up through the established performance monitoring mechanisms, although CHI could be involved in this process if agreed by the health authority or Regional Office. In cases of serious default in meeting statutory duties, or where confidence in the quality of local services has been compromised, the Secretary of State has powers to remove the Board altogether.

Second, the external mechanism is a new National Survey of Patient and User Experience. The aim here is to produce an independent data set on patients' experience. It is intended to inform local service managers and clinicians of the views of users and carers, to provide benchmarks on patient experiences showing scope for improvement and to demonstrate to users and carers that their views are important. The data set will be incorporated into the national performance framework and consistently poor results may trigger involvement of the CHI.

Third, the National Performance Assessment Framework is the major internal monitoring mechanism. Rather like HEDIS in the US, it comprises a data set across a range of significant fields. This initiative revives a concept which was discredited in the NHS in the late 1980s – performance indicators. However, it extends beyond quality issues to encompass the major principles of the NHS set out in the White Paper and incorporates measures of resource efficiency. Benchmarking, a management technique developed in the US corporate sector, will be a central mechanism for performance management.

THE MAJOR CHALLENGES FACING THE NHS

This policy has been developed in the face of a number of major challenges which face the NHS in the next millennium. We highlight three below:

- the impact of demographic change on the need for the most costly part of the NHS network – acute hospital care;
- relatedly, the management of chronic disease in the UK;
- comparative under-investment;
- fuelling further reform through consumer empowerment.

The acute hospital sector – demographics and access

The population of the UK is projected to increase from 57.6 million at the time of the last national census to just over 60 million by the year 2005. More significantly, the age structure is changing. Taking figures for England alone, 16 per cent were people aged over 65 – a proportion which will remain stable although their numbers will increase. The over-75s are projected to increase from 7 per cent to 7.6 per cent and over-85s from 1.6 per cent to 2.2 per cent.

There has been much debate about the impact of this demographic change on health care utilization. When the OPCS last surveyed primary care, people aged over 65 accounted for 21 per cent of GP encounters, significantly greater than their proportion of the population. However, the use of hospital services by this group is substantially disproportionate to their presence in the population as a whole. By way of illustration, in 1997/8 there were 9.75 million episodes of activity – admissions and day cases, but excluding births – in the general and acute sector. Thirty-six per cent of these people were over 65 and 22 per cent over 75 years of age. Just over 4.2 million of this total acute activity were emergency admissions. Of these 44 per cent were aged over 65 and 28 per cent aged over 75.

As well as being the largest group in admissions, elderly people stay in hospital longer. Again in 1997/8 all acute admissions occupied 1.1 million beds. People aged over 65 accounted for over 64 per cent and people aged over 75 44 per cent of this figure. The skewed utilization by the elderly of emergency acute hospital beds is still greater. Emergency admissions accounted for 64 per cent of all acute beds, with 68 per cent of emergency beds occupied by people aged over 65 and 49 per cent by people aged over 75.[12] This over-representation of elderly people in acute hospital utilization and bed use has increased significantly since we last reviewed it about four years ago.[13]

This reflects the fact that utilization of acute hospital services is increasing faster among people aged over 65 than in the general population both for all services and, particularly, emergency admissions. Between 1992/3 and 1997/8 total acute episodes increased by 25 per cent or about 3 per cent per year. The number of admissions among elderly people increased by 42 per cent or over 5 per cent per year. All emergency admissions went up by 27 per cent or about 3.5 per cent per year. Those of people aged over 65 increased by 37 per cent or 4.6 per cent per year.

One thing is certain, however: if we continue to manage current acute sector workload, the elderly will require increased bed numbers. The American experience of utilization management is instructive here. The acute hospital admission rate (defined as hospital spells) of people aged over 65 in England in 1997/8 was 277 per 1000 in the population.[14] An equivalent figure from US integrated delivery systems with utilization management techniques in place is 204 per 1000 (including acute hospitals, skilled nursing and other intermediate care facilities). This compares with 320 per 1000 in American health systems with no utilization management processes in place.[15]

There is a direct trade-off in hospital expenditure between emergency and elective care. Without more proactive management of emergency workload to hospital, and in the absence of a substantial injection of additional resources into the acute sector, emergency admissions will continue to constrain access to elective programmes thus perpetuating waiting list problems.

Severe chronic disease management in elderly people

One of the major causes of emergency admission to hospital is an acute exacerbation or complications of a severe chronic disease. The recent White Paper, *Saving Lives, Our Healthier Nation*[16] singled out ischaemic heart disease and stroke, where the UK has high mortality rates compared to other European Union countries, and accidental falls in the elderly. However, other chronic disease such as chronic obstructive pulmonary disease, and complications due to undetected or untreated diabetes, also figure highly in analyses of emergency admissions to hospital. Moreover, it has been estimated that schizophrenia gives rise to 60 per cent of mental health hospital admissions and bed utilization.

Improving the management of these conditions through primary and secondary prevention is a major agenda for the NHS into the next century. Chronic disease management requires integrated care strategies designed around the evidence base supported by protocols and care pathways linking primary and secondary care services. Success is dependent on patient compliance, collaboration and empowerment in the clinical management process.

There is, however, a wider user empowerment agenda which is reviewed in relation to the NHS Plan. We first address the under-investment issue.

From under-investment to resource bonanza

The NHS entered its second millennium with some of its more influential commentators crying crisis. With the UK population hit by a potent flu virus, accident and emergency departments were reportedly besieged mostly by elderly people requiring admission for chest infections, pneumonia, or simply because their general health status was so poor that a bout of flu put them at significant risk. The Chief Medical Officer declared an official flu epidemic (although the incidence was nowhere near the level required) and thereby merely fanned a smouldering suspicion in the media that the NHS was unable to cope. The New Labour government, modern guardian of Aneurin Bevan's great legacy, came under further pressure when a peer from its own side, also a celebrated doctor, demanded additional funding for the NHS from his office in a specialist London Teaching Hospital. He declared that more money was essential to deal with the 'shortage of acute beds' which he claimed had been made apparent both by the flu 'epidemic' and the continued problem of growing waiting lists which in June 1999 had showed 1.3 million people waiting for elective surgery. The Health Secretary announced yet another delay in the publication of a report from the Department of Health's

Chief Economist on the current and future demand for acute beds which had originally been scheduled for publication in September.

The government's senior medical critic was obliged to swallow a mandatory breakfast served up by the PM's Press Secretary, after which he felt inclined to qualify his earlier statement. But the damage was done. Journalists were already on the scent and accordingly plastered the media with case after case of people whose elective surgery procedures had been cancelled at short notice, sometimes after they had been admitted, fasted and even given pre-operative medication. All in all, the NHS seemed to be in the grip of a utilization crisis which the government appeared powerless to address.

According to the conventional wisdom, encouraged by high-profile interventions by leading healthcare commentators, the supply problems in the NHS were due to insufficient resources. Hence the 'crisis' in acute hospital utilization has been directly linked to the level of gross domestic product (GDP) which the UK devotes to healthcare expenditure. Since the case for utilization management rests on the need to make most effective use of any level of expenditure, we begin with a review of the topical debate of the adequacy or otherwise of current levels in the UK.

When the NHS was founded in 1948, the country was devoting just over 4 per cent of GDP to healthcare. This had risen to 5.5 per cent by the late 1970s and around 7 per cent when Appleby and Ham reviewed evidence from the OECD in the early 1990s.[17] This latter figure compared to an average of 8 per cent across the 23 countries and ranked Britain a lowly 17th. At that time, the OECD average was inflated by countries such as the US (spending 14 per cent) and Canada and Germany (around 10 per cent), all of whom have been endeavouring to constrain growth in healthcare expenditure recently. In the United States, for example, annual growth rates have fallen from 12 per cent in the heady days of the early 1990s to under 4 per cent in 1998, with managed care taking much of the credit (see Chapter 2).

However, the fact that the UK continues to lag behind the OECD average adds weight to the case that healthcare in the UK is underfunded; hence the waiting lists, inequity of access and, not least, the claimed bed shortages. In the mid-1990s, some commentators argued that the persistence of supply problems required that the NHS should abandon its objectives of comprehensive cover and equity in favour of some kind of formalized and officially sanctioned rationing system. Others called for the funding of the NHS to be supplemented by additional sources of revenue such as private health insurance and/or additional charges.[18]

When we reviewed this issue in 1996,[19] we argued that it was impossible to prove or disprove objectively whether the NHS was underfunded until it improved its current rudimentary understanding of the relationship between healthcare need, service utilization and costs. Nevertheless, it seemed clear at that time that whatever the objective case, the political pressure engendered by public belief and perceptions of underfunding was likely to continue to fuel real growth in the proportion of British GDP devoted to the NHS. Indeed, one of the Prime Minister's first responses to the winter 2000 so-called crisis was to state an aspiration to increase NHS expenditure as a proportion of GDP so that the UK might catch up with its European partners in the next five years. Given that GDP was projected to expand by well over 2 per cent per year over the same period, this would prove an expensive aspiration to fulfil, and therefore one which one would have expected to have pleased the healthcare community. In contrast, New Labour was to learn how sharper than a serpent's tooth it is to have a thankless child.

The PM's claim that the European average spend was 8 per cent was greeted by a chorus of criticism led by prominent health economists who formed an orderly queue to be interviewed on TV seated in front of computer screens. They argued that 8 per cent was simply an average of each country's net average spend and that if population weighting was used, the impact of the larger, higher spending countries such as Germany took the real average to over 9 per cent. Of course, not only does this reflect a certain tendency of the NHS never to be satisfied however much money is thrown at it, but it also warns us to be wary of health economists. As noted earlier, the higher European spenders are persuaded they are spending too much of their GDP on healthcare and, in any case, not one of the PM's critics had ever answered the critical question of whether 7 per cent, 8 per cent or 9 per cent is a sufficient, adequate or excessive level of spend to deliver a quality, comprehensive service.

Whatever European average is used, this PM's aspiration was always likely to prove an expensive one to realize. Even so, there was a degree of surprise across the NHS when the Chancellor of the Exchequer responded to the calls for greater funding by allocating nearly 30 per cent of real growth to the service over the four years from 2000/1 which would bring the spending in the UK to 7.7 per cent of projected GDP by 2004. This will be the year before the Prime Minister's target year of 2005 for 8 per cent, and is also likely to be the year before an election, allowing the prospect for his aspiration to be fulfilled early in any third Labour term. Meanwhile there was a political cost for Labour as other social programmes were deprioritized. With inflation low, the state pension increased by a measly 75p per week and the government's rapid decline in poll ratings over the summer of 2000 showed what pensioners thought about it.

What to spend it on? – The National Plan

Having promised the NHS this unprecedented real growth, the government rightly wanted to set clear targets for the NHS to deliver. The first NHS Plan[20] was published in July 2000. In order to convey a sense of national consensus, the Plan was signed by a slightly perplexing selection of interest groups including the NHS staff representatives of the

British Medical Association (BMA), Royal College of Nursing (RCN) and Unison, and a range of healthcare user lobbies and healthcare managers' associations. The list is as intriguing for its omissions as its inclusions.

The Plan restates the core principles of the NHS rehearsed by the White Paper within an expanded list of ten. Added to the previous list there is:

- services shaped around the needs and preferences of patients and carers;
- supporting and valuing staff;
- respect for patient confidentiality and providing open access to information on services and performance.

There is one conspicuous exclusion in that any reference to cost-effectiveness or value for money is omitted, perhaps in the search for the much-vaunted consensus or perhaps in the belief that the additional resources allocated meant that concern with such issues was no longer justified.

Leaving that aside, the Plan launches a radical and challenging attack on complacency in British healthcare with the identification of eight national fault lines:

- lack of national standards leading to wide variations in access and performance;
- demarcations between professional staff leading to delays, confusion and even inappropriate patient care;
- no clear strategic incentives, with failure often rewarded and success penalized;
- barriers to access such as inappropriate use of acute hospital beds and failure to use spare capacity in the private sector;
- lack of adequate performance data or assessment;
- over-centralization – which is perhaps ironic given the centralism implicit in nationally set targets and monitoring mechanisms which the government have reintroduced;
- disempowered patients – a brave and honest critique which as we argue in this book the Plan does little to address;
- underinvestment – which in contrast is resolutely addressed by the Plan.

The Plan draws together existing policies such as the three published National Service Frameworks (on cancer, coronary heart disease and mental health) and foreshadows the fourth on care of the elderly due for publication at the time of writing. It goes on to set some highly specific service delivery objectives for the NHS not just in relation to these programmes but in other areas. Selectively, these include reducing waiting times for outpatient referrals to five weeks and for elective surgery to the target of no more than six months by 2005 – particularly uninspiring if compared with publicly-funded managed care in the US or the performance of the better European systems. To be fair to the government, this seems to have been a compromise, and a more internationally comparable target of only three months is set for 2008. To facilitate the six-month target acute trusts are set targets of 75 per cent for the proportion of procedures undertaken on an ambulatory basis which is also conservative compared with over 80 per cent common in US managed care and already being achieved in some British acute hospitals.

As a result of the consultation on the National Bed Inquiry published in January 2000, acute bed levels are to be increased by a total of 2100, some adding to critical care provision. Meanwhile intermediate care beds will increase by 5000 including reuse of surplus capacity in private sector nursing homes. Additional bed provision will be integral to an ambitious and long-overdue modernization of the NHS capital stock and equipment including premises in primary care. The Plan also invests heavily in the quantity and quality of NHS staff. NHS professional staffing will increase by 35,000 or about 4 per cent, with a disproportionate growth of 30 per cent in consultant numbers to move towards a consultant-led service and bring the UK closer to European averages on doctors per head of population. More radically, the Plan challenges existing professional boundaries and demarcations which limit staff potential and cause delay and duplication for patients and lack of flexibility in workforce deployment.

Lastly, the Plan makes much of a new patient advocacy service to be built into the management structure of NHS Trusts as a mechanism for patient empowerment alongside other measures to survey patients' views and strengthen choice. It is perhaps one of the less convincing sections of the document, particularly disappointing when set alongside the conclusions of Chapter 3 of the Plan. This purports to review the arguments for alternative funding mechanisms for public healthcare in the UK. One of these is social insurance which is not only the predominant model in Western Europe but also the basis of the US Medicare programme. The alternative models are dismissed on the grounds that they fail to meet the key criteria of efficiency and equity. The ensuing argument is fundamentally flawed when applied to social insurance. First, the presumption that the NHS is efficient is open to challenge. Second, the Plan's own critique of the current service provides powerful evidence that equity is far from guaranteed under the present NHS system.

From a government with an ostensible commitment to radicalism the omission of consumer choice and empowerment as criteria for evaluation is disappointing. Labour remains hostile to social insurance because, as we have seen, it has been associated in the minds of the party's health policy advisers with commercialized medicine. However, the principles of the NHS would be simply preserved by guaranteeing cover to all citizens thus ensuring equitable access. In marked contrast to the tentative proposals in the Plan, a social insurance scheme in which the resources followed patient choice would offer a new phase of radicalism with patients truly empowered to make real and meaningful choices. Administrative costs might be higher, but could be offset by savings arising out of process re-engineering and information technology, which the Plan firmly

Elements of managed care	Currently in place	Partially in place or in current policy
Single payer system	▩	
Primary care base – provider	▩	
Primary care base – purchaser		▩
Integrated quality strategy		▩
Integrated prevention strategy		▩
Integrated delivery systems		▩
Utilization management		▩
Performance management framework		▩
Consumer empowerment		
Incentives aligned		

Figure 3.1   Is the NHS a managed care system?

advocates. A social insurance scheme would also be consistent with convergence within the European Union. Hence closing off the option for the future, as the Plan's Chapter 3 does, seems like an opportunity missed.

IS THE NHS ALREADY A MANAGED CARE SYSTEM?

Some leading commentators also argued that the NHS 'already had the major elements of a managed care system'.[21] We would dispute this view. Taking our optimum model of managed care from Chapter 1 we can see in Figure 3.1 to what extent the NHS has the major elements either in place or not within policy in the course of implementation over the next decade. The diagram is illustrative of the extent to which the New Labour policy takes the NHS closer towards our optimum model developed in Chapter 1. Two key elements are indeed in place – the single payer system and the provider base in primary care. A further seven are objectives of the new policy.

HOW CAN MANAGED CARE FURTHER THIS MODERNIZATION AGENDA?

Since the policy is taking the NHS closer to a managed care model, it follows that managed care techniques should facilitate implementation of the policy. We have therefore focused this book on the use of managed care techniques in the key following areas of NHS modernization:

- improving quality through disease management and evidence-based medicine;
- utilization management to improve both quality and resource use and extend access in primary, intermediate and acute in-patient care;
- case management to address key healthcare quality and resource challenges posed by an ageing population;
- the agenda for primary care;
- managed care and mental health to deliver the requirements of the National Service Framework;
- the use of benchmarking in healthcare performance management;
- modernizing the workforce to improve quality and supply;
- consumer empowerment to open up a new phase of modernization and reform for a future government of whatever political persuasion.

This leaves one area unexplored and that is the alignment of incentives with strategic objectives. It is a key component of any managed care system and, as highlighted by the National Plan, not always a feature of current NHS decision making. However, the move to Primary Care Trusts with budgets to commission secondary and social care creates a huge opportunity for the type of risk sharing and pooling of savings described by Robert Larsen in Chapter 2. If more clinically inspired, integrated healthcare management can generate savings, particularly in the secondary hospital sectors, some pooling system will be required so that all parties gain from the process. Otherwise, naturally protective of their budgets, the hospitals will frustrate shifts in resource deployment. It will therefore be a matter for PCTs working with their providers and health authorities to quantify any resources released and agree a working formula for fair and equitable distribution.

A SECOND TERM OF MODERNIZATION

With its second emphatic election victory, New Labour has been granted the benefit of the doubt over delivery on improving the NHS. Anxious not to be exposed on this issue in four to five years time, the government will accelerate its modernization agenda in state-funded healthcare. Hence 75 per cent of total NHS funding will be devolved to primary care trusts on the model of US primary care groups. Doubtless to guarantee delivery on NHS plan targets in elective surgery, trusts will have authority to purchase elective surgery from the private sector rather like a network HMO. There is even a stated intent to cross the thin red line between the public and the commercial in the provision of care with the proposed new privately-run surgical units. The Prime Minister has also re-emphasized his commitment to organizational and workforce reform within the NHS itself. A policy-drive which can only make the ensuing chapters still more relevant to British healthcare practitioners.

NOTES AND REFERENCES

1 H. Glennerster (1992) *The GP Fundholding Scheme*. Buckingham: Open University Press.
2 Department of Health (1989) *Working for Patients*, Cmnd 555. London: HMSO.
3 Glennerster, op. cit.
4 Department of Health (1994) *Developing NHS Purchasing and GP Fundholding*, EL 1994/97. London: Department of Health.
5 J. Posnett, N. Goodwin, J. Griffiths *et al.* (1998) *The Transaction Costs of Total Purchasing*. London: King's Fund.
6 Department of Health (1997) The Prime Minister's Foreword in *The NHS: Modern, Dependable*, Cmnd. 3807. London: The Stationery Office.
7 Ibid., para. 4.3.
8 Department of Health (2000) *The NHS Plan: A Plan for Investment, A Plan for Reform*, Cmnd 4818-I. London: Department of Health.
9 Department of Health (1998) *A First-Class Service: Quality in the New NHS*. London: DoH.
10 Ibid., para. 2.8.
11 Ibid., para. 3.2.
12 All data from *1997/98 Hospital Episode Statistics*, supplied by Department of Health.
13 M. Conroy and D.A. Cochrane (1996) *The Future Healthcare Workforce*. Manchester: University of Manchester.
14 *Hospital Epidode Statistics* 1997/8, supplied by the Department of Health.
15 Milliman and Robertson (1997) *Healthcare Management Guidelines*. Irvine, CA: Milliman and Robertson.
16 Department of Health (1999) *Saving Lives: Our Healthier Nation*, Cmnd 4386. London: Department of Health.
17 J. Appleby and C. Ham (1993) *The Future of Healthcare: A Report for Vision 2000*. Birmingham: University of Birmingham.
18 Vision 2000 (1995) *UK Health and Healthcare Services: A Report by Vision 2000*. Manchester: University of Manchester.
19 Conroy and Cochrane, op. cit.
20 Department of Health (2000) *The NHS Plan: A Plan for Investment, A Plan for Reform*, Cmnd 4818-I. London: Department of Health.
21 A. Maynard *et al.* (1998) *Managed Health Care*, Nuffield Trust Paper. London: Nuffield Trust.

Part two

MANAGED CARE IN PRACTICE

4

THE NEW PRIMARY CARE IS MANAGED CARE

David Colin-Thome

'Managed care' is a phrase which often engenders hostility due to its American antecedence, yet the National Health Service as a whole has always possessed many of the attributes of a managed care organization. It has a defined population and budget as well as primary care gate-keepers, but is encumbered in developing managed care principles by its sheer size. The new primary care organizations, taken together with their constituent general practices, offer a devolved version of managed care whose attributes would be primary care providers acting as gatekeepers, coordinators, utilization managers and budget holders, and a perspective that the registered practice population is viewed not only as patients.

All of the United Kingdom countries have developed similar primary care intermediate organizations. In England, we have Primary Care Groups (PCGs) which span 'levels' 1 to 5, with 'levels' 3 and 4 being also known as Primary Care Trusts (PCTs) as they are self-standing bodies with their own budgets. All are, in essence, building on the merits of fundholding and other practice-based budget-holding variants of total purchasing, as well as of GP commissioning where GPs, together with other primary health care workers, advised the health authority how to manage the local health system. All these forms of general practice organization were recognized as having merit, but the current government also felt that their patchwork arrangements led to increasing inequity of provision in primary care and in access to hospital, compounded by a fragmentation of services, increased bureaucracy and excess administration costs.

It was an attempt to address such problems and yet retain the benefits of the previous system that, in England, led to the formulation of PCGs/PCTs, whose remit is to improve primary and community services and improve the health of local people, as well as reducing inequalities in health, and to commission for secondary care services. Wales has come up with a similar model but as yet has shown no interest in moving to a

Trust status model. Northern Ireland has not produced its White Paper (at the time of writing), so the final form of its intermediate organization has not yet been defined, but it appears it will incorporate health and social services budgets as will the newly proposed level 5 PCTs in England. The Scottish model, although similar in principle, eschews the GP purchasing/commissioning model but gives GPs and other primary healthcare workers the opportunity to redesign care, including that of secondary care, through the medium of joint investment fund monies.

A 'new primary care' is developing, building on the various successes of the past, adopting and adapting to new government initiatives and in a response to demographic and societal changes. This new primary care could be described as a synthesis of the best of traditional general practice, a wider concept of primary healthcare, the new public health and a new public management. Let us explore these four facets in more detail with a particular concentration on traditional general practice, as it is key in helping to bring together the best of the old with the promise of the new.

TRADITIONAL GENERAL PRACTICE

UK general practice at its best has delivered personal care, coordinated care, continuity of care, longitudinal care and a gatekeeper function.[1] There are well-documented variations in general practice performance, but the general practice system together with comprehensiveness and relative cheapness continue to be the most envied parts of our National Health Service. These three attributes are interlinked as a consequence of the complementary effect of the general practitioner, the primary healthcare team and the registered practice population, the latter a relatively unique feature of British general practice.

It seems that much of the past needs to be retained given its success and continuing popularity. A common definition of the role of the GP in the 1960s was a doctor who provides personal, primary and continuing medical care to individuals and families. The GP may attend his patients in their homes, in his consulting room or sometimes in hospital. The GP accepts the responsibility for making the initial decision on every problem his patient may present, consulting with specialists as it seems appropriate to do so. The GP will usually work in a group of other general practitioners from premises which are built or modified for the purpose with the help of paramedical colleagues, adequate secretarial staff and all the equipment which is necessary. Even if in a single-handed practice, the GP will work in a team and delegate when necessary. A diagnosis will be composed in physical, psychological and social terms. He will intervene educationally, preventively and therapeutically to promote his patients' health.

This is still the essence of modern general practice. A key part of clinical care is the consultation. James Spence,[2] former Professor of Paediatrics in Newcastle, writing in 1960, defined, most eloquently, the consultation thus:

> The essential unit of medical practice is the occasion when in the intimacy of the consulting room or sickroom, a person who is ill seeks the advice of a trusted doctor. This is a consultation and all else in the practice of medicine derives from it. The purpose of the consultation is that the doctor, having gathered his evidence, shall give explanation and advice. If it be the purpose of medicine to give explanation and advice in consultation as a prerequisite of technical treatment, how are we to train our students? How are we to give them the understanding of the individuals who are needing consultation? How are we to maintain in doctors a sympathetic understanding of so many individuals without which their work becomes a weariness of spirit and of flesh? Can we, in fact, teach the art of consultation?

While recognizing his emphasis on the doctor and, again, the masculine gender, what Spence described then is relevant to clinical practice today. Both definitions do, however, bear the criticism of paternalism from which doctors have not progressed as much as they should if we wish to see a participatory model of care in the future.

General practice, however, is not only about individual care; it also has an organizational dimension. Starfield,[3] reviewing international primary care in 11 western nations, concluded that:

1 A higher primary care orientation is likely to produce better health of a population at lower cost.
2 Primary care is not necessarily synonymous with managed care. Managed care is explicitly aimed at restriction of medical choice of investigation and treatment. The essence of good gatekeeping is that of patient advocate. The patient–doctor relationship at a primary care level will be damaged if the doctor is perceived as simply an agent of his or her organization.

It seems essential, therefore, to retain the traditional role of general practice married to other aspects of the new primary care if primary healthcare workers are to manage resources, while retaining the trust of their patients.

Three discernible models of UK general practice have already been described, although they are essentially complementary:[4]

1 The *biomedical model*, where patients with perceived clinical problems seek advice and are offered advice, care and, where appropriate, cure.
2 The *humanist model*, stressing, once again, the importance of the patient–doctor relationship and given added force in the 1970s by Balint[5] in bringing a psychotherapeutic approach to the relationship.
3 The *preventive public health model*, best described in the UK by Doctor Julian Tudor Hart.[6]

THE WIDER PRIMARY HEALTHCARE

Primary, in the context of primary healthcare, can be defined as where the first point of contact between patient and clinical carer occurs. The provision of advice and first contact care for patients already do not necessarily come from general practitioners. The future should see a collaboration between daytime and out-of-hours general practice services, minor injury units, accident and emergency units, pharmacists, who for many years would regard themselves as a model of a walk-in-centre, and the new NHS initiatives such as walk-in-centres and the NHS direct telephone system. Making a coherent whole of such alternative contact points and initiatives is likely to ensure that if continuity of carer cannot always be achieved, continuity of care can be, through linked information systems. The general practice's role in the future would be that of a first contact for patients who choose that option, bringing continuity of care for episodic illness as well as ensuring continuity and coordination of care, often through care management for chronic disease sufferers.

Where then for primary healthcare? Melding the best of traditional general practice and community services with the lessons and achievements of budget holding produces four overarching, related areas of care:[7]

1 High-quality clinical care

This is the very stuff of clinical governance. Clinical transparency and accountability can be achieved through the open development of processes such as clinical guidelines, pathways and audit. As better clinical information systems develop, the general practitioner, or any other member of the primary healthcare team who refers on to other agencies, must utilize such information to be truly the patients' advocate by ensuring that wherever they are referred offers a defined and reviewed quality service. Clinical governance is the responsibility of both the providers of services and the referers to clinical care.

2 Coordination of care

This is one of the key attributes of good UK general practice. Such coordination now needs to be much more systematic and structured with clarity of roles, responsibilities and clear monitoring. For too long the aphorism that doctors see themselves as sole agents of success or failure, rather than part of a wider team, has hampered the development of quality integrated care.

3 Utilization management

This can be defined as ensuring better resource usage, both within primary healthcare itself and elsewhere. The new primary care intermediate organizations have a significant role to play in this, whether in challenging the variation in clinical practice itself or in clinical organization such as variations in referral patterns or lengths of stay in hospital.

4 The public's health

The maintenance and where possible the improvement of the public's health must be ensured. Primary care can play its full part in delivering this agenda by encompassing health needs assessment, anticipatory care, inter-agency working, community development and clinical governance.[8]

All these four facets of primary care are, in fact, underpinned by clinical governance, signifying its central role as follows:

- Where evidence-based clinical care has been defined, it must be implemented.
- Inappropriate clinical activity needs to be identified and ceased so as to protect patients from unnecessary interventions: an essential public health function. Resources thus released, although by necessity in a planned manner, can be utilized to effect wider health gain even beyond the NHS.

The National Health Service at its inception simply nationalized existing clinical practice, reinforcing the separation of function and budgets as well as reinforcing the reactive, curative model of care. A former US Surgeon General was quoted as putting such care into context by listing the general cause of premature death and disability as: 10 per cent due to inadequate access to medical care, 20 per cent due to environmental factors, 20 per cent due to genetic factors and 50 per cent due to behavioural and lifestyle factors. Health services, therefore, are important but essentially peripheral to health gain. By delivering the four aspects of primary care described, as well as ensuring that the individual clinician–patient consultation remains paramount, primary healthcare which abuts onto both the biomedical aspects of care and the wider community aspects of population health can be the catalyst for improving health and healthcare services.

A NEW PUBLIC HEALTH

This has been described as a synthesis of environmental and lifestyle change, together with appropriate medical interventions.[9] One of the unrealized potentials of general practice in the United Kingdom has been due to the reluctance to combine traditional one-to-one care with a population focus based on the registered GP population. A tension exists between these two dimensions, but for them to be addressed by one organization would bring a coherence and strategic importance to primary care by improving patient care and concomitantly achieving health gain.

If the National Health Service in general and primary healthcare in particular does not wish to be engaged directly in wider public health work, it should at least ensure the effective use of NHS resources so as to release resources to other agencies. The eradication of child poverty as a general aim, and the improvement of pre-school education as a particular aim, would do more to improve the health and wealth of our population than more money spent on healthcare. To be involved in both health and healthcare would be the ideal.

A NEW PUBLIC MANAGEMENT

The new public management has been described by Ferlie and Pettigrew[10] and seems to be overly concerned with monitoring and control, which is already much in evidence in the present NHS. Hunter[11] argues for a new third way in health management, which focuses on strengthening trust between organizations and encouraging a network approach, and seeks to restore a true sense of public purpose based on improving population healthcare. A question arises if the new primary care incorporates the best of traditional general practice, a wider primary care, coupled with the new public health and the new public management, and if primary care workers themselves provide better clinical care, coordination, utilization management and local initiatives in public health. How can primary healthcare begin to subsume these different aspects and dimensions into a coherent whole?

THE FUTURE OF PRIMARY CARE

It is often said that to predict the future one needs to look at current best practice. In that vein, the practice with its registered population will remain the bedrock of primary healthcare for the foreseeable future, but only if primary healthcare workers wish to play a more responsive, wider and proactive role as a resource to their communities. Population perspectives, therefore, need to be developed but a much more participatory approach to one-to-one patient care also needs to be developed, as it will contribute to improving care and managing demand by giving patients more confidence to be increasingly self-sufficient. A public health focus can also be brought to individual care, an approach currently being explored by Professor Jenny Popay[12] at Salford University through the medium of the public health referral. Current government initiatives, in particular Healthy Living Centres, can be the recipients of such referrals from primary healthcare.

Developing an holistic approach to the GP–patient consultation was described as far back as 1979 by Stott and Davies.[13] Their description of the ideal consultation encompassed managing the patient's presenting problem, modifying the patient's health-seeking behaviour, managing coexisting problems and opportunistically offering health promotion. To that model of the consultation can be brought the increasing knowledge about clinical effectiveness and appropriateness, developments in participatory care, and referral to specifically trained members of the primary care team who would offer enhanced systematic care for chronic disease sufferers. Whether a more participatory approach to care was achieved in the consultation can be assessed through questionnaires developed by the Department of General Practice at Edinburgh University.

There are, however, contrary views to such developments.[14] There are some general practitioners who feel that

> by placing a high value on the individual in context, the generalist approach to medicine may obviate the population perspective. Another challenge to the new general practice is how to achieve the benefits of delegation without exposing patients to unreasonable risk and how to ensure that general practitioners continue to develop their deductive, clinical reasoning skills.

They go on to say, in the context of resource utilization,

> one of the more important contributions clinical generalists can make to a health care system is to keep patients out of the expensive secondary health care system. The 'effect size' of appropriate gatekeeping has not been measured, but international comparisons by Starfield and others suggest a powerful effect.

Alternative views about primary care delivery abound. Patients increasingly may value easy access to any clinician above a long-term relationship with a personal doctor, who themselves may be increasingly difficult to recruit at a time when patient demand has increased. There is evidence that continuity seems to be more relevant to a more elderly patient, whereas younger people seek easy access. New suggested models of primary care are beginning to emerge. One is

> the development of the GP Hospital, purpose-built or set in existing building-stock, with no overnight beds, housing 50–80 better remunerated doctors providing, in addition to family medicine, specialist outpatient clinics, day-surgery and comprehensive diagnostic tests. The GPs will work closely with hospital consultants, with a much enlarged multi-disciplinary team and a 24-hour emergency service. No longer individual practice premises will be dotted around the town but there will be an emergence of a much more dispersed and accessible primary care service with health shops in places such as schools, malls, hotels and workplaces.[15]

Other developments are currently in place or being explored.[16] These include:

- the move to a practice-based contract, manifested currently in the Personal Medical Services pilots which have already taken 6 per cent of general practice outside traditional personal remuneration;
- law firm-type models with both partners and salaried professionals, who are not only doctors;
- the development of private models of care where either GPs charge patients or there are hybrid systems of private and state care.

Nevertheless, the desirability of continuity of personal care remains high in the public's mind. It manifests itself particularly by the high regard for small practices compared to larger ones. These various views and models often contradict. It seems the way forward is still to retain the practice as the building block around the registered population. The first contact clinician in the practice may be as likely to be a nurse as a doctor, but will still need to be perceived as a trusted personal carer for the patient.

The most important development which could further justify and ensure the retention of the registered population around the general practice would be for the practice to adopt a public health population perspective, while emphasizing that the registered population is also a prerequisite to effectively undertaking the traditional gatekeeper function.

To summarize, the new primary care[17] can be delivered from a practice-based service, serving a registered population who predominantly, historically, live mainly around the practice area, even in conurbations. A clinical generalist, not necessarily a doctor, but one who is perceived by the patient as a personal carer, will continue to provide many services but will also work within a system of varied first-contact points for patients which are information-linked. This clinical generalist will be part of a wider primary healthcare team that would ensure quality of individual care, systematized coordination of care, effective resource management including those of clinical resources, and working with others to address social determinants of health. The individual clinician, to remain trusted, must be seen as the patient's advocate while bringing wider skills to the consultation. The new primary care intermediate organization[18] must support individual care by being a resource to general practice, yet ensuring that primary care becomes more strategically important through being of sufficient population size to impact significantly both on the National Health Service and on the public's health. These organizations should also help to identify tasks suitable for different levels of primary healthcare or other organizations; to define, for example, what the practice should do; what the PCG should do, and so on. This approach will maximize effectiveness and involvement by rejecting rigid institutional functions and moving to a system where the most effective and competent organization is identified and charged with delivery of a particular aspect of care.

As an example, the practice or a group of practices may still be the most relevant organization to begin to redesign and challenge elective surgery, yet a much bigger organization may well be the focus for improving services such as forensic psychiatry. These organizations must also help to pull together and shape the various initiatives into a coherent and manageable entity such as the National Service Frameworks and, as already described, various out-of-hours services. Primary care organizations will also need to develop performance management of their constituent practices over whom they have no hierarchical control, quintessentially a 'new management for health' which would encompass two-way accountability and a development focus for performance management that measures movement as well as absolutes, and is built on relationships. These intermediate organizations will have to demonstrate good corporate governance, whole systems development and the improving of the public's health, an approach that will ensure high-quality care, but will also continue to ensure a comprehensive service that is more cost-effective than specialist-based healthcare delivery systems. To achieve this goal, well-developed infrastructure and systems need to be in place, various components of which are now described.

CLINICAL GOVERNANCE

A new entry to the National Health Service lexicon and, although perceived by some as having a threatening ring, derived from concepts of corporate governance. Clinical governance should systematize high-quality care, rather than care being the preserve of sporadically distributed centres of excellence. It will need to deliver three clear objectives:

1 High-quality care which, for primary care, patients have already defined:[19] availability and accessibility, technical competence, communication skills, interpersonal attributes of care, continuity and coordination of care and a range of on-site services. Such care should be ensured where primary healthcare is provided, but also where patients are referred, e.g. the hospital sector. There are three excellent, practical publications describing quality assurance and related methodologies.[20]
2 Evidence-based clinical care, where such evidence exists. Audit should be integral to all aspects of care, measuring all the components that patients value and emphasizing care as much as cure.
3 Management action to ensure that behaviour change takes place where the evidence indicates.

There are three strands essential to good clinical governance, namely accountability, internal and external mechanisms:

1 Through the new intermediate organizations, clinical accountability arrangements need to be in place for individual clinicians, the practice and the primary care group itself.

2 Internal mechanisms for improving clinical performance need to be in place, such as audit pathways, care pathways, research and development programmes, education and training which needs to be individual and practice-based, multidisciplinary and unidisciplinary. Such activity should be an essential part of the organizational development agenda of primary care organizations. It is imperative for the foreseeable future to keep the disciplining of clinicians as a separate process, so as not to damage the concept of clinical governance. If a critical mass of good-quality clinicians perceive governance as 'the quality police cometh', the realization of an enhanced clinical accountability will be doomed. Despite the misgivings expressed by many medical organizations, the Chief Medical Officer's consultation document[21] offers a sound way forward.
3 External mechanisms must be in place, such as a contractual framework or monitoring via, e.g., the health authority, the Commission for Health Improvement and professional bodies both of a professional and regulatory function.

An essential part of clinical governance is that of clinical risk management, defined as 'a means of reducing the risk of adverse events occurring in clinical care by systematically assessing, reviewing and then seeking views to prevent their occurrence'. There are two essentials to lessening clinical risk:

- through encouraging reflective thinking, a learning culture, systems development, by challenging clinical inappropriateness and by inculcating an accountability mindset in the individual clinicians who practise within the PCG;
- As advocated by medical defence organizations, undertaking a proactive risk assessment of both practices and individuals, and ensuring training programmes for administrative staff and clinicians alike.[22]

INFRASTRUCTURE

Premises are one of the most important aspects of primary care and an urgent priority particularly in London where GP premises are more substandard than in other parts of the country. New thinking but also good management information is essential.

1 There needs to be a constant updating of information regarding standards of practice premises and their suitability for development. Given the often changing demands of primary care, premises need to be flexible and expandable.
2 So-called hub and spoke models should be developed, so that small practices can refer patients to a central site, or to a larger general practice for certain aspects of their patient's care, e.g. physiotherapy, mental health groupwork, clinical investigations.

3 Intermediate care centres are needed, which build on hub and spoke models by also providing services more traditionally associated with acute hospital care such as outpatient services, day care and, where appropriate, low-technology in-patient care, all to lessen demand for acute hospital care. These centres could utilize existing hospital buildings, which will increasingly become surplus to requirements, as primary care continues to redesign healthcare. Is there, in effect, a long-term future for the present stand-alone outpatient department if we utilize primary care, its premises and information systems more effectively? These departments could then be taken over to become the intermediate or ambulatory care centres. The funding of such premises would need to be more flexible and imaginative including private–public partnerships for finance, ownership and management. GPs are increasingly reluctant to pay for premises that provide the whole panoply of primary and community services. Many younger GPs do not wish to buy into premises, leaving the existing GPs with the burden of a larger capital investment shared among fewer and fewer doctors.

4 Examples of new primary care developments within the Health Service are the Epsom Cottage Hospital Development, funded via a general practice, utilizing private monies and providing hospital services, and the Primary Care Resource Centres in the North West of England which provide extended primary care services and social care, and are a resource for community activities as well as hospital services. The Primary Care Trust could be the future owners and managers of primary care centres, although the staff could come from hospitals and other providers. Alternatively, the PCT could commission the private sector to fund, build and manage such centres, while retaining overall responsibility.

INFORMATION SYSTEMS

All practices need to be computerized and such information systems utilized in everyday practice. Practices should move away from paper-held records, encouraged by a proposed change in regulations to allow the cessation of paper records. Modern information systems need to be linked to other primary care providers, to secondary care as well as social care. They also need to incorporate clinical support systems, so that evidence-based practice is easily available at the time of clinical need. Patient-held records including smart cards will, increasingly, become the norm. Good information systems are essential for clinical care, not only to facilitate audit but also to provide a morbidity database as part of the public health agenda. General practices which are currently Information and Management Technology NHS 'beacons' will be a fruitful source of information and advice.

STAFFING

Recruitment and retention of general practitioners is currently a significant problem, especially in conurbations, and in London this is compounded by difficulties in recruiting community nurses. Gloomy predictions may, however, be allayed by more flexible and local approaches to employment, especially of general practitioners.[23]

INTEGRATED CARE

This can take various forms, e.g. care pathways developed across primary and secondary care and, for example in the care of the elderly and for mental health services, can include social services. The audit of such pathways would be across systems ensuring whole-system accountability.

Experience derived from health maintenance organizations involved in care of the elderly demonstrates that 6.5 per cent of the elderly population consume 60 per cent of healthcare resources due to the severity of their co-morbidities. Intensive case management for only a few months produces long-term benefits in quality of life, but also less use of resources, in particular those of the hospital. The Minnesota tool[24] can predict when patients are likely to require hospital admission and can be used by case managers to prevent such expensive in-patient care. We have now established this model in our own practice and to date seen quite dramatic reductions in service use by this group of patients. This service is described in more detail in Chapter 8.

UTILIZATION MANAGEMENT

Integrated care as described will ensure better utilization of resources but better clinical resource management should reap even more benefits. Hospital care is expensive and often wasteful, e.g. great variations in admission and readmission rates as well as length of stay, but primary care should look to itself in this respect, challenging current clinical practice through the wider use of skill mix, by adopting more participatory models of care so as to lessen the increased demand on primary care, and by the acceptance of wider and more varied first-contact points for patients such as NHS Direct and walk-in centres. The latter two initiatives are much derided by general practitioners but could lessen demand on general practitioner services, although evaluation is essential. Enhanced primary care will lessen the need for secondary care through the use of intermediate care facilities, case management and packages of care so as to lessen the need for acute admissions and to ensure shorter lengths of stay, but the biggest challenge is to tackle the clinical appropriateness agenda – a challenge which should be within the skills of primary care professionals, now to be in the lead in NHS care. There is much evidence of inappropriate or ineffective medical care:

1 Professor Eddy[25] of Dukes University of North Carolina, using the randomized control trial (RCT) as the gold standard for clinical care, estimated that only 15 per cent of medical activity is scientifically validated. Furthermore, as an instance, writing in 1991, he reviewed the evidence as far back as 1911 and could find no evidence of a randomized control trial validation for any treatment of glaucoma.

2 Medical practice variation is a problem throughout all healthcare systems. This has been demonstrated since at least the 1930s and yet little systematic work has been undertaken to address this problem. Medical practice variation can take several forms; two that are relevant to primary care are the fourfold variation in prescribing and referral patterns of general practice.

3 Professor Colin Roberts et al.,[26] of the now defunct anti-rationing group, estimated the scale of inappropriateness in the National Health to be in the order of 20 per cent, much of which is clinical practice. The thesis of this group was that rationing is the delay or denial of appropriate and effective care and that rationing may not need to take place if inappropriate and ineffective care is challenged and ceased.

Examples are many:

• Brendan Devlin and Gwynn Bevan[27] describe how since peptic ulcer operations have fallen surgeons have simply 'colonised the space' to undertake more cholecystectomies and laparoscopic interventions;
• the exponential growth in gastroscopies;
• the over-provision of tonsillectomies and insertion of tympanic ventilator tubes such as grommets;
• the over-provision of D & Cs for women below the age of 40 and, generally, of hysterectomies;
• the assessment by the the Royal College of Radiologists that 20 per cent of all X-rays performed in this country are unnecessary;
• the wide variation in follow-up appointments in hospitals.

These are all examples of interventions which have been shown to be not always related to clinical need. There is a further dimension in that many hospitals are under-utilizing day surgery and by so doing are wasting valuable in-patient resources.

4 Wennberg's work in the US demonstrated inter alia that in prostate care 50 per cent of men listed for prostatectomy for benign problems chose not to go ahead with the operation when given much more detailed information from interactive videos.

The advent of the National Institute of Clinical Excellence (NICE), by providing up-to-date information, will help to improve clinical effectiveness. This will supplement existing information from such as the Cochrane Database, Effective Healthcare bulletins (produced by the University of York, NHS Centre for Reviews and Dissemination), the *Bandolier* (http://www.jzz.ox.ac.uk/bandolier) and various Scottish products such as the Scottish Inter-Collegiate Guideline Network (SIGN) guidelines, obtainable from the Scottish Royal College of Physicians. It is up to clinicians to challenge care which, if inappropriate, has a public health dimension in that it could be harming patients.

As part of this agenda, the future may see the demise of outpatient clinics, as much of this work can be transmitted to primary care, where new technologies such as near-patient testing and tele-medicine, and, more importantly, a more sophisticated, confident, extended primary healthcare team, can provide more services and cease inappropriate clinical activity. The rest of traditional outpatient care could be delivered differently, e.g. direct admission from primary care, some cases to be seen in the wards of hospitals and the remaining outpatient care being delivered in premises needed for other services, e.g. GP premises, ambulatory or intermediate care centres. These facilities will be for the use of all general practitioners wherever such clinics are sited.

PRIMARY CARE INTERMEDIATE ORGANIZATIONS

I will use the English model of Primary Care Groups and Primary Care Trusts as an example, but similar opportunities arise within the other United Kingdom countries. The merits of fundholding, multi-funds and total purchasing are now accepted, in particular the merit of primary care professionals, especially GPs, having budgetary responsibility for NHS resources. There is now an acceptance that fundholding[28] and multi-funds improved clinical management, resulting particularly in increased cost-effectiveness of prescribing, increased responsiveness of hospital services and increased range of services at practice level. Budget holders also, in the vast majority of cases, unlike many other parts of the NHS, stayed within their budgets, although some have suggested that the budgets were not set appropriately. Total purchasing evaluation[29] seemed to suggest initially that small total purchasing pilots were the most effective in reaching their objectives, but later evaluation showed that, given sufficient management resources, larger total purchasing sites also achieved their objectives albeit taking a longer time and only if the larger sites had contiguous general practices. It was the work of the multi-funds and the total purchasers which seemed to have impacted most on government thinking in the development and progression of Primary Care Groups.

These intermediate organizations must continue to be a resource for the practice rather than becoming stand-alone bureaucracies. A Primary Care Group or Trust should devolve appropriate resources including budgets to the practices which can demonstrate managerial skills, while the PCG retains responsibility, hopefully temporarily, for practices that are unable or unwilling to accept such responsibility. Devolution to all practices should be the aim, as a sound principle of management is to devolve responsibility to where spending decisions are made. There will always be a justifiable fear, demonstrated in even some single practice fund-holders, that clinicians will remain disengaged even from clinical resource management; therefore, unless there is a local ownership of clinical resource management, there will also be a temptation for individual practices to cede responsibility quickly for such matters to the PCG/PCT, especially if the PCG/PCT is perceived as too discrete and distant from the practice. The Primary Care Group/Trust, therefore, needs primarily to be a resource to enable practices to improve their care as well as becoming more strategic organizations for their local population. The Primary Care Group/Trust, however, would retain responsibility for tasks best suited to that tier. Primary Care Groups and Trusts need to be:

- a management skills resource;
- a care knowledge and skills resource, in particular for clinical effectiveness;
- an information resource including the development of information management at the practice and at PCG/PCT level, as well as providing a library function;
- a vehicle for education, training and development whether at practice or supra-practice level;
- a management services agency, e.g. seconding practice managers to where needed, bulk purchasing of practice equipment, locum bank of clinicians;
- responsible for resource allocation to practices and negotiating with the health authority for Primary Care Group budgetary allocation;
- performing a financial function including financial risk management and a banking function for facilitating practice under/overspend;
- commissioning in the short term as a resource to the practices;
- the accountable body, even when in virtual form as a PCG;
- responsible for clinical governance.

The essential functions of a Primary Care Group or Trust should be finance, communication, management/planning, people management (human resources plus organizational development), clinical governance and public health development. These functions could be delivered not by recruiting full-time staff for each role but by identifying people with the requisite skills and competencies within the health system and to engage them on a part-time, occasional basis or shared basis. An inventory of skills across the health system is, therefore, an early task to be undertaken. To deliver such an all-encompassing agenda and work in a networking mode is currently unfamiliar to the NHS. A major organizational development strategy needs to be implemented by:

- determining the function of the new primary care organization, its roles and responsibilities, so that form can follow function in an iterative process;

- transitional planning via a diagnosis of the current state of affairs, mobilization of primary care leaders and natural work-teams;
- communication;
- education and training.

To ensure progress organizational development is necessary at all levels of the NHS and, for primary care, necessary at the practice, PCG/PCT and health authority level. The PCG/PCT corporate governance remit must include responsibilities for:

- health improvement and, in particular, addressing inequalities in health and health provision;
- financial control;
- value for money;
- ethics of decision making;
- internal and external accountability;
- ensuring that quality systems are in place;
- public involvement;
- clinical governance.

Good quality financial and information management is required, necessitating a much improved clinical information system. Through such information can better clinical decision making and utilization management be accomplished. A revenue-releasing strategy, mainly through tackling clinical inappropriateness, should be part of an investment strategy. Practice-level innovation can act as a laboratory for the wider Primary Care Group or Trust thus accepting temporary two-tierism coupled with a subsequent developmental programme, so as to spread good practice. The development of Primary Care Act pilots, now know as Personal Medical Services pilots, could provide a model for practice-based contracts placed with either the PCG or PCT, or alternatively PCG/PCT-wide PMS pilots accountable to the health authority, or in some cases the PCT. Such contracts will enable practices to be rewarded for quality rather than processes, will further their accountability to the parent PCG board and become a model for the incentivization of practices. PMS pilots include direct general practice remuneration and, once coupled to the unified budgets of Primary Care Groups, examples of primary managed care will emerge, as all budgets will be unified with an associated alignment of incentives and a clear management responsibility.

A six-point contractual framework could be applied to practices which would virtually cover all aspects of primary healthcare:

1 the defining and implementing of clinical quality standards;
2 consumerist or patient access criteria;
3 the quality of patient care. Enablement and empowerment of patients during the consultation are two measurable criteria;
4 organizational standards. Education and training opportunities are integral to this;

5 clarity of accountability to individual patients and the practice population;
6 a public health agenda.

CONCLUSION

The National Health Service Executive (NHSE) has stated that the objectives of Primary Care Groups and Trusts are to improve primary and community services, improve the public's health and to commission secondary care services. There is a view that purchasing and thereby commissioning, whether at practice-based levels such as fundholding or, even more so, at health authority level, became a bureaucratic exercise or, at best, concentrated on price rather than on a change in clinical behaviour. Primary Care Trusts will develop primary and community services, taking over many of the functions currently held at health authority level, and may well be able to develop clear strategies around primary care premises and primary care workforce development, currently in abeyance in many health authorities. Axiomatically they should also address the public health agenda by demonstrating improvement in health and the tackling of health inequalities among the resident population. They could and should also and innovatively be the catalyst not to commission services in the sense of purchasing, but to integrate and redesign healthcare across the primary/secondary care interface and, where possible, incorporating social services. The Primary Care Trust holding the NHS budget should be the key player with the health authority, in bringing people together. This should not be a model of comfortable collusion, but rather using the power of the budget to ensure that, where appropriate, clinical behaviour alters, and that services become much more cost-effective, coordinated and more efficient and, even more importantly, that patient services are of a higher quality.

The Primary Care Trust can be the organization which ensures that managed care principles, enunciated at the beginning of this chapter, can be delivered at both practice and Primary Care Trust level. This will deliver the responsive, information-rich, systematized care of the best of US managed care while delivering the public health population focus which British primary care has so far failed to develop significantly. All this can be delivered while retaining the British National Health Service values, so treasured by the British and envied by many Americans, of social justice within a healthcare system. There is a cultural dichotomy between the US and UK approaches made practically most manifest in whether the public has a choice in moving easily from one managed care organization to another. In essence, a competitive market model may increase responsiveness but damage the population public health focus. The UK model, of availability of choice between general practitioners who will nevertheless retain a registered population while the Primary

Care Trust boundaries remain sacrosanct, seems the best way forward to achieve the best of managed care; the best of British general practice underpinned by ensuring the continuance of social justice within healthcare.

NOTES AND REFERENCES

1 B. Starfield (1993) 'Primary care', *Journal of Ambulatory Care Management*, 16 (4): 27–37.
2 J. Spence (1960) The need for understanding the individual as part of the training and function of doctors and nurses, in *The Purpose and Practice of Medicine*, pp. 271–80. London: Oxford University Press.
3 B. Starfield (1992) *Primary Care, Concept, Evaluation and Policy*. Oxford: Oxford University Press.
4 P. Toon (1994) *What is Good General Practice?* Royal College of General Practitioners Occasional Paper 65. London: Royal College of General Practitioners.
5 M. Balint (1964) *The Doctor, His Patient and the Illness*. London: Pitman.
6 J. Tudor Hart (1988) *A New Kind of Doctor*. London: Merlin Press.
7 D. Colin-Thome (1998) *The Third Way (or How to Love Primary Care Groups)*, Occasional Paper. Manchester: University of Manchester Health Services Management Unit.
8 D. Colin-Thome (1999) Primary care perspectives, in S. Griffiths and D. Hunter (eds) *Perspectives in Public Health*. Oxford: Radcliffe Medical Press.
9 J. Ashton and H. Seymour (1988) *The New Public Health*. Milton Keynes: Open University Press.
10 E. Ferlie, A. Pettigrew, L. Ashburner and L. Fitzgerald (1996) *The New Public Management in Action*. Oxford: Oxford University Press.
11 D. Hunter (1999) *Managing for Health. Implementing the New Health Agenda*. London: Institute for Public Policy Research.
12 J. Popay (1998) Personal communication.
13 N.C.H. Stott and R.H. Davies (1979) The exceptional potential in each primary care consultation, *Journal of the Royal College of General Practitioners*, 29: 201–5.
14 Royal College of General Practitioners (1996) *The Nature of Medical Practice*. Report from General Practice 27. London: Royal College of General Practitioners.
15 L. McMahon (1999) Personal communication.
16 K. Manning (1999) *Fast Forwarding Primary Care*. London: Newchurch and Co.
17 D. Colin-Thome (1999) *A Vision for Primary Care. Visions of Primary Care*. London: New Health Network, King's Fund.
18 D. Colin-Thome (1999) *The New Primary Care and the Role of Primary Care Groups and Primary Care Trusts*, Occasional Paper. Manchester: University of Manchester Health Services Management Unit.
19 S. Buetow (1995) What do general practitioners and their patients want from general practice and are they receiving it? A framework, *Social Science and Medicine*, 40: 13–221.
20 M. Roland, J. Holden and S. Campbell (1998) *Quality Assessment for General Practice*. Manchester: National Primary Care Research and Development Centre, University of Manchester; M. Roland and R. Baker (1999) *Clinical Governance: A Practical Guide*. Manchester: University of Manchester National Primary Care

Research and Development Centre and Leicester University; T. Greenhalgh and J. Eversley (1999) *Quality in General Practice*. London: King's Fund.

21 Chief Medical Officer (1999) Supporting *Doctors, Protecting Patients*. Consultation paper. London: DoH.

22 MDU (1999) *Risk Assessment for General Practice*. London: Medical Defence Union.

23 B. Leese *et al.* (1999) *Disappearing GPs*. Manchester: National Primary Care Research and Development Centre, University of Manchester.

24 HMO Workgroup on Care Management (1999) *Chronic Care Initiatives in HMOs*. Robert Wood Johnson Foundation website, http://www.rwjf.org/.

25 P. Eddy, cited in R. Smith (1992) Where is the wisdom?, *British Medical Journal*, 303: 798–9.

26 C. Roberts *et al.* (1995) Rationing is a desperate measure, *Health Service Journal*, 12: 15.

27 G. Bevan and B. Devlin (1994) *Social Market Foundation Memorandum*. London: Social Market Foundation.

28 D. Colin-Thome (1997) *Why fund holding should stay*. London: Social Market Foundation.

29 N. Mays (1998) *Total Purchasing: A Step towards PCG's*. London: King's Fund.

5

EVIDENCE-BASED MEDICINE IN PRACTICE

David Cochrane

The higher quality managed care organizations (MCOs) have spearheaded the practical application of evidence-based medicine in the United States during the last decade. Along the way they have encountered anxious, defensive and even hostile elements in the American medical profession who, initially at least, viewed guidelines as a means of limiting clinical freedom and controlling access to care. These concerns also surfaced in the UK as the concept became widely discussed in the mid-1990s and guidelines were caricatured as 'cookbook' medicine among the more conservative sections of the profession. Fortunately, the debate has largely moved on and it has become widely recognized by healthcare professionals that guidelines are central to improving and standardizing quality in clinical practice. The counter-arguments have retreated but pockets of resistance and paranoia remain. So, if and when this is encountered it is worth remembering the words of one American medical colleague in defence of guidelines who pointed out once that 'people will eat cakes baked without a cookbook but they would think twice about flying in a jet aircraft which had not been maintained as specified in the manufacturer's manual.'

As the current government has developed and refined its modernization programme, clinical guidelines have become central to both the national quality strategy and programme-specific policies such as the National Service Frameworks, each designed to improve performance and support greater consistency in service delivery in the NHS. All local health communities in the NHS are now tasked to develop integrated care guidelines and pathways. The National Institute for Clinical Excellence has established an extensive programme for guideline development over the next few years with specific clinical areas led by respected national authorities. However, its current list is far from exhaustive and, even as these national guidelines become available, each health community will need to interpret them to reflect local circumstances such as patterns of need, demography and local service configurations.

Evidence-based guidelines and pathways of care not only provide a basis for standardizing quality, they can further other key management agendas. First, the evidence base can promote value for money since cost is a perfectly legitimate discriminant between two treatments of equal clinical efficacy. Second, by incorporating the patient's experience in the prescribed process, they can improve user satisfaction. Third, with the appropriate content and structure, guidelines can also serve as a currency for more clinically informed service-level agreements than conventionally used in the NHS. Fourth, they constitute the building blocks for planning integrated delivery systems both within care programmes and more widely across and within sectors of care. Finally, by empowering local groups to undertake the work, guideline development can facilitate what is otherwise one of the most difficult challenges in healthcare management: changing clinical practice.

This chapter therefore sets out a practical approach to developing guidelines and pathways at local level, spanning the following domains, each essential to the process of development:

- which clinical areas to select and prioritize;
- a disease management framework of primary, secondary and tertiary prevention;
- distinguishing and defining commonly used terms such as guidelines, protocols and pathways;
- the process and working structure for local development work;
- the content and structure of the documentation.

The last section of the chapter goes on to illustrate how guidelines and pathways can be used to develop a more sophisticated currency for service-level agreements and integrated delivery systems.

WHICH CLINICAL AREAS TO SELECT

The development of evidence-based guidelines and pathways is a time-intensive process. It needs to involve both service and resource managers as well as busy clinicians who will use the documentation and implement the prescribed processes. Given everyone's time pressures, it will rarely be practical to undertake this work for every type of medical condition or surgical procedure. Accordingly, a number of relevant criteria can be used to prioritize a guideline work programme.

- Work should focus on procedures and conditions where there is scope for significant improvements to clinical outcomes evidenced by comparative morbidity or mortality data.

- They should be high volume to maximize the number of patients for whom care will be improved.
- There should be a concentration on those which are high cost due to high admission rates or length of stay in order to explore the scope for more effective resource use.
- There may be similar opportunity to reduce unit cost and improve access within a specific programme, hence surgical procedures with significant waiting lists are often early priorities for review.
- Since chronic disease accounts for 80 per cent of resource use in any healthcare system, the major causes of chronic morbidity should therefore be included in early programmes of work.
- Any national priorities, such as ischaemic heart disease, will also need to be reflected at local level.
- They should span the typical workload of providers so that they can also serve as the currency for planning services. Hence in the acute sector, medical conditions and both emergency and elective surgical procedures should be included.
- They should include care processes where user feedback is consistently negative and hence there is scope to improve the patient experience.
- To minimize the research involved for project participants, clinical areas which have recently been subject to extensive evidence review by national or international authorities should be tackled first (see below).

By way of illustration, the following conditions meet most of these criteria, including accounting for current high levels of utilization of hospital services as evidenced by more regional admission and morbidity data.

- *Ischaemic heart disease*, prioritized in the first National Service Framework and which accounts for 21 per cent of emergency admission in the Camden and Islington Health Authority in London.
- *Stroke* where the UK has the highest incidence among women of any EC country.
- *Chronic obstructive pulmonary disease* (COPD) which accounts for 12.5 per cent of admissions in the former Mersey Region and is a major cause of early death in men.
- *Diabetes type II* which when poorly managed causes vascular disease, accounting for 11 per cent of admission in South Glamorgan.
- *Osteoporosis* which leads to 200,000 fractures in the UK of which 30 per cent are hips or neck of femur, projected to increase by 50 per cent in the European Union in 20 years if management is not improved.
- *Schizophrenia* and other psychotic conditions which account for 60 per cent of all adult hospital bed-days in mental health providers.
- *High-volume elective surgical procedures* such as hernia repair which readily lend themselves to day procedures but where current local performance has proved otherwise difficult to improve.

USING DISEASE MANAGEMENT AS A FRAMEWORK

According to Plocher,[1] the aim of disease management is take a more proactive approach to managing a disease in order to improve the likelihood of favourably altering its natural history. It is a comprehensive and integrated approach. The outcomes should include improving the quality of care and thus quality of life for the individual and reducing the cost of management of each individual – in particular by reducing their need for hospital-based care. The content of a disease management programme is specific to the condition, however the following components are common:

- Care is devolved from hospital- to primary care-based as far as possible consistent with quality.
- It should be 'patient focused' or coordinate all elements of the care process around the individual with the particular condition.
- It should include a detailed assessment of the aetiology and management of each condition extending beyond the medical to include social, cultural, psychological and environmental factors which can impact adversely or favourably on the condition.
- For high-volume conditions such as diabetes or COPD, it may be led by an expert practitioner with a specific caseload to which other healthcare workers refer appropriate cases.
- The role of each element of care is specified within an overall package.
- Treatment compliance and monitoring strategies are core elements.
- Patient awareness and education are central components so that he or she is skilled in self-management as far as possible.
- The patient is an active participant in the care plan design and goal setting.
- It should include an agreed, evidence-based, integrated set of documentation comprising guidelines, protocols and pathways from which all healthcare professionals work.
- Each set of documentation is structured around three phases of management – primary, secondary and tertiary prevention.

PRIMARY PREVENTION

This level seeks to prevent onset of the disease principally by influencing contributory lifestyle factors. Diet, lack of exercise, smoking, excessive alcohol use and stress are all contributory factors and/or causes of exacerbation in most of the chronic conditions listed above. They also all have some hereditary or genetic factor predisposing individuals to fall victim in later life. Effective primary prevention campaigns among people with high-risk behaviours can significantly reduce in the future the hospital bed usage which these conditions currently cause – thus freeing up resources within the NHS to meet other needs. For example, and in the ideal universe, COPD could be virtually eliminated in the UK if every person who smokes regularly gave up.

The problem is that it is exactly those groups in the population among whom incidence is highest and chronicity is most severe who have proven the least likely to change unhealthy lifestyle choices in response to health promotion campaigns. The professional and managerial classes have responded well, consequently fuelling the current market explosions in health centres, organic and low-fat foods, and vitamin and mineral supplements. The next major challenge for British public health therefore is to extend this success to the less affluent sections of society. It is not enough to provide people with information on healthy lifestyle choices if they lack the economic power or motivation to act on them. Technical advances will assist, such as the recent wide-scale introduction in the NHS of medication which controls the symptoms of nicotine withdrawal, thus helping to take the willpower out of smoking cessation. However, even these technical advances must be promoted through culturally sensitive health education programmes at community level with primary care as a key player. Such collaborative projects with local community groups can begin to address the primary preventive agenda at the micro-level. Structurally, and in the longer term, ultimate success is likely to require more fundamental change such as the elimination of child and family poverty and economic and social marginalization.

SECONDARY PREVENTION

Secondary prevention is targeted at people with early onset of the disease. The objectives at this stage are to prevent or slow deterioration of the condition. Management will be aimed at changing causal lifestyle factors as with primary interventions, and will also include active medical management of the early symptoms. Evidence is emerging from the US that the proactive management of severe chronic diseases at early onset stage can dramatically improve prognosis and thus hospital utilization later on. In some conditions – such as the mild symptoms of COPD or angina – it is evident that a secondary preventive strategy is required. The patient will often present to his or her GP with mild chest pain, or coughing. However, some chronic conditions such as osteoporosis or diabetes type II are asymptomatic at early onset. Similarly, raised blood pressure which substantially increases the risk of heart disease and stroke may not trouble the sufferer in the slightest. This has three implications which are significant for health service provision:

- Asymptomatic conditions require a 'case finding' strategy to locate those individuals for whom secondary preventive interventions would be beneficial. This approach usually identifies key risk factors and targets

Diary of an osteoporosis victim – currently aged 82	Hospital record
1986 fell off ladder – multiple knee and shoulder fracture	18 weeks length of stay + procedures
1990 – fell when out shopping – arm fracture	1 week + procedure
1997 – back pain reported to doctor – hairline fracture neck of femur	1 week + procedure
1997 – hairline fracture – total fractured neck of femur	4 weeks plus procedure
1997 – admitted to psychiatric hospital with depression due to 'slow' progess with 'rehabilitation' at home	6 weeks in hospital on prozac while mobilized by physios
Invalidity benefit 1998	
Invalidity benefit 1999	
Invalidity benefit 2000	
Cost to date	£48,500
Next major fracture need nursing home care?	£25,000

Figure 5.1   Cost of re-active management of osteoporosis

an objective diagnostic test at those individuals who fall into the high-risk category.
- Since the management of the condition at this stage is often through some form of drug therapy, patients with no symptoms of illness need to be persuaded of the benefits of taking medication – which may even have mild side effects – in order to guarantee better health at a future stage.
- Since most secondary prevention is delivered by primary care, immediate investment needs to be made to resource case finding, and also in higher drugs budgets.

Let us take the case of osteoporosis as an illustration. An example of the cost to the NHS and social security of fractures due to osteoporosis is illustrated in Figure 5.1 by the case of one elderly woman, now in her early eighties but aged only 75 when she sustained her first fracture. Cases like this are worth citing whenever anyone suggests that the NHS cannot afford better quality and more proactive management. The costs of re-active and poor quality care are enormous, leaving aside the trauma and disability of its victims.

As noted above, the management of osteoporosis requires a case-finding strategy. It onsets mostly in women (four female cases to every one male)

Box 5.1   Case finding Stage 1 – identifying risk factors for osteoporosis

- Maternal family history of hip fracture
- Low body mass
- Oestrogen-deficient
- Early menopause
- Amenorrhoea (especially if exercise-induced)
- Women who have had hysterectomy
- Cortiscosteroid therapy
- Other disorders associated with osteoporosis (listed)
- Age
- Nulliparity
- Smoking
- Sedentary occupation
- Low body weight
- Excessive alcohol
- Calcium deficiency in diet (prolonged)

---

around the time of the menopause. Diagnosis can only be confirmed by the measurement of bone mass density through a special 'dexa-scan'. It would be both uneconomic and also impractical to send all women aged, say, 40–55 for a dexa-scan. Therefore, in order to narrow the field, the Royal College of Physicians listed a number of risk factors to help identify likely candidates, in its recent guideline on the management of osteoporosis (Box 5.1).

Individuals who are high risk are referred for a dexa-scan which is the objective test for the condition. A measured bone density two or more standard deviations below that found in healthy young adults confirms a diagnosis.

Until recently scanning machines have been available only in hospital outpatient departments. Technology is changing, however. Ultrasonic scanning equipment is now on the market small and economic enough to be provided in the larger health centres and GP surgeries, making it possible for the diagnostic process to be managed entirely within primary care. Treatment includes addressing lifestyle issues such as calcium and vitamin D supplementation in diet, smoking cessation, reducing alcohol consumption and taking more weight-bearing exercise. However, the progression of the disease is halted completely by medication – primarily hormone replacement therapy (HRT). This medication needs to be taken consistently for at least 10–15 years to halt long-term disease progression. Hence the patient must agree to take a powerful drug which may give her some unpleasant side effects to treat a condition which poses no problems to her at this point in her life.

This requires the active participation of the patient in the treatment process. Currently the number of women compliant with long-term HRT who would benefit in terms of prevention of osteoporosis is estimated at about 16 per cent in the UK. Evidence from the US indicates that this compliance rate is increased to around 60 per cent provided:

- all the long-term risks and the patient's own perceptions and anxieties are fully explained by healthcare professionals – including the increased risk of cancer from long-term HRT use;
- the results of the objective diagnostic tests – in this case the dexa-scan – are shown to and discussed with the patient;
- a range of alternative drug therapies is available should the first line of treatment prove difficult to tolerate for the patient.

At the end of the day, however, it remains a matter of informed patient choice whether she proceeds with treatment. Whatever the views of healthcare professionals, people retain the right to forgo medication today and run increased risk of chronic disease in later life. *In secondary prevention, therefore, it becomes the primary role of the healthcare system to empower the patient to make that informed choice.*

Tertiary preventive interventions are those aimed at treating more people with more advanced disease. Since most guideline work to-date in the UK has been based in and focused on secondary care, it has been primarily concerned with tertiary prevention. Our approach, however, is not only to seek to integrate service delivery, but also the three levels of prevention into the management of any condition. The guidelines and pathways prescribed here are therefore both treatment- and prevention-oriented.

GUIDELINES, PROTOCOLS AND PATHWAYS – SOME DEFINITIONS

Since these terms are often used interchangeably, some clarity of definition is required.

Guidelines in our terms are documents which capture the patient's overall journey through the healthcare system, beginning and ending in primary care. It has been the practice in some health communities for the acute hospital consultant to produce referral guidelines and send them out to GPs on the assumption that they will employ them. Not only is this an unsound assumption, but these documents have tended to be narrowly focused on guidance for specialist referral and prior patient 'work-up' (diagnostic tests etc.). It is more advantageous for guideline development work to be based in primary care provided there is secondary care input to the process. Hence *primary care management and referral guidelines* should be developed by project teams of clinicians and resource managers in facilitated group work. This approach has the following advantages:

- patients begin and end their healthcare pathway in primary care;
- an aim of the approach is to facilitate devolution of management to primary care and therefore the approach needs to fully reflect the local context;
- it is an action learning experience in evidence-based medicine and clinical governance for the primary care team itself;
- guidelines developed in primary care are more likely to be used by primary care teams;
- they can be used to devolve care from the GP to other members of the primary care team.

Using this approach should also allow scope for individual clinical preference and individual patient need to be built into the guideline within the evidence base (see section on evidence review below) and thus avoid the 'cookbook' criticism. Basing the work in the primary care team also facilitates capture of the following key components in the process:

- early recognition and treatment including case finding, initial recognition and assessment which will begin in primary care;
- the management objectives and treatment process in primary care thus defining its clinical role;
- criteria for secondary referral and admission can be specified and agreed so that most appropriate use is made of these services by the primary care team, including any patient work-up required by the specialist prior to referral;
- in the case of conditions sometimes requiring in-patient stay, they will include the expected length of stay drawn from the agreed in-patient pathway (see below);
- criteria for discharge are set out and defined as the stage of improvement the patient should have reached;
- referral criteria to more specialist assessment and diagnostics, agreed with the secondary sector clinicians;
- an agreed investigation plan including clinical criteria for admission to hospital;
- finally, guidelines should incorporate after-care, secondary preventive work and periodic patient review; functions most appropriately led and managed at primary care level.

Pathways are most useful where the process of care can be described and documented on a day-by-day basis, hence:

- they are a particularly useful process for a period of in-patient care or day procedure;
- they list the activities required by the patient on each day and who is responsible for delivery (doctors, nurses, discharge planner etc.);
- they should encompass both treatment and discharge planning and can therefore be used to define an optimal length of stay for a given condition;

- hence they can provide both a means of ensuring that everything that should happen during the in-patient episode does so at the right time and the baseline for contracting expected length of stay for given conditions and auditing out-turns.

An example of a care pathway for the acute management of a patient with a neck of femur fracture is given in Box 5.2.

In our terms, *protocols* are highly specific documents governing the use of diagnostic procedures or treatment interventions such as for medication

---

Box 5.2 Clinical pathway

Procedure/diagnosis: *Fracture neck of femur*
Objective: *effect repair, manage patient to orthopaedic stability, begin mobilization and decide next stage of care – length of stay 4–6 days*

Activity	Day of admission/ surgery	Day 2	Day 3 to discharge
Medical	1 History/exam 2 X-ray 3 Anaesthesia assessment 4 Medical assessment 5 Direct to ward 6 No more than 2 hours in A & E 7 Repair and instruct ward team	1 Heart lung 2 Wound evaluation 3 Post-anaesth. assess. 4 Review need for transfer to ortho-geriatrics	1 Discharge summary for GP 2 Changes medication on discharge
Nurse	1 Admission assessment (skin/pressure points, pain, home/social conditions) 2 Prior mobilization 3 Bowel/bladder assessment 4 Obs. etc. 5 Pre-op. assess. 6 Pre-anaesthesia 7 Accompany patient to theatre 8 Wound assessment	1 Physical assessment 2 Drain out 3 Wound check 4 Obs. 5 Skin care 6 Turning 7 Write care plan	1 Implement care plan 2 Wound check 3 Skin care 4 Turning 5 Obs. etc.
Diagnostics	1 (Lab tests) 2 X-ray in A & E 3 X-ray of hip in recovery room	1 Check X-ray if not already done	

Activity	Day of admission/ surgery	Day 2	Day 3 to discharge
Medications	1 Pain management pre-anaesthesia 2 Post-op. angioplasty epidural 3 Antibiotics pre/post op.	1 Pain management	1 Pain management
Nutrition	1 Nil by mouth p. midnight 2 Diet as tolerated 3 IV fluids as required	1 Diet as tolerated	1 Diet as tolerated
Physio./ occupational therapy	1 Bed rest 2 Obtain pre-injury history 3 Physio. assess.	1 Weight bearing and mobilization begins	1 Continue mobilization 2 Home assessment by community rehab. team ('Fast trackers')
Education/ communication	1 Explain process to patient 2 Explain process to family 3 Expectations of recovery and timescales incl. injury process 4 Reading material to relatives	1 Plans/goals/ expectations of therapy 2 Reading material to patients	1 Discuss goals/ expectations of recovery with patient and relatives 2 Reading material to patients
Discharge planner	1 Assessment 2 Notify rehab. team for home rehab. 3 Notify GP	1 Discuss discharge plans with family, and patient 2 Assessment 3 Referral to ortho-rehabilitation	1 Discuss discharge plans with family, and patient 2 Assessment 3 Referral to community rehab. teams (if applicable)

or use of oxygen therapy for people with advanced COPD. They set out the range of options, clinical criteria for selection, the process of obtaining a therapeutic dosage, any therapeutic combinations and the relative costs – particularly in the case of medications of equal therapeutic efficacy. They also set out how and by whom the treatment or diagnostic procedure should be administered. Hence guidelines and pathways will

---

Box 5.3   Medication protocol for the management of congestive heart failure in primary care

During first two weeks
- Frusemide 40 mg daily and sparing diuretic such as co-amilofruse
- Increase dosage to 80 mg

Then
- Reduce dosage to 40 mg
- Stop postassium and diuretic
- Add ACE inhibitor
- Start ACE inhibitor at low dose and build up to therapeutic dose as tolerated
- Preference for ACE which is once a day and licensed for GP use (hence *not* captopril)

N.B. NSAID, oral steroids, beta-blockers, and verapamil in general make CHF worse

Monitor for
- Shortness of breath
- Orthopnea
- Urea – concern if creatinine rises more than 30% from (patient specific) baseline
- Electrolytes
- Liver function
- Weight *and* oedema
- Exercise intolerance
- Signs of depression
- Cognitive capability

---

include appropriate protocols. An example of a medication protocol for the primary care management of congestive heart failure is given in Box 5.3.

THE GUIDELINE DEVELOPMENT PROCESS

Who coordinates?

The development programme for guidelines across the major medical conditions and surgical procedures is usually vested with clinical governance leads within the health authority public health function and Primary Care Groups and Trusts. The assumption here is that clinical staff in management positions will have more credibility with practising clinicians, especially doctors. However, whoever leads the process, the important competencies are:

- the ability to facilitate groups in an open and challenging working environment;
- a comprehensive understanding of the roles of each sector of healthcare delivery;
- good research skills including the ability to sift and present often extensive literature searches into concise, informative formats.

Since we are also seeking to inform commissioning, planning and cost-effectiveness the work programme should be coordinated by a steering group which incorporates representation from these management functions.

Setting up the project team with the relevant clinical staff

Each set of documentation is developed by a project team tasked by the steering group and comprising the clinical staff with a major direct role and expertise in the management of the condition under review. By way of example, a guideline group reviewing angina will typically comprise:

- GPs;
- practice nurses with special interest in ischaemic heart disease;
- consultant cardiologist;
- hospital-based nursing staff from coronary care;
- health promotion staff;
- cardiac rehabilitation staff.

A hospital-based group reviewing fractured neck of femur would include:

- orthopaedic surgeon;
- ortho-rehabilitation consultant;
- ward-based nursing staff;
- physiotherapy and occupational therapy from secondary and community providers;
- GP;
- district nursing.

The choice of medical staff is relatively easy. For other professional staff, it is important to avoid the tendency for departmental heads such as the head occupational therapist to nominate themselves to the group, especially if they are not experts in the field under review. There can be a tendency for staff in managerial roles to be less inclined to change practice if they perceive it could have implications for the current size of their departments. For example, moving the rehabilitation of stroke or fracture patients out of the acute hospital closer to, or into, the patient's home will inevitably reduce the workload of centralized therapy departments and, logically, the resource base of those departments.

Follow good project management procedure

All meetings should be documented and the results fed back before the start of the next meeting to agree each stage and allow group members to comment and amend at key points in the process. Ground rules for the group's procedure are set and would typically include the following:

- All participants are of equal status within the group regardless of relative status outside.
- There should be no substitutes in case of a member's absence since this can take the whole group back to square one to brief the newcomer and also unbalance an established group dynamic.
- There should be a comfortable working environment.
- Meetings should be at times convenient to staff, even if this means lunchtime or early evening.
- Do not let individuals dominate; invite into the discussion those who are naturally reticent or who tend to defer to more senior staff such as consultants.
- Facilitate the group and keep to the timescale by placing a limit on the number of meetings.

Initially a group may need four to six meetings to complete a guideline, particularly for complex conditions such as stroke; however, as it becomes more skilled the work can be largely completed in three.

Begin with a critical review of the current care process

The first stage is to undertake a critical appraisal of the current management of the condition under review. This is achieved by tracking typical patients through the process and capturing the role of each service sector and clinical staff group. This stage allows each member to be informed of the current role of all the others and also warms up the group dynamic by getting everyone contributing early on. It also identifies key issues and concerns with the existing care process to be taken forward into the review.

Evidence review

The second stage is to undertake a thorough review of current evidence in the condition. There are a number of good practices in the use of evidence-based medicine.

Identify all authoritative sources of evidence
There are a number of sources of evidence for guideline work. These include:

- the National Institute for Clinical Excellence (NICE);
- the British Royal Colleges and their journals;

- *Effective Healthcare Bulletins* (University of Leeds);
- specialist medical societies and associations such as the British Rheumatological Society and British Thoracic Society and their publications;
- the Scottish Intercollegiate Guideline Network (SIGN);
- the Cochrane Library;
- the World Health Organization;
- the American Colleges and professional associations and their publications;
- the US Agency of Healthcare Policy and Research (AHPR);
- specialist user representative organizations such as the Stroke Association or the National Schizophrenia Fellowship.

First port of call is the websites of these organizations. Also, a search on MEDLINE will generally provide a list of the most recent internationally authoritative evidence reviews and guidelines that have been produced for the condition. As a general rule, material produced in North America, Europe or Australia can be downloaded direct. However, most of the material produced in the UK is only available in abstract on the Web and has to be purchased from source. An honourable exception here is the Scottish Authority SIGN whose publications are provided free of charge from its website.

The best guideline material includes a thorough evidence review, and a structure for the management of the condition. This can be used to draft local guidelines. Some also include a model guideline or concise guide which can be easily adapted if the project group agrees to this. The material produced in the UK over recent years commands maximum respect from British clinicians and is also among the most thorough and comprehensive in terms of the evidence reviewed and cited. The American evidence is also of high quality and often leads its European counterparts by six months to a year in revising recommended practice. Some excellent starting points produced over the last three years or so include:

- the Royal College of Physicians' guidelines on stroke and on osteoporosis;
- the American Psychiatric Association practice guideline on the management of schizophrenia;
- the British Thoracic Society's guideline on the management of COPD;
- the AHPR guideline on the management of depression;
- the World Health Organization (WHO) guideline on the management of hypertension;
- the American Diabetic Association and American Association of Endocrinologists' guidelines on diabetes;
- the Bethlem and Maudsley prescribing guidelines.

Use levels of evidence to reduce the 'grey zone'
One of the major issues in evidence-based medicine is the availability and quality of the evidence itself. Clinical evidence is classified as follows:[2]

Ia   Based on meta-analysis of randomized controlled trials (RCTs).
Ib   Based on at least one RCT.
IIa At least one well-designed, controlled study but without randomization.
IIb At least one-quasi-experimental study.
III At least one well-designed, non-experimental descriptive study such as comparative studies, correlation studies or case studies.
IV   Expert committee reports, opinions and/or experience of respected authorities.

Evidence can also be graded A (encompassing Ia and Ib), B (II–III) and C (IV).

In general the aim in any clinical area should be to use these levels of evidence to reduce the 'grey zone' by eliminating those interventions for which the evidence is weak, as shown in Figure 5.2. This implies that level I and II evidence should certainly be incorporated however much of the evidence in some conditions is level III or IV in the darker grey zone. To resolve the dilemma of what to include from these categories, one group followed a guiding principle simply stated as: 'What would group members wish to see included were the care process to be implemented on themselves and/or their significant others?'

Leave scope for legitimate variations in individual clinical practice
The inclusion of less definitive evidence also has the advantage of leaving scope for individual clinical judgement within the evidence base, thus alleviating any residual 'cookbook' concerns.

The patient's experience of a process of care is a critical component
All guidelines should be drafted from a 'patient focus' perspective. Not least, negative experience such as unpleasant side effects of medication will reduce patient compliance with treatment programmes and compromise outcomes. Therefore scope for variations in patient experience and choice of treatment alternatives should be reflected in the documentation. Implementation of guidelines should also incorporate feedback from patients on their experience of the process to inform audit and review.

Cost is a factor
Where two alternatives are of equal efficacy and generate equal patient satisfaction and compliance, cost is a factor.

Figure 5.2   Reducing the 'grey zone'

Content of the guidelines

Although the content of guidelines is governed by the clinical condition itself, it is advisable to work to a common structure and format. The following is a useful framework, illustrated by a worked example in unstable angina.

Box 5.4 Alerting symptoms, condition description and risk factors, including guidance on how to eliminate conditions with similar symptoms

Chest pain of ischaemic heart disease origin
- Praecordial chest pain
- Exertional pain
- Severity of pain
- Breathlessness and sweating
- Associated with pain into neck, jaw or left arm
- Presence of risk factors

Other causes of chest pain (muscular/skeletal, dyspepsia, anxiety etc.)
- Local tenderness
- Relation to meals
- Relation to perspiration
- Anxiety
- Response to conservative treatment

Diagnostic tests required to confirm a diagnosis and/or inform treatment

Aim to
- Clarify underlying cause
- Identify risk factors for myocardial infarction (e.g. diabetes, ECG changes, hypertension, age)
- Inform need for anti-thrombotic therapy (Aspirin)
- Identify patients with poor prognosis

Procedures
- Diagnostic trial dose of nitroglycerine (GTN)
- Electrocardiogram (ECG)
- Haemoglobin and blood sugar
- Lipids
- Chest X-ray
- Exercise ECG for stable patients aged under 70 (to identify 30–40% of patients with poor prognosis)

  - 10 minutes tolerance indicates 90% chance of 5-year survival
  - 3 minutes tolerance indicates 20% chance of 5-year survival

---

Box 5.5   Management in primary care including criteria and objectives for patient management. This will also prescribe who leads the patient management process at each stage (GP, nurse specialist, community mental health professional etc.)

Manage in primary care if
- Clear diagnosis (exercise-induced pain that responds to nitro-glycerine)
- Moderate- or low-risk patients with no evidence of myocardial infarction

Aims of therapy
- Pain and other symptom control
- Prevent myocardial infarction
- Manage risk factors
- Anti-thrombolytic therapy
- Lipid control
- Treat hypertension
- Monitor every 6 months

Lead clinicians in primary care
- GP confirms diagnosis and initiates therapy continued and monitored by heart nurse

Box 5.6   Criteria for referral for specialist opinion including those diagnostic tests which will need to have been completed by primary care prior to referral

Refer to cardiologist if
- Fail to control rest pain
- Uncertain of diagnosis
- Condition is specific to work (e.g. manual workers, drivers etc.)
- Risk factors
- Previous myocardial infarction, chronic cardiac failure, murmur

Provide details to cardiologist of
- Exercise tolerance ECG result
- Copy of resting ECG
- Chest X-ray
- Glucose
- Lipids
- Thyroid function test
- Risk factors

Box 5.7   Agreed investigation plan by cardiologist: this should be set out and agreed with the expected number of outpatient visits specified

- Clinical assessment
- Exercise stress test
- Stress echocardiagram
- For angiogram with a view to establishing need for coronary artery bypass graft or angioplasty
- Consider for cardiac catheterization

Complete and feed back in two outpatient visits

Box 5.8   Criteria for emergency referral and admission

- Frequency
- Increasing severity or sudden deterioration
- Patients with rest pain continuing for 20 minutes
- Need I/V heparin
- Expected length of stay 4–7 days

Box 5.9   Agreed criteria for discharge (i.e. what stage of improvement will the patient have reached upon discharge?)

- Stable ECG
- Discontinuation of heparin
- Symptom control
- Pain free without medication
- Investigation plan agreed and in place

Implementation, audit and review

Once implemented, guidelines should be monitored and audited on outcome measures. Some examples of audit measures might include:

- percentage of patients with angina with blood pressure at or below prescribed levels (defined by WHO);[3]
- number of patients prescribed and taking appropriate anti-lipid medication;
- rate of hospitalization for unstable angina;

Box 5.10   Agreed process and frequency of monitoring patients, plus case management

Treat and monitor
- Diet
- Lipids
- Cholesterol
- Hypotension

Advise on
- Diet
- Adverse lifestyle (lack of exercise, smoking, poor stress management etc.)
- Refer to appropriate health promotion services

Develop strategy for drug compliance
Educate the patient and carers on early symptom recognition and appropriate self-referral
Refer to cardiac rehabilitation as required

- average length of stay;
- rates of angioplasty, CABG, cardiac catheterization.

New evidence is constantly emerging, and best practice recommendations are to be reviewed six-monthly. Operationally, however, time constraints may allow only annual review unless of course there is a major development in treatment, diagnostics or other stage of management.

PLANNING INTEGRATED DELIVERY SYSTEMS

Guidelines and pathways provide a clinically based currency for commissioning and planning integrated care over operational and strategic planning timescales. Strategic planning spans the timescales for major service changes, such as new capacity building or professional staff training, usually taken as five years. Operational planning works within this strategic framework and includes those changes which can be implemented in the next year or two. This can be illustrated by stroke and fractures.

Operational planning

In the short term, secondary preventive programmes will have little impact on incidence. However, guidelines and pathways can have a major impact on service delivery and configuration. In the case of stroke, for example,

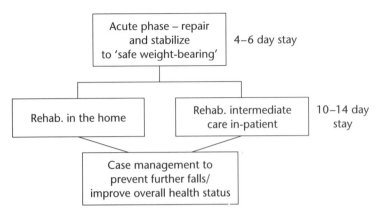

Figure 5.3   Integrated care model for fractured neck of femur

there are two major service changes prescribed by the Royal College of Physicians' guideline:[4]

- the evidence base supports an increase in the number of mild to moderate strokes managed without admission to hospital at all;
- the rehabilitation of stroke patients is as effective in the home as it is in a hospital setting provided the community and in-patient rehabilitation services have appropriate neuro-rehabilitation expertise.

Similarly a traditional model for fractured neck of femur repair would involve the patient staying on the orthopaedic ward about three weeks until mobile on crutches. However we now have ten years' experience of the care model developed by clinical staff in Peterborough for the 90 per cent of patients who benefit from active rehabilitation. This has been extensively evaluated and prescribes the following.

- The rehabilitation stage is initiated at the end-point of the acute phase when the patient is medically stable post-surgery and has begun mobilization, usually between four and eight days.
- In-patient rehabilitation is moved from the acute setting into specially designed and staffed rehabilitation centres. These can be located on acute hospital sites in urban areas where transport links are good, or in more rural settings in community hospitals.
- However, it is equally effective to rehabilitate those who were fully mobile prior to the fracture, or about half of the cases in the home.

The implications for contracting and delivery are a reduced need for acute in-patient stay and a requirement for a community-based rehabilitation team with the skills to manage these patients at home. Teams can also provide complementary services such as stroke, cardiac and pulmonary rehabilitation (for patients with COPD). Increasing the numbers rehabilitated at home will further reduce the need for beds. Resources released can be transferred to services with supply problems within the acute sector and/or to support secondary preventive services which need to develop simultaneously.

Strategic planning and contracting

Over a more strategic period, secondary preventive programmes should begin to impact on incidence and severity of chronic conditions, further reducing the proportion of acute and rehabilitation in-patient days. In this way activity levels and the requisite capacity can be planned to reduce on the basis of revised expected utilization specified in the guidelines and pathways (expected length of stay, number of outpatient visits etc.) and a reducing incidence rate per thousand head of population over the next five years or so based on the outcome of secondary preventive services. Similarly, expected costs can be ascribed either for an individual case or on a programme basis for an entire population served by a PCT and thus provide a clinically based contract currency for service-level agreements.

NOTES AND REFERENCES

1 D.W. Plocher (1996) *Disease Management*, in P.R. Kongstvedt, *The Managed Care Handbook*. Gaithersburg, MD: Aspen.
2 Royal College of Physicians (2000) *National Clinical Guidelines for Stroke*, p. 10. London: Royal College of Physicians.
3 World Health Organization (1999) *Hypertension Guideline*. Geneva: WHO.
4 Royal College of Physicians, op. cit.

FURTHER READING

Agency for Health Policy and Research (1997) *Clinical Practice Guideline Number 10. Unstable Angina: Diagnosis and Management*. AHPR website, http://www.ahcpr.gov/.
Commission of the European Union (1998) *Building Strong Bones: Summary and Report on Osteoporosis*. Brussels: European Commission.
P.D. Fox (1996) *Managing Chronic Care*. Gaithersburg, MD: Aspen.
North American Menopause Society (1999) *Achieving Long-term Continuance of Menopausal HRT/ERT, Consensus Statement*. NAMS website, http://www.north americanmenopausesociety.healthandsupplements.com/.
Royal College of Physicians (1989) *Fractured Neck of Femur, Presentation and Management*. London: Royal College of Physicians.
Royal College of Physicians (1999) Osteoporosis: *Clinical Guidelines for Management and Treatment*. London: Royal College of Physicians.
K. Sethi *et al.* (1995) HRT uptake and compliance, *European Menopause Journal*, 2(4): 33–4.

6

UTILIZATION MANAGEMENT IN PRIMARY AND COMMUNITY CARE

David Cochrane

The primary objectives of utilization management (UM) are to reduce the requirement for services and lower unit costs within any given programme of expenditure. In any healthcare system, UM processes can therefore extend access and thus mitigate service gaps, inequity and supply problems. This sounds fine in theory, but fully exploring the potential of UM is essential in the NHS which is bedevilled by supply problems, in turn interpreted as symptomatic of expenditure constraint. Turning this theory into practice is therefore the central theme of this and the next chapter. This first one sets out the practical techniques of UM in primary general and ambulatory care; the next does likewise for in-patient care. They both focus on general and acute services. UM in mental health is covered in Chapter 9.

The NHS is enjoying unprecedented real-terms resource growth which will have increased expenditure by 30 per cent above inflation during the four financial years beginning April 2000. There is no scope for complacency, however. The population is getting more numerous, older and more demanding. These trends will guarantee steady growth for current acute in-patient expenditure and workload which risks consuming the additional resources unless we change the way we manage that utilization. The service must continue to strive for improved cost-effectiveness from its resource base in order to address rising demand within the objectives set by the 1997 White Paper and the National Plan. For not even the NHS can now legitimately ask politicians for more money over the next five years. It has to get more productive.

UTILIZATION MANAGEMENT DEFINED

So what is utilization management, and why is it a core activity of any managed care organization? Adapting Kongstvedt's definition to the context of the NHS, utilization management refers to 'those activities of a health-care system which are designed to reduce the overall need for health care services' by the population covered.[1] It seeks to manage healthcare resources in any system *which cannot ration* services. Utilization management developed in the US managed care sector in the State of California, where waiting lists are now unheard of. Even if funded by Medical – the state programme for those without employer or Medicare cover – HMO members have rights defined by state legislation including to be seen by a specialist within a month of referral by the primary care physician and for any elective procedure to be carried out within a month of the specialist's decision that it is required. Two further practical objectives of UM are:

- to reduce the unit cost of services while maintaining clinical efficacy and user satisfaction;
- to provide a service at a lower level of intensity within an integrated delivery system mitigating the clinical need of the patient or client.

As shown in Figure 6.1, an integrated delivery system provides health-care interventions at all levels of intensity from acute hospital in-patient care – the most resource-intensive – through to primary prevention which when successful can eliminate the need for any other healthcare intervention. It is a fundamental aim of utilization management, therefore, to shift the balance of health service provision down this vertical continuum. In practice, we need to invest most of the new growth money in the NHS into the services which prevent admission to hospital.

VALUE FOR MONEY VERSUS COST REDUCTION

In the US managed care sector there is no attempt to conceal the importance of reducing unit costs.[2] However, there is also a governing principle that quality and member satisfaction should not be compromised in the process. In a service with major supply bottlenecks such as the NHS unit cost reduction is a perfectly legitimate strategy since within the same programme budget it enables the potential volume supplied, and therefore access, to increase. However, it feels more comfortable in the NHS to adapt the objectives of utilization management by being less concerned with cost reduction as a single factor and more focused on improving *value for money* defined by the relationship shown in Figure 6.1.

Quality improvement may be measured according to the standard typology of the *structure, process and outcomes* of the clinical process but also as improved patient experience and satisfaction for a given level of clinical quality. However, if we can increase volume and/or quality for the same cost, or maintain volume and quality while reducing cost, we have increased value for money. Volume of service needs to be assessed against need since we should not be increasing volumes *per se*. As a general

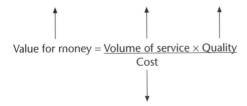

Figure 6.1   The value-for-money formula

objective in reviewing healthcare processes we should be looking for improvements on all three parameters at once which, as we shall see, is perfectly feasible.

The definition of utilization management is more usefully given by its component processes. In terms of primary and ambulatory care there are three major categories: primary prevention, secondary prevention, and demand management of tertiary preventive services.

PREVENTION IS EVERYONE'S BUSINESS

Health maintenance is utilization management at its most fundamental level, and as such has been a central objective of managed care organizations in the United States since their inception. Clearly the optimum approach to reducing need for services and thus overall expenditure is to seek to prevent illness and injury in the first place. There are three levels of prevention: primary, secondary and tertiary.

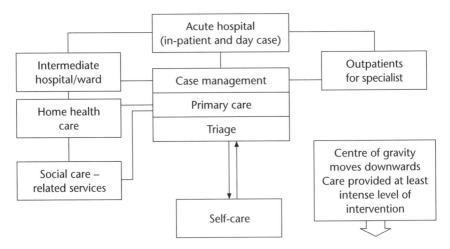

Figure 6.2   An integrated delivery system

Primary prevention

This level seeks to prevent any onset of the disease, principally by influencing contributory lifestyle factors such as diet, exercise, smoking, alcohol consumption or stress management.

Of course, although the NHS has always had a philosophical commitment to primary prevention it has consistently devoted most of its resources to sickness response services. The first formal attempts to bring policy and provision more into line with this intent were made in the 1970s when protected budgets for prevention were created and health promotion departments began to spring up in district health authorities. These services ran campaigns at local level to persuade people to quit smoking, take exercise or improve their diet. However, they were disconnected from both primary and secondary care and therefore the rest of the management of those conditions whose incidence they were striving to reduce.

Although the impact of the early health promotion activities was significant, particularly on the lifestyle choices of professional classes, it was the example of HIV/AIDS in the 1980s which demonstrated – in the absence of any effective sickness response options – that effective prevention could effectively control prevalence. Highly targeted and culturally sensitive campaigns, often initiated, designed and implemented by self-help groups drawn from the communities who were most affected at the time, seemed to be dramatically impacting on prevalence rates which by the early 1990s were out-turning well below the projections of the mid-1980s. Driving home the message of safer sex and needle-exchange schemes broke numerous taboos in terms of the content of leaflets and other promotional material which public authorities could fund and even produce directly. For once the conservative British led the world in explicit and direct communication. It is yet to be proven, but the decision in the 1990s to discontinue safer sex campaigns with the sexually active heterosexual population may have been short-sighted, particularly as the number of new infections of HIV is now highest among that group.

So as the experience of managing the AIDS pandemic reinforced the role of preventive healthcare, the next major initiative from the NHS was more systematic. *Health of the Nation*[3] identified the major clinical areas which gave rise to early deaths and/or high morbidity in the population – coronary heart disease, stroke, cancer, mental illness, accidents and (added later) HIV/AIDS. The policy was to set targets not only for reducing incidence but also for changes in lifestyle which were correlated with increased risk of contracting these conditions. For example, to reduce the longer term incidence of heart disease and stroke, health authorities were to secure reductions in smoking rates, reduce systolic blood pressure among the adult population, reduce the proportion of people drinking more than 21 units of alcohol and the proportion of food energy derived from saturated fats.

This list of targets highlights two key aspects of primary prevention:

- the health system must have influence over the primary causes of disease to make a favourable impact on incidence;
- most of the major chronic illnesses which afflict people in later life – and thus clog our hospitals – have common lifestyle choices as risk factors.

Diet, lack of exercise, smoking, stress and excessive alcohol use are all contributory factors and/or causes of exacerbation in most of major disease areas. These diseases also seem to have some hereditary or genetic factor predisposing individuals to fall victim in later life. As with HIV and AIDS, effective primary prevention campaigns among people with high-risk behaviours could reduce incidence and thus future hospital bed utilization – freeing up resources within the NHS to meet other needs.

Secondary prevention

Secondary prevention targets people early in the disease process to prevent or at least slow progession. Secondary prevention is central to any disease management process which is described more fully in the previous chapter. Key components include:

- Asymptomatic conditions require a 'case finding' strategy to identify those individuals for whom secondary preventive interventions would be beneficial. This approach usually identifies key risk factors and targets an objective diagnostic test at those individuals who fall into the high-risk category.
- Since the management of the condition at this stage is often through some form of drug therapy, patients with no symptoms of illness need to be persuaded of the benefits of taking medication which may have even mild side effects for the sake of better health in the future than they would have had if they had not taken the drugs at all.
- Since most secondary prevention is delivered by primary care, immediate investment will be needed, giving rise to higher drugs budgets for primary care in the prospect of reduced medium-term expenditure in the hospital sector.

This therefore needs to be recognized in the resource allocation decisions which support strategies such as the National Service Frameworks on coronary heart disease. It is crucial that a significant amount of the unprecedented growth allocated to the NHS over the next few years is devoted to secondary prevention.

DEMAND MANAGEMENT OF TERTIARY PREVENTIVE SERVICES

Primary and secondary prevention offer medium- to long-term strategies to reduce the need for sickness response services. However, once an illness, injury or other disease process is relatively advanced, be it a head cold or a major pathology, we are in the domain of tertiary prevention or delivering care to the sufferer. In this domain, the techniques of demand management can reduce the need for service provision, the levels at which it is required, and its intensity, in the short to medium term.

DEMAND MANAGEMENT IN PRIMARY CARE

We will begin our typology of demand management techniques at the least intense level of service delivery in primary care.

NHS Direct and walk-in centres

Despite our long tradition of a primary care-based service, which has inspired reform all over the world including in the US managed care sector, it is perhaps characteristic of the British love of amateurism that we still have no national database on workload in primary care. Estimates of the numbers of consultations with GPs in the UK reported to the General Household Survey hover around the 200 million mark. The Office for National Statistics (formerly OPCS) undertakes a ten-yearly survey based on a 1 per cent sample of the population which may be more accurate and which produced a somewhat lower figure than the above when last completed in 1991. This database also shows activity in primary care growing at about 1 per cent per year due to demographic changes such as the ageing population. When we projected the likely impact of nationwide implementation of GP commissioning – as is the New Labour policy – we envisaged that that growth rate could either double or triple in ten years.[4] Given that the numbers of GPs is projected to grow at under 1 per cent per annum over the same period, there will be a crisis if some of this workload is not managed in other ways.

There is a clue within the same OPCS report which also analysed the case mix in primary care and concluded that 35–45 per cent of all consultations with GPs were for trivial or self-remitting illnesses which do not need a medical intervention. Indeed, most analyses of the ten most frequent diagnostic codes in primary care show Upper Respiratory Tract Infection (URTI) and back pain in the top three or four. In the US managed care sector these clinical facts have given rise to an explosion of nurse-led telephone triage services, some run by large practices themselves or 'carved out' by large companies specializing in this service. Based on the success of this US experience in convincing many people they do not need to leave the comfort of their own homes to bother the doctor, the current government has opted for a public sector version of the second model – i.e. a large organization separate from primary care – NHS Direct.

Where available, NHS Direct employs senior nurses at the end of a phone working to protocols to advise members of the public who ring in with concerns about their health. The nurse advisers offer the patient three options:

- self-care including advice on what type of medication he or she needs and how to administer it. An example here for our URTI patients would be to take aspirin or some other commercial cold remedy and take to bed for 24 hours, only consulting the GP if symptoms persist beyond a week;
- based on the symptoms described, a recommendation that the person should indeed see the GP at the nearest available appointment;
- a recommendation that the symptoms sound so serious that a self-referral to hospital is appropriate, perhaps via 999.

NHS Direct is being implemented nationally with concurrent evaluation. Hence even if it proves not to have the desired outcomes of reducing primary care workload, the national infrastructure and concomitant costs will still have been committed.

There are a number of issues which NHS Direct raises.

- First, it is yet another service which is currently not integrated with primary and secondary care. This could be addressed if at some stage there was one phone number through which the user accessed the NHS at any level.
- Second, since it is currently on a different phone number from that of the patient's GP, it is questionable how many members of the public routinely keep the NHS Direct number to hand alongside that of the local practice.
- Third, a triage service actually based in the GP practice would offer advantages of a separate, centralized model for the following reasons:
  - the clinical staff taking the calls would know the patient or at least have his or her records to hand or on computer;
  - clinical staff from the patient's own practice may command more credibility with the callers in the first place;
  - staff on the phones could be rotated to other duties, both providing a break from what will inevitably become a routine job and not least maintaining their hands-on practitioner skills.
- Fourth, with all the staff on senior grades (mostly nursing grade G) it is an expensive service and one which is seen by many in primary care as diverting resources which are urgently needed at practice level;
- Fifth, and not unrelated to the last point, in some parts of the country NHS Direct has been creating staffing shortages for senior nurses. In outer London, for example, the creation of the service has drawn practice nurses away from otherwise popular posts in primary care, thus adding to already acute supply problems for clinical staff in that sector.

The jury is currently out on NHS Direct. Some of the early evaluation indicates that, along with walk-in centres which are another alternative to primary care for minor complaints, additional workload is being generated from among those who may not otherwise have bothered the NHS and might have managed perfectly well through self-care management. Some PCGs are already creating alternative triage services in the face of findings, after a year of the service, of no reduction in local primary care workload. In some areas they have stopped advertising the NHS Direct. phone number. That said, consumer satisfaction rates are high, perhaps reflecting the 15 minutes or so of time each caller receives from the nurse at the end of the phone. Whatever their future, however, these initiatives need to be integrated into the rest of the NHS so that there is no fragmentation, duplication or creation of additional and unnecessary workload which inevitably drains resources away from more pressing needs.

Self-care

Self-care goes beyond simply advising a patient to take aspirin or rest up for a few days. Most of the larger HMOs in the US take a much more proactive approach to self-care, extending the principles which are well established in diabetes management in the UK. The patient is provided with an individualized treatment programme, usually written down in non-technical language in a step-by-step format. The patient will also be given information on his or her disease symptomology and how to monitor symptoms such as rapid weight gain in congestive heart failure, as well as ongoing management and how to administer treatment including self-administration of intra-muscular medication in diabetic patients. Information on how and under what circumstances specialist clinical services should be engaged is also given in the event of exacerbations. Self-care is neither simply an attempt to save resources nor an abrogation of responsibility. At its best it can release the patients from the traditional 'sick role', giving them greater control over their medical condition and empowering them to live more normal lives.

Moreover, in the United States, systematic and more proactive self-care management programmes have been evaluated and shown to bring a return of 250–400 per cent on the investment *needed to finance them properly*,[5] with no reduction in clinical outcomes or patient satisfaction. Indeed, performance on both of these indicators can and should improve.

Shared decision making through patient participation and collaboration

These outcomes cannot however be achieved without full patient participation and collaboration. Diabetes is one field of management where in the UK we currently fully involve the patient in care planning and implementation. This is not simply a matter of devolving care processes which patients prefer and record in positive feedback to satisfaction surveys. In most disease areas, patient collaboration is critical to a successful clinical process. This involves providing relevant information. As previously mentioned, in order to prevent the progression of osteoporosis in women – who account for 80 per cent of cases – patients need to take medication for ten to fifteen years from the point of onset of the condition which in some women can be as early as age 35 to 40. The most cost-effective medication is hormone replacement therapy and this may produce side effects which cause discomfort or generate concerns about increased risk of cancer. As a result, compliance rates in the UK to long-term HRT are as low as 15 per cent. However, research in the US has shown that engaging the patient, sharing the results of the bone density test which confirms onset of the disease, and discussing the implications of advanced osteoporosis in old age, including risk and implications of a major fracture, increases compliance rates threefold or fourfold. The patient has taken the decision to follow the course of treatment having had all the facts put before her. Lack of tolerance of side effects is another major cause of non-compliance and should be discussed, and alternatives tried.

Re-engineering within primary care

The average GP in the UK sees about 5,000 patients per year with an average consultation time of about eight minutes. Projected growth rates in primary care activity of 2 or 3 per cent per year will, if realized, outstrip the expected rate of increase in the numbers of GPs. The growing numbers of women in the GP workforce, plus the increasing tendency for family doctors to opt for part-time working or early retirement, are creating supply problems already in some parts of the country. At the same time devolution of workload from the secondary sector, combined with the impact of triage which should remove the more trivial cases, is likely to increase the intensity of the average GP consultation, necessitating more time input than the current eight minutes.

The only way to manage this challenge is to re-engineer workload in primary care so that other clinical staff can manage patients. From our experience, the OPCS finding that a significant proportion of current GP workload does not need a medical consultation is supported when caseload is reviewed in detail at practice level.[6] Figures of 40 per cent or more are a common finding. Distributing this work to nurses, counsellors, physiotherapists or other practitioners will greatly alleviate future pressure on GPs themselves. However, more recent experience in the United States indicates that these types of strategies are becoming relatively conservative.

The development of primary care in the managed care sector has run alongside the growth of nurse practitioners in a wide range of clinical areas in the US. By the mid-1990s, it was already commonplace to find nurses working alongside family doctors, each with his or her own patients. The nurses were very popular with the patients. Indeed, some HMOs had a 'quality control' mechanism in place whereby if a patient had not seen a doctor for five visits in a row, then he or she would be automatically scheduled a medical appointment on the next visit. The patient satisfaction surveys and quality audits of nurse practitioners in primary care continued to provide such positive results, however, that in 1998 American nurse practitioners were able to persuade the Clinton administration, supported by Congress, to give each state a discretionary power to grant nurse practitioners the right to work across the entire scope for practice for primary care without medical supervision. The scope for practice includes prescribing all medication used in primary care and referral rights to specialists in hospitals. Initially about one-third of states took up the measure and there are now a number of nurse-led primary care practice pilot projects running across the country.

Re-engineering to nurses or other clinical staff is only cost-effective, therefore, within controlled productivity parameters. Costs can rise if this issue is not carefully monitored. With nurses paid between a third and half the salary of a GP in the US, these initiatives are likely to prove cost-effective in the States. However, the cost issue is less clear-cut in the UK. One of the reasons why patients prefer to see the nurse is that, *even within the US system*, they get a longer consultation – usually 20 minutes. The practice is similar in the UK. Therefore, if we decide to take 40 per cent of GP consultations in practice and refer them direct to nurse practitioners on senior nursing grades, and it takes the nurse twice the time per consultation, we need to bear in mind that the differential in salary is only around 2:1 between the two staff groups. Hence the differential in cost will be nil – although if it costs the same and the clinical outcomes are the same but patient satisfaction improves, then so does value for money.

However, we can take the example of the management of mild to moderate depression in primary care which figures high among GPs' current workload as an illustration of cost parity of re-engineered workload. Currently in primary care, most people with depression will be put on medication, sometimes for up to six months at a cost of around £50 per month for an relatively expensive new generation anti-depressant such as Prozac, perhaps with four to six GP consultations over the period of therapy. Total cost would be about £400. According to the evidence base, however, psychotherapy is just as effective in managing the symptoms and may produce a better long-term prognosis in some patients. This will require an average of 12 sessions over a three-month period. However, if each counselling session is costing £35 a time for a 50-minute consultation, both the staffing time per case and the cost comes out at around £400. Hence, in this case, re-engineering may offer quality benefits for the same unit cost, thus bringing an improvement in value for money.

DEMAND MANAGEMENT OF SPECIALIST OUTPATIENT SERVICES

During the first year of the various GP commissioning pilots, including fundholding, many practices were able to reduce outpatient attendances by their patients – in some cases by as much as 40 per cent.[7] Financial incentives were important here. Fundholders who were paying up to £150 for each attendance were understandably zealous scrutineers of the clinical necessity of it. We can therefore expect PCGs and PCTs to take a keen interest in promoting techniques of demand management directed at specialist outpatient services, not least because the more they spend in the secondary sector within a fixed budget the less is available for investment in primary care.

There are three questions to consider in the demand management of specialist, usually consultant-led, outpatient services:

- What are appropriate levels of activity and how do we monitor it?
- Is it clinically necessary against the evidence base?
- If so, can it be re-engineered consistent with patient-focused care, either by locating the service closer to the patient by providing it in primary care or by reducing the number of outpatient visits for each episode of specialist care?

Monitoring

Monitoring outpatient referral and attendance rates may be sufficient in itself to motivate GPs and consultants to review their current practice. Data on two indicators should be routinely collected and analysed:

- referral rate from each practice – defined as first attendances per 1000 population on the list;
- ratio of new to follow-up attendances.

The first measure gives an indication of how appropriate the use made by the practice of the consultant service is and throws light on complaints by the latter that there are GPs who refer cases they should be managing themselves – the amount of chest pain of non-cardiac origin referred to cardiologists is one case in point. The second indicates the propensity or otherwise of consultants to bring back patients for unnecessary repeat visits and explores the validity of the complaints by some GPs that certain of their specialist colleagues 'adopt' patients or insist on managing them for the medium term rather than refer back early to primary care – a common tension in diabetes management, for example. Data may also be disaggregated by GP and consultant to identify any significant variations in individual practice. Comparative data by practice and clinician can be simply reported back with no commentary or interpretation in the hope that the figures will speak for themselves.

It is important to monitor for under-utilization as well as over-utilization since the latter may indicate a quality problem. Levels are monitored within a range which has a maximum and minimum defined as acceptable. This 'utilization range' can be defined by benchmarking, evidence review or process re-engineering – or, optimally, all three.

Defining the utilization range through benchmarking

Benchmarking is a technique now strongly advocated by ministers for managing performance. However, it is a useful demand management technique also. By gathering referral data on practices which have similar age, sex and socio-demographic profiles such as one would largely expect within a PCG, for example, an acceptable range can be defined from current practice. One approach, for instance, is to take the inter-quartile range of that within which the 50 per cent most representative values lie. Benchmarking in this way should be used to identify significant variations from common professional practice and thus stimulate discussion of any service or population-need factors which explain them. In the case of consultant practice we need to be mindful of the different case-mix with individuals managed within a given specialty which may require differential reattendance rates. If these legitimate factors are not present then there is likely to be a utilization issue. The working methods of GPs and consultants with the most efficient and clinically appropriate patterns of utilization can also be studied with a view to passing on their approaches to the outliers. Generating the data within the PCG will require a special exercise. However, comparative databases for outpatient attendances by specialty at higher levels of aggregation are often available from the health authority, or in published statistical returns such as those produced by the Department of Health, which has provider and regional aggregates, and the Welsh Office's *Health Statistics Wales* 1998.[8] For a more detailed discussion of how to use benchmarking, see Chapter 9.

Defining the utilization range through clinical review

Benchmarking alone is commonly criticized as a purely statistical process which is unrelated to clinical need and, relatedly, as rendering all practice to the lowest common denominator. Although these criticisms caricature the process, we need to recognize the genuine concerns that underlie them. These can be addressed by defining the requirement for specialist outpatients in evidence-based, integrated care pathways or referral guidelines. These documents are produced by multidisciplinary groups of clinicians from primary and secondary care. It is advisable to develop them with the clinical staff who will use them in those conditions where volumes and/or case costs are high (see Chapter 5 for how to develop them). The documentation should specify, as clearly as the evidence allows, the agreed criteria for referral to specialist opinion, the number of outpatient visits each patient is likely to need, usually stated as a range, say up to two repeats, and the investigation plan which the specialist will follow.

It thus becomes a kind of contract between primary and secondary care in clinical and resource-specific terms.

Reducing outpatient attendances by re-engineering

The development of referral guidelines can reduce the number of out-patient attendances by extending the role of primary care in the diagnosis and management of many common and costly conditions. First, much of the 'work-up' or diagnostic tests required can be coordinated from primary care (see Chapter 5 for an extract from a referral guideline for unstable angina).

In a conventional outpatient service, many of these tests will be instig-ated by the cardiologist at the first attendance, with the results only becoming available for the second. Hence the re-engineered process im-mediately cuts out one visit. However, the guideline should also assist the GP to interpret the results of tests and inform the decision as to whether the patient's condition is severe or complex enough to need a specialist or whether he or she can be managed by the primary care team. In this case if the patient tolerated 15 minutes on the treadmill – the stress test – then the GP could retain management. Five minutes or less indicates a definite need to refer. Between five and fifteen minutes the GP would speak to the cardiologist on the phone and discuss the case before deciding one way or another. This approach therefore further reduces the need for outpatient attendances by devolving care to the primary care team, thus increasing its clinical acumen and confidence in the management of angina.

Of course, these processes require the primary care team to have direct access to a wide range of diagnostic tests such as 12-point ECGs, bone density scans for osteoporosis, and spirometry for lung function tests, which have previously only been available in hospitals. As technology renders the diagnostic equipment needed both smaller and less expensive, it will be increasingly feasible to make groups of GPs self-sufficient, avoid-ing any need for many patients to go up to the hospital at all. Critical mass will clearly be an issue since it is not economic to provide diagnostic equipment which is only used two or three times per week. The strategy, therefore, should be to develop interim diagnostic centres in larger health centres or other premises of large group practices, or even to have some of this equipment in a mobile unit. In some of the larger primary care centres in the managed care sector in the US it is not uncommon to find X-ray rooms, an endoscopy room, and a small laboratory where 90 per cent of tests can be carried out.

An alternative re-engineering approach being developed in some outpa-tient departments in the UK is the 'rapid diagnostic centre'. This approach is designed to reduce the number of visits by patients by integrating the diagnostic testing, diagnosis itself and instigation of any management into one half-day during which time the patient may see the consultant or one of his team two or even three times. Again, an evidence-based protocol agreed by primary and secondary care is put in place to define the process followed in any condition. The centre itself will be designed so that all the necessary diagnostic tools are within a short distance of the consulting rooms themselves for rapid throughput of patients. Given the need for patient focus and critical mass, this model is most suitable for incorporation into a community hospital well located to serve a clearly defined population of, say, 50,000–100,000 people, with good transport access, and which is eventually transferred to management of the local Primary Care Trust. Otherwise, where much of the care process is retained by the secondary sector it may be seen as less attractive than models which devolve to primary and community care.

Using standard referral forms – from monitoring to audit

Finally, compliance with the guidelines should be kept under constant review. A mechanism for this is to replace the traditional referral letter with a standard referral form which includes the agreed referral criteria as well as an open section for other comment. This would generate a more clinically specific or audit database which will greatly increase the legitimacy of any monitoring process in the eyes of clinical staff. Audit reports can then be discussed by GPs and consultants alike as part of the routine review process of the guidelines themselves. The aim is to empower the GP to consider all the options and make specialist referrals 'count'. Outliers can then be discussed and either the guidelines amended if too tightly drawn or the practice of the outlying clinicians reviewed. As Kongstvedt puts it: 'This often means breaking old habits, but then that is what medical management is about.'[9]

NOTES AND REFERENCES

1 P.R. Kongstvedt (1996) Managing basic medical–surgical utilisation, in *The Managed Care Handbook*, p. 249. Gaithersburg, MD: Aspen.
2 Kongstvedt, op. cit., p. 199.
3 Department of Health (1992) *Health of the Nation: Specification of National Indicators*. London: Department of Health.
4 M. Conroy and D.A. Cochrane (1996) *The Future Healthcare Workforce – First Report*. Manchester: University of Manchester.
5 Kongstvedt, op. cit., p. 200.
6 M. Conroy, D.A. Cochrane (1999) *The Future Healthcare Workforce – Second Steering Group Report*. Bournemouth: University of Bournemouth.
7 Castlefields Health Centre (1998) *Annual Report 1997/98*. Runcorn: Castlefields Health Centre.
8 Similar databases exist for Scotland and Northern Ireland.
9 Kongstvedt, op. cit., p. 207.

UTILIZATION MANAGEMENT IN ACUTE IN-PATIENT CARE

David Cochrane

As British health professionals, we are gradually coming to terms with the reality that most people do not like being in hospital. It is not because they are ungrateful. It is not simply because the food can be of variable quality, sleep is often disrupted on open wards and, unless there is personal TV service available, one rarely gets to see one's favourite programmes. Nor is it just because of the risk of cross-infection. More significant, perhaps, the general public tends to associate admission to and extended stay in hospital with severity or seriousness of an illness or procedure. Most people are understandably less inclined to worry if their condition does not lead to hospital admission or, if it does, the stay is only one or two days. There is also good objective evidence for this preference. Study after study has shown that people recover more quickly and require less medication such as analgaesia in their familiar surroundings, partly because of the need to return to familiar routines, and partly because they are less likely than in hospital to assume the passive and dependent 'sick role'. Moreover, it seems reasonable to assume that admission rates to hospital and average length of stay are in some part proportionate to the general state of ill health of our population and also to accept how invasive and debilitating our medical procedures are. Since we are constantly striving to improve performance in both these domains, minimizing the use of hospital stay is not just a resource concern; it should be an inevitable by-product of any quality strategy.

The £12 billion the NHS is spending on acute hospital care in 1999/2000[1] seems insufficient to avoid bed crises, over 1 million people on waiting lists for elective surgery, and over 50,000 cancellations of booked surgery each year.[2] The aim of demand management in in-patient care needs, therefore, both to mitigate supply problems and to release resources for secondary and primary prevention. However, before we get too ambitious, the first question which arises is the scope for further acute bed reduction, if any, over the next five to ten years. At first sight this looks challenging.

- The number of acute beds in the NHS in England has been declining steadily from just under 150,000 – excluding maternity – in 1990 to 113,000 by 1997/8.
- In contrast, acute hospital activity as measured in finished consultant episodes was increasing by over 3 per cent annually over the same period.
- This figure of 3 per cent masks a wide variation in the growth of surgical and medical admissions to hospital; whereas surgical admissions remained relatively static, medical admissions were increasing by 8 per cent annually.
- Chronic diseases in elderly people dominate emergency medical admissions and the population is ageing.[3]

Acute hospitals have been managing these seemingly conflicting trends by reducing average length of stay while also running closer to full capacity, which in some places has meant occupancy levels of over 90 per cent. A key question in the current debate about acute bed levels therefore is whether this process has gone as far as it can.

Figure 7.1 shows the growth in general and acute hospital activity since the early 1980s projected through to the year 2005 when we can expect over 12 million episodes of hospital care on current management practices. This rising demand is fuelled partly by the tendency of medicine continually to extend the range and scope of conditions which can be cured or alleviated. Hence yesterday's breakthrough in medical care becomes tomorrow's mainstream acute service. The other major factor is of course the changing demography and particularly the increasing numbers of elderly people in the population. The population of the UK

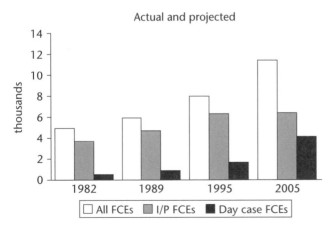

Figure 7.1   General and acute hospital activity 1982–2005

is projected to increase from 57.6 million at the time of the 1991 census, to just over 60 million by the year 2005. Figures for England show that in 1991 just over 16 per cent of the population was aged 65, 7 per cent over 75 and 1.6 per cent over 85. Now, although the proportion over 65 will not change greatly over the next five years or so, their absolute numbers will increase in line with the general population. Moreover, the proportion over 75 will rise to 7.6 per cent and those over 85 to 2.2 per cent.

These trends have major implications for hospital care in particular. Taking figures for the mid-1990s, over 20 per cent of consultations with GPs were with people aged over 65, however, over 50 per cent of bed use in the acute sector was by this age group. More recent data shows that the impact of the ageing population is an increasing proportionate use of acute hospital services.

In 1997/8 there were 9.75 million episodes of activity – admissions and day cases, but excluding births – in the general and acute sector. Thirty-six per cent of these people were over 65 and 22 per cent over 75 years of age. Just over 4.2 million of these acute episodes were emergency admissions. Of these, 44 per cent were aged over 65 and 28 per cent aged over 75. As well as being the largest group in admissions, elderly people stay in hospital longer. Again, in 1997/8 all acute admissions occupied 1.1 million beds. People aged over 65 accounted for over 64 per cent and people aged over 75, 44 per cent. The skewed utilization by the elderly of emergency acute hospital beds is still greater. Emergency admissions accounted for 64 per cent of all acute beds, with 68 per cent of emergency beds occupied by people aged over 65 and 49 per cent by people aged over 75.[4] This apparent over-representation of elderly people in acute hospital utilization and bed use had increased significantly since the early 1990s.[5]

Do these statistics indeed reflect over-utilization of acute hospital care either in terms of avoidable admission or excessive length of stay? Most elderly emergency admissions are referred by their GPs rather than self-referred direct to accident and emergency. There has been no national audit of the appropriateness of emergency admissions, however myriad local studies have tended to report conflicting and inconclusive findings of the propensity of junior medical staff in hospital emergency departments to admit patients whom their more experienced consultant colleagues may have sent home. In such cases there are usually three clinical reviews involved – the GP, the A & E doctor and nurses, and the receiving department medical staff at ward level. So it would seem unlikely that significant numbers of inappropriate admissions slip through. However, the term *appropriate* in this context has tended to mean in need of admission either because of undeniable clinical need of acute hospital care at the time or, in many cases, because the elderly person is clinically vulnerable and at risk and no suitable alternative care is available. Moreover, when admission rates are compared internationally and internally in the UK, there is some evidence of over-hospitalization. The recent National Beds

Inquiry found that admission rates for all older people have been either flat or falling in the US, Canada, the Netherlands, and even Scotland. It also reported wide variations in admission rates and bed use within the UK with over 25 per cent of all health authorities more than 20 per cent higher or lower than the mean average. These variations show no correlation with needs profile or the effectiveness of local bed management systems.[6] The one factor which did correlate, however, was the availability of NHS community care and social services for elderly people.

There is even further evidence of excessive length of stay. Various reviews from the Audit Commission, the University of York and medical bodies such as the Royal Colleges have consistently reported that the proportion of acute beds occupied by elderly people no longer in the acute phase of illness ranges from 20 to 50 per cent.[7] According to the National Audit Office, delayed discharge alone results in the loss of 2.2 million bed days or 7500 available beds at current average occupancy of 80 per cent. Lastly, despite perceptions in some quarters to the contrary, this average suggests that the NHS does not use its current acute bed stock to a reasonable capacity. As the National Audit Office also found, average bed occupancy in 70 per cent of acute trusts in the UK was below the optimum level for access and efficiency of 85 per cent.[8]

DEMAND MANAGEMENT THROUGH INTERMEDIATE CARE

In conclusion, therefore, there is scope for reducing our reliance on hospital in-patient care. The techniques of demand management for achieving this fall into two categories:

• avoiding the admissions;
• minimizing acute length of stay for appropriate admissions.

AVOIDING ADMISSIONS

One of the most effective ways to minimize the use of in-patient beds is to avoid the admission in the first place. There are three mechanisms for doing so:

• day surgery and hospital hotel schemes;
• admission diversion schemes;
• admission prevention schemes such as case management.

Day surgery

In 1998/9, the average acute hospital in England was undertaking 60 per cent of its elective surgery on an ambulatory basis. This average masks a wide range of variation, with the percentage in some hospitals still as low as 40 per cent and day surgery rates per 1000 varying between 20.3 and

102 in 1997/8.[9] When day surgery first began to be actively promoted to patients by the NHS, it was done so rather apologetically. It saved money and increased access, yes, but many health service managers assumed the public would prefer to have their operations on an in-patient basis. However, as day surgery units began to offer scheduled appointments which suited the patient, as well as lead on the use of anaethetics and minimum invasive techniques from which people recover quickly, so day surgery has become popular with patients and GPs alike.

The National Beds Inquiry used a planning assumption of 70 per cent of elective surgery undertaken on a day basis in five years' time. The recent National Plan increased this to 75 per cent. However, both figures are conservative for most surgery programmes. For example, Kingston Hospital and its medical staff have been national leaders in day surgery and now undertake 85 per cent of all elective procedures including ear, nose and throat (ENT) and ophthalmology without admission through the hospital's purpose-built day surgery unit. This local experience, which mirrors performance in the better US managed care schemes, is now being planned into other new acute hospital developments.

Achieving these results requires the following:

- providing a purpose-built and designed day surgery unit (DSU) with sufficient theatre capacity, a range of recovery areas reflecting the varying invasiveness of surgical procedures and separate access for patients pre- and post-surgery;
- a team of surgeons and anaesthetists who are committed to and skilled in techniques which require minimum post-operative nursing care and rapid patient recovery;
- scheduling appointments so that the service retains patient support and demand;
- a 12-hour working day including scheduling systems so that patients requiring eight hours' recovery are operated on in the first morning theatre sessions;
- rapid pre-operative medical review procedures to assess fitness for surgery on the day of surgery;
- in some cases, devolution of these procedures to primary care so that the patient arrives with the results already available to the DSU's staff and can go straight in;
- a good after-care support service, with patients given sufficient post-operative medication, fully informed of the post-operative recovery process including the progress of the wound itself, and a phone-line for patients with concerns. Apart from good quality, this minimizes the nuisance levels of day surgery for GPs – such as out-of-hours calls by patients in pain or unduly concerned about their wounds – and hence helps maintain the support of local general practice;
- a policy allowing immediate hospital admission for patients with adverse outcomes.

Eight-five per cent of day surgery targets may not be generalizable given the range of elective procedures carried out in tertiary referral centres – such as open heart surgery – which require in-patient care. However, even if the NHS achieves 75 per cent in the next ten years, sufficient in-patient beds should be released to accommodate both the in-patient work of current waiting lists and any natural growth.[10]

Hospital hotel

Some patients, such as isolated elderly people who cannot fend for themselves during the first day or so after surgery, may not be able to go straight home. To achieve 85 per cent at Kingston, therefore, these patients are offered accommodation overnight in a hospital hotel on discharge. This is a facility usually on or close to the hospital site offering good quality hotel-type accommodation. An unqualified nurse or receptionist will be on duty at all times, accessible by guests in case of any concerns. Any problems are immediately referred to the hospital A & E department. The hospital hotel can also reduce length of stay for some elective and emergency in-patients.

Admission diversion schemes

As noted earlier, many emergency admissions arise because GPs and admitting clinical staff are concerned that some elderly patients would be at risk if sent home since they are unable to fend for themselves during illness or be monitored for any exacerbation of their condition. These patients typically include those with a chest or urinary tract infection, or those who have suffered a minor cardio-vascular event or an unexplained fall which would not greatly trouble a younger, fitter person, or would give rise to less clinical concern in older people with relatives and other carers to hand. Initiatives that reduce the risk threshold for these patients can consequently reduce admissions.

First, evidence-based, integrated care pathways produced and agreed by secondary and primary care can themselves through both the process of development and the wide availability of the documentation support the primary care team in managing more patients without referral to A & E. As with outpatient referrals, clear and graduating criteria can be drawn up which govern whether and when referral is needed. Again, these can be audited over time and practice kept under constant review. In the case of a home-sitting service, a health or social care staff member simply stays with a patient for up to 72 hours, allowing the GP to monitor daily until any danger has subsided. It is important to remember that this service is a substitute for a relative or friend. Consequently trained non-professional staff or volunteers are just as effective as qualified staff and will keep down relative costs.

Step-down facilities

Alternative in-patient facilities which are less intensive in resource terms than acute care are another alternative. These include both beds in NHS sub-acute or community hospitals or, to avoid capital outlay, use of specialist private sector nursing home places. A multi-agency scheme based in North Mersey Community Trust has demonstrated the effectiveness and quality of care which can be delivered from private sector nursing homes with spare capacity.[11] Successful projects such as this doubtless inspire the National Plan's recommendations that some of the proposed additional intermediate care beds will derive from partnerships with the private nursing home sector.

These services need to be carefully planned and designed to avoid them simply functioning as respositories for elderly people with little or no active care input. Typically the case mix therefore is likely to comprise people undergoing rehabilitation after the acute phase of stroke or fractured neck of femur, and medical cases such as the less severe exacerbations of congestive heart failure and chest or urinary tract infections which do not require the intensive diagnostic and clinical interventions of an acute hospital. A useful starting point for reviewing the likely case mix of step-down facilities is the Milliman and Robertson Recovery Facility Guidelines which specify expected length of stay and admission rate by diagnosis or procedure.[12] Rehabilitation beds should be planned within the growing body of evidence that rehabilitation can be just as effective in the home environment as in hospital. Moreover, one of the key objectives of step-down is to provide appropriate care at a cost per day lower than the acute sector. In the US managed care sector, the cost of these 'step-down' facilities is substantially less than acute hospital care. This partly reflects the high costs of hospital stay in the US but also a competitive process since the step-down facility would not get the business if its costs were not significantly lower. In any case, the staffing input to patients in the post-acute phase is far less intense. In the UK the cost differentials tend to be smaller but nevertheless should show the interim care facilities costing between 50 and 70 per cent of the acute hospital costs. To give an indication of what should be achieved some comparative costs are as follows:

Acute hospital	£170–220 per day
Community hospital	£115–145 per day
Specialist nursing home	£70–110 per day

Hence for any Primary Care Group or Trust, high-volume use of intermediate care facilities offers significant scope for resource release from the acute sector as well as bargaining power to keep the daily rates within bounds. However, clear criteria drawn from care pathways prescribe which type of patients under which circumstances are appropriate, with clear boundaries set for the expected length of stay. Otherwise patients can linger in these facilities, adding to costs, for no further clinical benefit.

Admission prevention through case management

Analysis of acute admissions and bed use by elderly people reveals one group with potential for more proactive management. This group subdivides into the following:

- those with an acute exacerbation of a condition (such as COPD or unstable angina) already known to the healthcare system;
- those with a relatively minor problem such as urinary or chest infection which becomes serious because of the generally poor health status of the patient;
- those who have an acute exacerbation of a condition not previously known to the system;
- those who are retained in hospital for protracted periods because, having dealt with the acute problem which presented on admission, hospital clinical staff find a number of pre-existing co-morbidities which have been suboptimally managed and which require sorting out prior to discharge.

For this group, the potential to mitigate the need for admission and stay in hospital lies in the US model of case management. Case management is a total quality management approach to people whose poor health status causes them to use high levels of healthcare resources. The programme in the US was developed in the mid-1990s following federal government concerns that expenditure on its Medicare Programme, which funds healthcare provision for retired people, would be unsustainable as the population age structure changed over the next ten to fifteen years. Analysis of resource use at that time by the Health Care Financing Administration (HCFA) and the American Hospital Association showed 10 per cent of 30 million beneficiaries accounting for nearly 70 per cent of expenditure.[13] This group of patients is identified and targeted for short-term but intensive case work usually by senior nurses with some social work support.

Case management employs secondary prevention to improve health status and prevent acute exacerbations of chronic conditions common in elderly people such as stroke, angina, fractures and COPD as well as serious illnesses such as cancer or renal failure in younger adults. Case managers assess and plan packages of care and ensure resources within the healthcare system are deployed to meet the needs of each individual. Specific areas of work include ensuring medical problems are sorted out, educating the client and significant others about the disease process including awareness of early warning signs and how and when to access the healthcare system, reviewing current medications, and facilitating compliance with treatment programmes.

The out-turns from the first case management pilots in the US showed very significant reductions in emergency hospital admission rates (up to 25 per cent), reduced length of stay in hospital, improved functioning for the individuals and high patient satisfaction rates.[14] The programme has therefore been 'rolled out' to millions of elderly Americans from all cultures and socio-economic backgrounds. Sherry Aliotta describes the service in detail in Chapter 8 and reviews out-turn studies including the first pilot in the UK. These support the consensus between the managed care literature and operational experience of MCOs which attributes continued reduction in hospitalization rates in the US during the 1990s to case management.

Unlike in the US where community nursing staff had to be specifically recruited and trained, the UK has an established infrastructure of district nurses and health visitors who could perform a case management role. Recent evidence from the Audit Commission has shown scope to re-engineer the workload of district nurses with the senior qualified staff being released to a more specialized and focused role.[15] The evidence base for the core role of health visitors in the twenty-first century in relation to mothers and babies not in at-risk groups is questionable. The productivity of both groups is subject to wide variations unrelated to population needs profiles. With positive results now showing that case management may prove as effective in the UK as in the US, it could become a high-priority service for current community nurses providing a central and leading role within the primary care team.

MINIMIZING LENGTH OF STAY ON ADMISSION

To date in the UK most demand management activity has been focused on managing and reducing length of stay for existing in-patients. Techniques include care pathways, systematic discharge planning, and process re-engineering to optimize throughput during a hospital stay.

Care pathways

Care pathways are designed to capture on a day-by-day basis the optimum care process for any stay in hospital, including expected day of discharge, and point at which action is needed to deliver this. Pathways tend to be most useful where the length of stay is predictable, as in the case of most elective surgical procedures which require in-patient care. However, even common causes of emergency medical admission such as myocardial infarction or unstable angina have fairly clear management processes which can be prescribed over the course of a four- to seven-day hospital stay. Care pathways are working documents and each stage of the care process should be signed off by the member of clinical staff prescribed to deliver it. For elective procedures such as a hip replacement or coronary artery by-pass graft, discharge planning including the provision of any services or aids needed in the home can be planned as part of the pre-admission process.

When care pathways are developed, they should reflect any scope for re-engineering acute bed-days out of the care process either by using hospital hotels, step-down facilities such as community hospitals or nursing home beds or providing clinical or rehabilitation services in the home. We give more detail on the development and content of care pathways in Chapter 5.

The role of the utilization nurse or discharge coordinator

Kongstvedt describes the utilization nurse as 'the one individual who is crucial to any managed care programme'.[16] This is a full-time job in American hospitals and the role is to ensure the pathway is followed and that any problems or delays are addressed immediately. The utilization nurse is also the discharge planner. This function should not be left to ward managers since it is bound to be interrupted and deprioritized in the face of more urgent clinical work required by other patients. The utilization nurse has the following functions.

First, the nurse gathers a database on each admission during morning rounds. This database will include diagnosis on admission, admitting consultant, appropriate care pathway, expected length of stay and, if the person is elderly, any social care package currently in place. In the United States the utilization nurse will use statistical databases to generate an expected minimum and maximum length of stay for the patient's type of case. Where no discharge plan has been put in place prior to admission, the utilization nurse starts the process immediately. The discharge plan will include:

- any special requirements on discharge such as aids to daily living provided direct by the NHS;
- immediate scheduling of case conference with social services if required;
- ensuring that move-on placement in a step-down or nursing facility is organized;
- ensuring community-based staff are geared up to assume management if the patient will be going straight home and will need further NHS support;
- educating the patient and carers on what to expect during the course of the hospital stay, prior to and after discharge.

In the more aggressive systems of utilization management, the utilization nurse does not work for the hospital but is an employee either of the HMO itself or the primary care purchasing organization such as the IPA. This had a dual advantage:

- It benefits the hospital by taking the responsibility for discharge planning and coordination off the staff delivering the in-patient care. Any disputes about length of stay or delayed discharge are thus not laid at the hospital's door.

- The commissioning group is incentivized to minimize use of acute hospital stay and is fully informed of the reasons for causes of any delays or divergence from agreed pathways.
- The commissioning group contracts with other providers whose co-operation is critical to rapid and effective discharge and who therefore have more bargaining power with which to address recurrent difficulties than the acute hospital itself.
- In joint commissioning models for elderly people, it is will be easier for the commissioning group or Primary Care Trust level 5 to ensure that social care packages are in place as required.

Up until recently, this model would have seemed too much of an intrusion on the prerogative of the acute hospital staff in discharge planning. However, North Cornwall PCG has instigated a system of discharge nurses based in the community working in the acute hospital setting with full and welcoming cooperation from the hospital staff and, not least, successful outcomes for patients.

Coordinating key processes needed for discharge

A number of hospital-based processes need to be in place before the patient can be discharged. These include:

- medical review;
- assessment by other professional staff such as physiotherapists;
- provision of medication;
- organizing transport.

It is therefore important that these services are available 12 hours per day, seven days per week. If a patient with a fracture is medically fit for discharge on Saturday morning, it is no longer acceptable practice for the patient to have to stay in until Monday because the physiotherapy service only works five days per week.

Ensuring bed management and throughput is efficient

There are a number of simple bed management mechanisms which the National Audit Office highlighted in its recent report.[17] These include:

- planning elective admissions around known seasonal peaks in emergency workload;
- separating bed management as a function and supporting it with an IT-based bed availability database and management system such as the one at the Royal Shrewsbury Hospital;
- ensuring elective surgery patients are fit for the procedure;
- ensuring elective surgery patients are admitted on the day of surgery, not before, and not admitted to a bed if the procedure is safe for day surgery;

- ensuring adequate theatre time is scheduled and coordinated;
- providing discharge lounges where final care processes are undertaken so that the bed itself is cleared as early as possible.

MONITORING AND AUDIT

Since admission rates to hospital vary widely by health authority it can be expected that variations of similar magnitude exist between referring GPs and admitting consultants. As with outpatient utilization, emergency referral and admission rates may be influenced simply by gathering data on individual practices and clinicians and reporting back with no commentary or interpretation in the anticipation that the figures will speak for themselves. Similarly, it is important to monitor for under-utilization as well as over-utilization since the latter may indicate a quality problem. Levels are monitored within a range which has a maximum and minimum defined as acceptable. This range of acceptability is defined by benchmarking, evidence review or process re-engineering – or, optimally, all three (see Chapter 10). In the case of in-patient care, indicators monitored will include (by health resource group or other case-mix measure):

- emergency admission rates per 1000;
- elective admission rates per 1000;
- day surgery rates;
- length of stay per finished consultant episode;
- length of stay per hospital spell where more than one consultant is involved in the in-patient management (such as in a neck of femur repair when a patient may transfer from the care of an orthopaedic to an ortho-rehabilitation consultant).

Guidelines and care pathways will define the expected and optimum hospital utilization for high-volume, high-cost cases. These can be used as the basis for audit of reported utilization data.

CASE STUDY – FRACTURED NECK OF FEMUR

We illustrate the utilization management process overall with the case of neck of femur fracture. Current incidence in the UK is about 60,000 per year and costs the NHS £5000 per case. According to the European Union, we can expect this incidence to increase by 50 per cent by 2020 if current management practice remains unchanged (see Chapter 5). This is largely responding after the event and providing emergency orthopaedic surgery and recovery in acute hospitals with a length of stay of about three weeks. In contrast, a comprehensive utilization management programme would offer the following services:

- **Secondary prevention of osteoporosis.** Since 80 per cent of current and projected cases are among women with advanced osteoporotic bone damage, the first line of attack, therefore, is to provide secondary prevention for peri- and post-menopausal women.
- **Case management of elderly people with advanced osteoporosis to prevent falls and fractures.** The second stage is to try and prevent the accidents which cause the fractures. For example, it is estimated that people who fall and break their hip have fallen on average twice before. Hence, the next line of attack is case management of elderly people at risk. This programme would identify frequent fallers – defined as those who are known to have fallen twice – and seek to remedy any medical causes of falling and fainting. At the same time, there would be a home safety evaluation which would seek to minimize accidents in the home due to loose stair carpets, exposed hard-surface flooring, or other domestic hazards. Clients can also be advised to require protective pads which are now small and discreet so they can work comfortably with ordinary clothing.
- **Re-engineering the management of NOF fractures.** The third line of attack is to reduce the unit cost of repairing a fractured NOF. The UK now has over ten years' experience of a re-engineered care process known as the Peterborough Model. Under this model the role of the acute orthopaedic services is simply to repair the fracture and stabilize the patient post-surgery. This is governed by a care pathway which prescribes surgery within 24 hours of admission – a clinical quality standard and an average acute hospital length of stay of about six days. Just over half the patients are transferred after four days to an ortho-rehabilitation in-patient service in a step-down, rehabilitation unit such as a community hospital for a further 10–14 day stay. The others are discharged after six to eight days with rehabilitation services provided on a 'hospital at home' basis. The general rule for selecting these patients is that they will have been fully mobile prior to the fracture. With rehabilitation in the home, patients recover more quickly and avoid the adjustment difficulties arising from becoming competent on crutches in a hospital physiotherapy department only to find on discharge that the challenge of the home environment is very different. Hence under this model 40 per cent of the hospital beds are eliminated and a further 30 per cent move to intermediate care at a lower cost per day. Investment in the hospital at home can be minimized by using support workers for the mobilization once professional staff have designed and initiated the care plan.

In the case of one locality of 300,000 people which had an incidence of 300 hip fractures per year, average length of stay fell from 21 days to 10 days with half of the bed-days in less expensive intermediate care facilities. The cost released from this re-engineering of hip fractures alone was £200,000 (hospital costs saved minus community costs incurred) or sufficient resource within an orthopaedic programme to provide an additional annual 100 hip replacement operations, consequently reducing waiting lists for this procedure.

INCENTIVIZING COST RELEASE THROUGH 'POOLING'

Whatever the potential cost savings to the system there will always be impediments to their release unless all parties share a common interest in the process. Incentives and strategic objectives must be aligned and congruent between purchasers and providers. If the NHS is successfully to re-engineer processes across providers it too requires an appropriate incentive structure. In managed care 'pooling' formulas are employed. According to this mechanism providers and purchaser of healthcare are open and honest about the potential for resource release. A formula is then agreed between the parties such that each of them gets a share of the benefit and therefore a pay-off from implementation.

Contracting on the basis of activity levels – the convention to date in the NHS – inhibits this process. In the managed care sector, therefore, hospitals are 'capitated'. This means that they are contracted to provide *an acute service* to the population enrolled in the plan which in a UK context would equate to the resident population of a PCT area. The provision of care is governed by quality standards and a utilization range set to avoid both under- and over-utilization of services. So long as the provider meets the standards and falls with the range, the balance of in-patient and ambulatory care is discretionary and there is no financial penalty if workload shifts from the former to the latter. In contrast, any resources released would go into the pool and be shared according to the agreed formula. Hence the acute provider and PCT as purchaser have congruent incentives.

THE ACUTE BEDS ISSUE REVIEWED

Finally, let us review the debate about the potential for further acute bed reductions in the NHS. In the late 1980s and early 1990s some leading analysts projected substantial reductions in acute bed provision by the turn of the century of up to 40 per cent. This issue was most recently reviewed by the National Beds Inquiry using a more rigorous methodology for projecting workload growth and a range of assumptions about its management. The conclusions were that a small growth of 1.8 per cent beds could be required in the short term to provide capacity to eliminate waiting lists. However, in the longer term the outcome would be dependent on the provision of other infrastructure and services to reduce reliance on acute in-patient beds. On a 'closer to home' scenario which assumed development of alternative care, the Beds Inquiry envisaged a slow reduction of about 10 per cent by the year 2020.

These figures seem a little conservative and indicate an underlying lack of confidence in the NHS to match Canada, the Netherlands and the more advanced parts of the United States. When we first reviewed this issue in 1996, our scenarios envisaged a rate of reduction of between 15 per cent and 25 per cent, including projected growth in intermediate care beds by the year 2005. The lower figure assumed full implementation of primary care commissioning, in turn maximizing incentives to minimize use of hospitals through utilization management which we envisaged would reduce projected growth in medical admissions by 25 per cent. When we reviewed this work in 1999, it was apparent that the more conservative scenario of 15 per cent reduction in the ten years to 2005 seemed the more likely outcome for the medium term.

The conservatism of the National Beds Inquiry may reflect a tacit recognition of two political realities in the NHS. First, the acute hospital sector is a powerful interest in the NHS and likely to resist any measures which at first sight appear to reduce its resource base. Second, the extension of primary care purchasing to encompass all GPs is a major organizational development agenda. PCGs with large complements of non-fundholders may require a longer lead-in time to move to Trust status. Not least, the NHS has a track record of preoccupation with organizational change which if left unchecked turns into inertia and stifles a radical national policy drive.

On the more positive side, there is evidence from the evaluation of Total Purchasing Pilots that GPs do reduce their use of hospital services if this is agreed as a prime objective.[18] Moreover, we believe the NHS can rise to the challenges posed by utilization management, to flatten the current growth rate in emergency admissions among elderly people and thus equal best performance in the US, Canada and Holland. Not least, by reducing hospital admission rates and length of stay in emergency workload, resources could be released from within existing acute hospital programme budgets which could be redirected to elective care and thus impact favourably on waiting lists.

The government's agenda for the NHS envisages a ten-year timescale. Minimizing the need for acute in-patient beds through utilization management should be a central objective in the NHS. It will require a major policy drive from the centre through regional offices and the strengthened district health authorities if inbuilt inertia is to be overcome. If successful, we would envisage that one implication of modernization would be for the out-turn for acute hospital bed levels to be significantly lower than envisaged by the National Beds Inquiry. There is demonstrable scope for the service to release resources, improve access, extend scope for equity and, not least, for both quality and user satisfaction. Accordingly the government has directed the NHS to give a particular emphasis to the development of intermediate care services.[19]

NOTES AND REFERENCES

1 Department of Health (1999/2000) *The Government Expenditure Plans*. London: Department of Health.
2 National Audit Office (2000) *Inpatient Admissions and Bed Management in NHS Acute Hospitals*. London: HMSO.
3 Statistics drawn from three sources: Department of Health, *Hospital Episode Statistics*; Department of Health, *Ordinary and Day Admissions for England 1997/98* and Department of Health, *Bed Availability and Occupancy, 1997/98*.
4 All data from *1997/98 Hospital Episode Statistics*, supplied by Department of Health.
5 M. Conroy and D.A. Cochrane (1996) *The Future Healthcare Workforce*. Manchester: University of Manchester.
6 Ibid., pp. 19–25.
7 M. Goddard *et al.* (2000) Avoidable Use of Beds and Cost-effectiveness of Care in Alternative Locations. York: Centre for Health Economics, University of York. Audit Commission (1992) *Lying in Wait*. London: HMSO. Royal College of Surgeons (1996) *Report of the Joint Working Group on Graduated Care*. London: RCS.
8 National Audit Office, op. cit., pp. 7–9 and 38.
9 DoH (2000) *The National Beds Inquiry – Supporting Analysis*. London: Department of Health.
10 M. Conroy and D. Cochrane (1999) *The Future Healthcare Workforce – Second Steering Group Report*. Bournemouth: University of Bournemouth.
11 S. Last (2000) Bed spread, *Health Service Journal*, 110 (5717): 22–3.
12 Milliman and Robertson (1997) *Healthcare Management Guidelines – Recovery Facilities*. Irvine, CA: Milliman and Robertson.
13 US Department of Health and Human Services *Health Care Financing Administration (HCFA), Statistical Supplement*, February. Washington, DC: HCFA Offices of Research and Demonstrations.
14 Data from first three pilot years in FHP Healthcare, California, USA, provided by Care Continuum.
15 Audit Commission (1999) *First Assessment*. London: Audit Commission.
16 P.R. Kongstvedt (1996) Managing Basic Medical–Surgical Utilisation, in *The Managed Care Handbook*, p. 255. Gaithersburg, MD: Aspen.
17 National Audit Office, op. cit.
18 R. Robinson, J. Robinson and J. Raftery (1998) *Contracting by Total Purchasing Pilots, 1997–98*. London: King's Fund.
19 DoH (2001) *Health Service Circular HSC 2001/01, Intermediate Care*. London: Department of Health.

8

CASE MANAGEMENT OF 'AT-RISK' OLDER PEOPLE

Sherry L. Aliotta

Case management is one of the most successful patient management initiatives developed in the managed care sector in recent years. It is widely credited in the American managed care literature with maintaining the continued trends in reducing service utilization over the last ten years. Managed care practitioners also ascribe a central role to case management in any effective quality and utilization management system. Moreover, recent research studies on outcomes have increasingly demonstrated that the perceptions of commentators and managed care organizations are well founded. Case management also offers a major opportunity to the UK, particularly in helping to address the disproportionate utilization of hospital services by older people and the annual winter bed crises that still plague the NHS.

This chapter describes the service, tracks its history in the US, then addresses the problem of measuring outcomes. It then goes on to review outcome studies to date including a first UK pilot.

WHAT IS CASE MANAGEMENT?

Case management is a total quality management approach to individuals, mostly people aged over 65, with very poor health status. It is a proactive, community-based service delivered by senior nurses and often social care workers working in teams. The programme in the US was accelerated in the mid-1990s following federal government concerns that expenditure on its Medicare programme, which funds healthcare provision for retired people, would be unsustainable as the population age structure changed over the next ten to fifteen years. Analysis of resource use at that time by the Health Care Financing Administration (HCFA) and the American Hospital Association showed 10 per cent of

30 million beneficiaries accounting for nearly 70 per cent of expenditure.[1] Clinical analysis of these individuals showed them to be at the core of 'at risk' groups in the population with severe and chronic conditions such as heart disease, stroke, untreated diabetes type II, cancer, COPD and osteoporosis which had led to serious fractures such as neck of femur. They commonly have a combination of chronic and severe clinical problems and sometimes inadequately met social care needs. However, their primary needs profile is clinical and hence the high utilization of healthcare resources.

Case management employs secondary prevention to improve health status and prevent acute exacerbations of chronic and/or 'catastrophic' conditions. It is an 'assertive outreach' service *based in primary care* and targeting people who are known to be high utilizers of healthcare services or at risk of becoming so. Case managers assess individual needs and plan packages of care, and seek to ensure resources within the healthcare system are deployed to meet the needs of each individual. It is thus not a hands-on care-giving role. Specific areas of work include ensuring medical problems are sorted out; educating the client and significant others about the disease process including awareness of early warning signs and how and when to access the healthcare system; reviewing current medications; and facilitating compliance with treatment programmes. In the US, the case management service is also extended to younger people with catastrophic diseases such as HIV/AIDS, cancer, or renal failure.

The service is delivered by senior nurses largely because the needs of this group of patients are predominantly clinical. Models vary, but typically each full-time equivalent nurse can manage about 50 elderly patients on the caseload at anyone time. Clients stay on the programme for an average of seven weeks. The case managers track the utilization of their cases both before and after having been on the programme to audit the impact they are having not just on cost but also on patient quality of life and satisfaction.

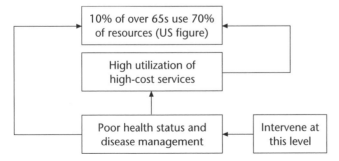

Figure 8.1   The case management rationale

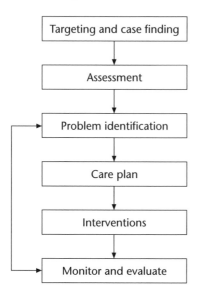

Figure 8.2   The case management process

About 10 per cent of people aged over 65 are candidates for case management. Most of these people can be identified by reviewing current hospital and primary care utilization records. The rest will not as yet be known to the healthcare system and can be identified by a screening questionnaire, the Pra Plus, devised by the University of Minnesota Department for Ageing. This simple schedule which can be completed by the patient has been validated to show the probability of someone being admitted to hospital over the forthcoming six months if no action is taken. It also allocates people to high-, medium- and low-risk categories, with the first group being assessed by the case management service. Once identified as high-risk, individuals are subject to detailed assessment across the domains such as medical, functional, psychological, nutritional and mobility status, and their ability to access healthcare services at the appropriate times. Only after this assessment process are patients brought into the programme, and only then if they agree to participate in the goal setting. The process is set out in Figure 8.2.

ORIGINS OF CASE MANAGEMENT

The origins of case management as practised in the United States today came from the workers' compensation system. Case managers assigned to ill or injured workers were able to affect return to work, and reduce the total cost of the episode. The indemnity-based US accident and health insurance industry began to speculate on whether case management could provide similar outcomes for them. Therefore, case management was first introduced as a cost control measure.

Since managed care was virtually non-existent at the time, case managers spent much of their time on negotiating rates and fees. For example, if a subscriber to an insurance plan needed intravenous antibiotics, the case manager would identify potential providers. Once the providers were identified, the case manager would negotiate for the best rates, document the agreement, and initiate the treatment. The case manager would then report back to the insurer the amount of money saved by comparing costs and negotiating with the providers.

Second opinion programmes were another early intervention conducted by case managers. Insurers identified certain surgical procedures where there was the potential for variability of practice, or alternatives to surgery. Case managers would often be assigned to assist the insured patient to obtain a second opinion. If the second opinion resulted in prevention of the surgical procedure, this was noted as savings realized as a result of case management efforts.

Examination and evaluation of the medical plan became another fertile area for case managers. Case managers quickly developed expertise in the medical management of catastrophic illnesses and injuries. Conditions such as traumatic brain injuries, spinal cord injuries, amyotrophic lateral sclerosis and neonatal prematurity became a prime focus for case managers. This area served as the foundation for the case management programmes of this decade. Case managers assumed the role of a neutral third party. They worked to advocate for the needs of the insured, and achieved cost-effectiveness via improved continuity, reduction of duplication, effective sequencing of care, and coordination.

For example, a 5-year-old child was struck by a motor vehicle. The child sustained a closed head injury, facial and jaw fractures, and a fractured femur. The child's parents were not involved in the child's care due to issues of substance abuse. The case manager was brought into the case to find a permanent placement for the child. The treatment team had concluded that the child was not a candidate for rehabilitation due to the severity of the brain injury. The case manager's assessment revealed that the child was indeed a candidate for rehabilitation. She arranged for evaluation and transfer to a rehabilitation facility. Additionally, the case manager secured the approval from the insurance company for the rehabilitation treatment, and arranged for the completion of the forms needed to enrol the child in the state medical insurance programme to pay for the treatment long term. There is much more detail to the case, but the example illustrates the change in the case management focus. The case manager did negotiate with the rehabilitation facility for the best rates, but focused on advocating for the child, ensuring that the medical benefits were used in the most effective way possible, and securing an outcome that reduced the likelihood that the child would suffer repeated episodes of exacerbation.

THE MANAGED CARE INFLUENCE

In the mid-1970s and early 1980s there was an emergence of a utilization review model. This model primarily focused on the necessity of the in-patient hospital and admission and the limitation or reduction in length of stay. This model evolved in response to several legislative initiatives.[2]

- the HMO Act of 1973 which created a favourable economic environment for the creation of 'federally qualified' HMOs;
- the TEFRA (Tax Equity and Fiscal Responsibility Act) of 1982 that supported the development of Medicare risk plans; and
- the Medicare Peer Review and Prospective Payment System (diagnostic-related groups creating set payments for the treatment of hospital patients with particular diagnosis.

Hospitals and managed care organizations hired nurses to evaluate each hospital admission for appropriateness, and to ensure that patients were discharged as soon as their condition could be managed outside the hospital. From 1981 to 1987 there were real decreases in in-patient days. By 1985, the savings accrued from these days had all but disappeared, and by 1987 even in-patient days were not significantly impacted.[3] Similar tactics were applied to elective admissions, diagnostic testing and outpatient procedures.

Hospitals quickly noticed the impact these measures were having on their occupancy rates. The hospitals responded by changing the charge structure for their outpatient services, therefore much of what had been gained via the shift to outpatient care was lost for a time.

THE CHANGING ROLE OF CASE MANAGEMENT

As the landscape of healthcare changed, payers and providers looked to more effective strategies to manage care and costs. Alone, traditional utilization review began to produce less dramatic results. The easily obtainable reductions in admissions and lengths of stay for hospitals had been realized. Further, as a single strategy, utilization review failed to account for patients who need to be hospitalized, and need to be in hospital for a certain period of time. Simultaneously, the public began to express concern openly over practices that seemed to discharge people 'quicker and sicker'.

The concept of the insurance case manager model captured the interest of managed care. Case managers had developed a positive image in the healthcare community. Their roles as advocate, assessor, facilitator and planner had cast the case manager as a 'kinder, gentler' managed care strategy. Unfortunately, some managed care programmes adopted the title and benefited from the image without changing the approach or the duties of their utilization review staff. Utilization review departments were renamed case management departments, and went on with the usual business. Suddenly, everyone was a 'case manager'. This paradoxical relationship with case management resulted in blurring the lines between utilization and case management.

THE RE-EMERGENCE OF CASE MANAGEMENT

Many physician groups began to look at the promise of case management as a powerful tool. These groups realized that a system of care management that addressed the demand for healthcare services and focused on the needs of the individual could be the missing piece of the equation. Traditional utilization management had focused on the 'supply side' of care. It looks at the amount and type of care rendered, its cost and appropriateness. The needs of the patient are considered in relation to the appropriate amount and level of care needed to meet the needs. Certainly, this is a significant component of care management. However, it lacks emphasis on anything but the current episode of care. Controlling the immediate episode of illness is clearly an important aspect of effective medical management, but it fails to address future episodes.

THE PREVENTIVE MODEL

The emerging model of case management is focusing not only on the management of any current episode, but prevention of future episodes. This shift in focus has occurred as both providers and payers have been faced with caring for populations. As the fee-for-service method of reimbursement has been eclipsed by managed care 'at-risk' arrangements, prevention and controlling demand has been essential in management of a population of patients. The strategies show promise in the reduction of overall cost of care while achieving favourable patient ratings and improved quality of care. Case management has been an integral part of these strategies. Before discussing the literature, it is necessary to discuss some of the issues in the measurement of case management outcomes.

ISSUES WITH CASE MANAGEMENT OUTCOMES

Case management practitioners began with the belief that they were saving money by making things better. Payers, especially, began with the belief that case managers made things better by saving money. Case managers quickly came to understand that they could continue to 'make things better' if they could demonstrate that they were able to save money. This led to a focus on the 'bottom line'. Case management outcome measures quickly became oriented towards their ability to save money. Rather than establishing the practice of case management, its ability to effect improvement, and the impact of the improvement, case management concentrated on justifying its existence as a cost saver. Those outside case management established the paradigm by which case management would be evaluated, and case management has not been able to escape.

Debate continues on the value of case management. Many of the more common indicators are process-focused. They scrutinize what has been done, but not the difference that was made. The payers and providers that employ case management continue to insist on data that demonstrates the return on their investment.

LACK OF CLEAR DEFINITIONS AND STANDARDS

One issue with regard to case management outcomes is the lack of common definitions and standards. Case management is defined by the Case Management Society of America as 'a collaborative process which assesses, plans, implements, coordinates, monitors, and evaluates options and services to meet an individual's health needs through communication and available resources to promote quality, cost-effective outcomes'.[4] As described in the previous section, many practitioners of utilization review changed their titles to case manager. Providers, patients and the general public became confused over the role of the case manager, and who were case managers.

The definition above is from the Standards of Practice for Case Management published in 1995 by the Case Management Society of America. Its creation was, in part, to establish clearly several key foundations of case management:

- the purpose and goals of case management;
- the functions of case management;
- the settings of case management practice;
- the case manager's relationship to the client;
- standards of care;
- standards of performance.

Although published in 1995, the standards have not been widely integrated into the process or structure of organizations engaged in case management.

The American Accreditation Healthcare Commission has established standards for case management organizations, and plans to begin surveys and issue accreditation to qualifying organizations. Despite these recent efforts to standardize, very little standardization exists. Most of the enforced regulations and standards dealt with utilization management. Surveys by the National Committee for Quality Assurance (NCQA) address case management under standards for quality management and improvement and utilization management. There are no specific case management standards.[5] Even the HCFA reviewer guidelines do not contain specific headings for case management.[6]

Legislative and accreditation inattention has allowed case management practice to develop with relatively little oversight. This has allowed case management innovation to proceed unfettered, but has also created a substantial amount of variation. While there is common ground, even the core functions of case management may be practised differently by different organizations. For example, most case management practitioners have an assessment process. However, one group may have case managers conduct a home visit where a complete medical history is obtained, a physical examination is performed, multiple assessment instruments are administered and completed, and numerous practitioners are involved. Another group may call an individual on the telephone and ask a series of case manager-generated questions. Because of the variation in process and interventions, each programme must be evaluated individually. It is virtually impossible to decide if outcomes are produced via the individual components of the case management programme, or the programme as a whole. This creates problems both with measurement and with potential replication. What is it that we recreate, the programme or one or more of its component parts?

FAILURE TO ISOLATE INTERVENTIONS

Case management is to some extent a victim of its own success. The early measure of case management success – cost savings – was enough, therefore neither case managers nor those employing them bothered to establish more rigorous evaluations. Practice was allowed to evolve with little evaluation beyond cost savings.

Case managers tend to be resourceful people. Sixty-five per cent of the members of the Case Management Society of America have 11 years or more of clinical experience. This clinical experience brings an extensive knowledge of interventions that can effectively address a comprehensive list of problems and issues. The case manager often uses multiple interventions to address the problems that are identified in the individuals in their practice. When a positive outcome results, it is difficult to identify the intervention or combination of interventions that culminated in the positive outcome. Further, when distinct interventions are isolated, they are often implemented in an individualized way. For example, home care services are a common intervention. Some case management models dispense home care services from a home care agency,[7] and other models have the home care provided by the case manager. Both methods of home care delivery seem to produce positive results. Another frequent intervention is coordination of care. Very rarely is the methodology precisely described. Coordination of care can vary widely in practice, from a telephone call to schedule an appointment to an elaborate care plan with multiple components.

Most often, the case manager implements as many interventions as possible and in multiple combinations. An appropriate metaphor would be a chef that is asked to create a spectacular recipe. The chef is high skilled in cooking techniques and combining ingredients. He begins to employ numerous techniques such as stirring, sautéing, chopping, whipping and more. In addition he adds numerous fine ingredients in various portions. He tastes his work as he progresses, and adds ingredients here and there. He starts again several times, and eliminates some things. The resultant dish is spectacular. However, the chef doesn't remember all the ingredients used, the order in which they were used, or all the techniques. He can't tell us how to recreate the dish, or what makes it work. The chef continues to produce reasonable approximations of the dish time and again without documenting what he does or how he does it. Other chefs begin to make the dish as well. The results may vary and we can't really compare the quality because every version is slightly or dramatically different. This describes the current state of affairs with regard to case management interventions. Everyone is claiming reasonably good results and, though the results are verifiable, the process of achieving the results is less certain.

METHODOLOGIES AND PROPRIETARY INTERESTS

Many of the organizations that are on the cutting edge of outcome measurement have made strides in clarifying their definitions, interventions and processes. Those that have been successful are often reluctant to reveal their findings completely for fear of losing a proprietary edge. Thus, they report their results without fully defining their interventions. This leads to others using trial and error when proven actions are available.

Methodologies for the calculation of outcome results vary widely. Some standard measures have evolved. These standard measures include:

- reductions in hospital admissions;
- reductions in overall cost per episode;
- quality of life;
- patient satisfaction;
- achievement of optimal physiological parameters (peak flow readings, haemoglobin A1c etc.);
- achievement of certain standards of care (rate of diabetics having annual retinal examinations, percentage of asthmatics on inhaled steroids, congestive heart failure patients on ACE inhibitors etc.).

The problem with using these measures of outcome for case management lies in their 'multi-factorial' nature. For example, reducing hospital admissions requires several factors. Case management interventions are just one of the factors. In one situation, a hospital received full payment for anyone admitted to the hospital. If a patient presented in the emergency room, it is likely that the patient would be admitted. Although the case manager could work with the patient to maintain his or her health and prevent exacerbation that may lead to an emergency room visit, the hospital had little incentive to avoid admission once the patient had arrived. The outcomes listed above can best be described as 'end outcomes'.[8] The key for clear case management outcomes lies in the ability to describe the direct outcomes of case management and correlate their direct impact on the end outcomes. Examples of direct case management outcomes include improved adherence, increased coordination of care and increased empowerment.[9] A current initiative called the Council for Case Management Accountability is undertaking the exploration of measures and indicators for these outcomes, key interventions to achieve these outcomes, and how these outcomes help to produce the end outcomes desired by the healthcare system.

Direct and end outcome measures of case management can be found in several general categories including:[10]

- clinical measures – physiological measurements, recovery times, presence or absence of symptoms, improvement or decline of clinical status etc.;
- functional measures – activities of daily living, ability to work, ability to participate fully in chosen lifestyle activities etc.;
- process measures – educational efforts provided to patients, discussion of care plans with physicians, problem identification and resolution etc.;
- productivity measures – number of assessments completed, caseload size, caseload acuity etc.;
- management measures – patient demographics, types of problems encountered by case management, diagnoses handled by case management etc.;
- financial measures – decreased cost, level of care comparisons, reduction in frequency and duration of admissions etc.;
- quality assurance measures – repeat referrals to case management, cases which are declined by case management and suffer decline in status, adherence to the standards established for the programme etc.

To be effective, evaluation of case management must include measurements and outcomes from a variety of perspectives.

THE RESULTS

There is a growing body of evidence that case management results in cost savings and other favourable outcomes. Sund and Sveningson[11] describe a 'community nurse case management program' that provided a home visit and telephone follow-up to clients, individual plans of care, linkage to community resources, and coordination of care across the continuum. The hospital admissions for the case management group decreased by 54 per cent compared to their six months' experience prior to case management. Emergency department visits decreased by 52 per cent, and costs decreased by 30 per cent. There was a very small sample size of 21 patients, but 50 per cent of them had a diagnosed mental illness. The programme did little to improve physical functioning, bodily pain, general health or social functioning. Mental health and emotional **role** was improved.

McKenzie, Torkelson and Holt report lower average billed charges, costs and length of stay for case managed patients. There was also evidence that patient satisfaction, adherence to treatment regimens and nursing satisfaction were improved. The programme revolves around the case management plan, a detailed set of desirable outcomes expected through the episode of illness and the clinical process required to obtain these outcomes successfully.[12]

Bradford Medical Center in Pennsylvania, USA, established a clinical resource programme staffed by registered nurse case managers. They were able to drop length of stay from 6.3 days to 5.8 days, and produced $430,944 in savings. There is also evidence that they reduced the total cost per case, and reduced variation in care. This model is more accurately described as a utilization management initiative, but includes family support and discharge planning.[13]

Delma Huggins and Kay Lehman describe three studies over a three-year period that compare nurse case management outcomes – resources, service cost and nurse case management costs. In-patient visits decreased from 102 to 42 and costs of services for the payer declined from $22,600 to $7428. Decreases were also noted in outpatient visits, emergency room visits, length of stay and cost of services for the institution.[14]

Beck *et al.* demonstrated fewer emergency room visits, fewer visits to sub-specialists, and fewer repeat hospital visits in a programme where patients with high health services utilization and one or more chronic illness had monthly group visits with their physician and a nurse. The visits included health education, prevention measures, opportunity for socialization, mutual support, and one-to-one consultation. Although not traditional case management, this model demonstrates the impact of challenging the traditional patient–physician dyad.[15]

Naylor *et al.* demonstrated fewer readmissions, increased length of time between readmissions, decreased hospitalization rates, decreased charges for admissions, and lowered health services after discharge. Patients in the intervention group received a comprehensive assessment, an individualized discharge plan, validation of patient and caregiver education, coordination of the discharge plan throughout hospitalization (and for two weeks following discharge), interdisciplinary communication, and ongoing evaluation of the effectiveness of the discharge plan. Although not called case management in the article, the study interventions met all four key case management functions:[16]

- assessor;
- planner;
- facilitator;
- advocate.

Rich *et al.* describe the impact of a nurse-directed multidisciplinary intervention on readmissions, quality of life and costs of care for high-risk congestive heart failure patients over 70 years old.[17] Ninety-one per cent of patients in the study remained free of readmission for 90 days compared to only 75 per cent in the control group. The overall cost of care for the study group was $460 less per patient.

A smaller, rural programme where case managers coordinated information from fragmented treatment sources and articulated a plan of care joining patients' medical and social needs, keeping the plan of care on track and encouraging both providers and patients to take action to improve care, resulted in reduced hospitalizations. The case managed group was 43 per cent less likely to use the hospital and 44 per cent less likely to go to the emergency room than the control group.[18] The cost of care for the study group was $596,211 (per annum) less than the control group.

With such results it is understandable that, to date, most managed organizations have been concerned to ensure that all their senior members who meet the criteria are brought into case management. However, one HMO in San Francisco was determined to test the service on more scientific criteria. Accordingly the first randomized control trial of case management reported in February 2000. After two years the programme had showed significantly lower utilization in both acute and intermediate care in-patient services. We now have Level 1 evidence from the US at least of the effectiveness of case management.[19]

FUTURE DIRECTIONS IN THE US

Future directions include the need to isolate the interventions or combinations of interventions that are most effective in producing the results. The 'bottom line' orientation needs to be broadened. No other medical practice has had to endure such scrutiny of its cost-effectiveness. At some point, the cost-effectiveness of case management must be accepted in order to allow for a full exploration of its capabilities. However, if a cost saving is to be a key, there needs to be standard guidelines for measurement and reporting. Only then can real comparisons be generated.

On balance, however, out-turn studies demonstrate case management as an effective intervention to improve quality and control cost. The programme has therefore been 'rolled out' to millions of elderly Americans from all cultures and socio-economic backgrounds. Continued research will allow the fine tuning and explication of the most effective practices.

UK EXPERIENCE

There is evidence of a similar pattern of a small percentage of elderly people accounting for a large proportion of healthcare resource use in the UK. For example, the acute hospital admission rate (all NHS hospitals excluding mental health) of people aged over 65 in England in 1997/8 was 277 per 1000 in that age group in the population.[20] An equivalent figure from American health systems with little or no utilization management processes in place[21] is 320 per 1000. However, in the managed care sector with integrated delivery systems incorporating case management in place, the admission rate is 204 per 1000 (including acute hospitals, skilled nursing and other intermediate care facilities). At the micro-level, admission data from a number of large GP practices to acute hospitals showed similar findings to the US experience.[22] In one large GP practice in the North West, for example, 4 per cent of the patients aged over 65 on the GP's list accounted for 80 per cent of the emergency acute bed-day usage by all patients from the practice – 100 individuals from an elderly population of 2500.

In the UK to date, however, the approach has been largely confined to the management of people with severe and enduring mental health problems. The effectiveness of assertive outreach has led to its inclusion as part of the national programme for development of mental health services in the UK through the National Service Framework. This is described more fully in Chapter 9. However, in terms of older people, there has also been one British randomized control trial of a similar approach to integrated case management across health and social care. In this programme, case managers were trained in geriatric assessment and care planning and implementation. Utilization in terms of accident and emergency attendances and hospital admission was compared between the clients and a control group. A & E attendances fell by 60 per cent and hospital use by 40 per cent in the study group compared to the control group during the 12 months of the study.[23]

THE CASTLEFIELDS CASE MANAGEMENT PILOT

The first US-inspired pilot targeting the high-utilizing elderly has been implemented in Castlefields Health Centre in North Cheshire Health Authority. In this model a district nurse trained in case management spends half her working week in the role and works closely with an attached social care manager and community psychiatric nurse. During the first nine months of the pilot, 40 older people have been on the

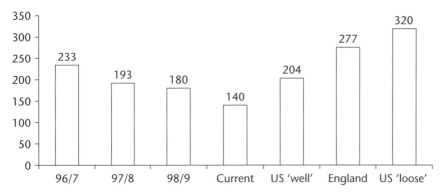

Figure 8.3   Admissions rates per 1000 over-65s, Castlefields – 1996/7 to 1999/2000 v England and US averages

programme, staying on for between four weeks and three months. The clients were all high-risk patients mostly aged over 75 with two or more active chronic diagnoses. They were mostly high utilizers of all services including in-patient care, regular visitors to accident and emergency and among the top 3 per cent of consultation rates with the GPs.

Following assessment and care plan implementation, the service utilization of these patients, including consultation rates with GPs, has reduced significantly. Figure 8.3 shows the out-turn for hospital admissions per 1000 people aged over 65 compared to the England averages and two US comparators: the 'loosely managed' systems with little or no utilization management in place and the well-managed systems with utilization management and case management in place.[24]

Castlefields had been employing demand management techniques prior to the case management pilot and was already at a relatively low base for admission rates to hospital. However, arrival of the case management service has brought a further 30 per cent reduction in admission rates. Patient satisfaction rates are high and there has been a paradigm shift, the primary team now viewing admission as a last resort once all other options are exhausted.

ACKNOWLEDGEMENT

The last section of this chapter owes gratitude to the wonderful work of Jayne Woodward, case manager at Castlefields Health Centre.

NOTES AND REFERENCES

1 US Department of Health and Human Services (1995) *Health Care Financing Administration (HCFA), Statistical Supplement.* Washington, DC: HCFA Offices of Research and Demonstrations.

154   Sherry L. Aliotta

2 K. Gervais, R. Priester, D.E. Vawter, K.K. Otte and M.M. Solberg (eds) (1999) *Ethical Challenges in Managed Care: A Casebook*, pp. 42–68. Washington, DC: Georgetown University Press.
3 Case Management Society of America (1997) *Unpublished Training Manual*. Care Continuum. Little Rock, AR: Case Management Society of America.
4 Case Management Society of America (1995) *Standards of Practice for Case Managers*. Little Rock, AR: Case Management Society of America.
5 National Committee for Quality Assurance (NCQA) (2000) *2000 Survey Guidelines for the Accreditation of MCO's*, Effective 1 July. Washington, DC: NCQA.
6 Department of Health and Human Services Health Care Financing Administration (1999) *Interim Monitoring Guide*. Washington, DC: DHHS/HCFA.
7 S. Aliotta (1996) in P.D. Fox *Chronic Healthcare Management*. Gaithersburg, MD: Aspen.
8 Council for Case Management Accountability (1997) *A Framework for Case Management Accountability*. Little Rock, AR: Case Management Society of America.
9 Ibid.
10 S.A. Squared, Inc. (1997) *Case Management Program Measures*. Farmington Hills: S.A. Squared, Inc.
11 J. Sund and L. Sveningson (1997) Case management in an integrated delivery system, *Nursing Management*, 2 (5): 183–91.
12 C. McKenzie, N. Torkelson and M. Holt (1997) Care and cost: nursing case management improves both, *Nursing Management*, 20 (10): 30–4.
13 Editorial (1998) CM program helps make hospital profitable, *Hospital Case Management*, September: 174–6, 181.
14 D. Huggins and K. Lehman (1997) Reducing costs through case management, *Nursing Management*, December: 34–7.
15 A. Beck *et al.* (1997) A randomized trial of group outpatient visits for chronically ill older HMO members: the cooperative health care clinic, *Journal of the American Geriatric Society*, 45: 543–9.
16 Case Management Association of America, op. cit.
17 M.W. Rich *et al.* (1995) A multidisciplinary intervention to prevent readmission of elderly patients with congestive heart failure, *New England Journal of Medicine*, 133 (18): 1190–5.
18 J. Battaglini and J. Czerenda (1999) Advanced practice nurses as system-wide case managers for internist, in E.F. Netting and F.G. Williams (eds) *Primary Care for Elderly People*, 65–83. New York: Garland Publishing.
19 D.M. Fick *et al.* (2000) Advanced practice nursing care management model for elders in a managed care environment, *Journal of Care Management*, 6 (1): 28–49.
20 Department of Health (1998) *Hospital Episode Statistics 1997/98*. London: Department of Health.
21 Milliman and Robertson (1997) *Healthcare Management Guidelines*. Irvine, CA: Milliman and Robertson.
22 Conrane Consulting professional database.
23 R. Barnabei *et al.* (1998) Randomised trial of impact of model of integrated care and case management, of older people living in the community, *British Medical Journal*, 316; *Evidence-based Health Policy and Management*, December.
24 Data from Milliman and Robertson, op. cit., Department of Health, and Castlefields Health Centre (2000) *Case Management Project Interim Report*, June.

9

MANAGED CARE AND MENTAL HEALTH

David Cochrane

When we first became interested in the potential of the American managed care experience to further the aims of the NHS, we accompanied senior NHS managers and clinicians on study tours of a number of California-based HMOs. The consistent feedback at that time was that the model seemed excellent for general and acute services but unsophisticated in relation to mental health. Indeed, at that time, many HMOs placed strict limits on the benefits provided to people with mental health problems and often 'carved out' provision to specialist providers. After exhausting a fixed benefit allowance of 20 days per year of hospital treatment, the member would be left to the vagaries of the residual public sector provisions. Also, the experience of deinstitutionalization, particularly in California, home of HMOs, was notorious worldwide for its poor quality.[1] The managed care sector seemed to lack interest in mental health, and was ill-suited to it.

To be fair, however, the US had led the world in the development of case management and assertive outreach programmes for clients with psychosis who were otherwise high utilizers of hospital care. Indeed, the models and approaches so successfully implemented with the at-risk elderly were pioneered in mental health in the US in the 1970s. Stein and Test's original study and its subsequent replication demonstrated such impressive reductions in hospitalization and costs that the service model spread rapidly.[2] More generally, managed care had not turned its attention to mental health until the mid-1990s, or two decades after its first interest in the general and acute sector. It is ironic therefore that of all fields of healthcare delivery in the UK, managed care techniques are more developed in mental health than in the general sectors. Indeed, when Boland began in 1994 to set out the implications of managed care for the American mental health service sector,[3] he unwittingly foreshadowed the agenda now firmly set for the NHS under the National Service Framework for Mental Health (NSF):[4]

- the importance of mental health promotion and early intervention;
- evidence-based practice;
- practice guidelines playing an increasingly important role in determining the right mix of services and care settings;
- mental health practitioners adapting and changing practice away from patient management on an in-patient basis and reducing admission rates;
- the integration of secondary and primary care with appropriate devolution of patient management through evidence-based protocols;
- collaboration and indeed more structural integration between agencies;
- designing new staff roles to span a wider spectrum of patient need than is possible under narrowly defined professional demarcations.

The focus of this chapter is the major cause of chronic and severe morbidity and hospitalization in the UK – adult schizophrenia. Not only is this the most challenging management issue in mental health; it also illustrates how major objectives of the NSF can be facilitated. These include a focus on the needs of people with severe and enduring mental health needs, access to 24-hour services on an emergency basis and, not least, given that people with schizophrenia are nearly 20 times more likely to take their own lives than the average population, reduction in the incidence of suicide.[5]

THE CASE FOR MANAGED CARE IN UK MENTAL HEALTH

Schizophrenia management also provides an excellent model for demonstrating how the components of managed care come together in a relatively discrete service. It offers plenty of scope to re-engineer services to improve clinical effectiveness, value for money, patient focus and responsiveness to the users.

There is also scope to reduce hospital utilization. Among younger adults (aged less than 65) schizophrenia is by far the major cause of admission, accounting for about 60 per cent of bed days. In 1998 for all case types there were 210,000 admissions to just over 35,000 psychiatric beds in England,[6] reflecting a sustained and continued trend in reducing bed levels which had started in the mid-1950s (when there were over 150,000). This sustained decline in bed provision has been slowing in recent years despite a growing body of evidence that much of this bed usage is both unnecessary and undesirable. In an end-paper to the Department of Health *National Beds Inquiry*, Goddard *et al.* estimated that 29 per cent of admissions to acute psychiatric beds (based also on 1998 data) were avoidable, with 58 per cent of bed days inappropriate for a continued stay on an acute psychiatric ward. Shortages in special needs and staffed housing and community support were the most common causes of discharge prevention (44–68 per cent). Rehabilitation was required for a further

22–36 per cent of cases and only 11–13 per cent needed a higher level of NHS care.[7] Other recent evaluation studies of alternative interventions to hospitalization in the UK have demonstrated both economic and quality benefits in terms of clinical outcome and client satisfaction. In this context Strathdee, a prominent psychiatrist and mental health policy analyst, has stated that most schizophrenic patients prefer to be managed outside hospital and that in most cases this approach is just as effective clinically.[8] Indeed, in a recent survey of acute hospital services, the Sainsbury Centre concluded that 'hospital care is a non-therapeutic intervention'.[9]

This chapter therefore illustrates how to develop a managed care system in mental health and thus deliver the government's mental health modernization agenda. The main elements are as follows:

- disease management in mental health;
- development of an evidence-based, integrated care model including
  - utilization management techniques to reduce reliance on hospitalization
  - developing therapeutic partnerships with clients
  - focusing the role of specialist services
  - defining the role of primary care in the service and integrating this with the secondary sector;
- developing new staff roles designed around service need to replace narrowly defined professional demarcations.

DISEASE MANAGEMENT

The management of schizophrenia lends itself well to a disease management model:

- It is a severely disabling, chronic disease which, alongside other less common psychotic illnesses, is one of the major causes of reduced disablement adjusted life years or DALYs.
- Suicide rates among sufferers are nearly 20 times higher than average.
- It is relatively high in volume with an estimated prevalence rate of 1 per cent of the population.
- It is the single highest cause of resource in mental health, accounting for around 60 per cent of psychiatric bed-day usage by people aged under 65, high medication costs, substantial time commitment from secondary mental health community services, and high consultation rates with GPs.
- If poorly managed it leads to disablement and high service costs in social care, subsidized housing, and social security benefits.
- There are distinct phases of the condition which respond well to primary and secondary preventive interventions.

- There is substantial scope for more proactive management to replace the conventional reactive approach to crises and recurrent and disabling psychotic episodes – both features of suboptimal management.
- Not least, and in common with other conditions where disease management is effective, client and carer collaboration in treatment is essential to good clinical outcomes, reduced relapse rates, improved quality of life and functioning for patients and thus lower hospitalization rates.

The disease management approach should therefore be central to any evidence-based integrated care model for schizophrenia.

DEVELOPING AN INTEGRATED MODEL IN SCHIZOPHRENIA

Evidence-based management of schizophrenia needs to be planned around the distinct phases of the condition:

- the early warning signs or prodromal phase which requires early detection and early intervention;
- the acute phase;
- the stable phase requiring secondary preventive interventions and case management.

The model set out here is drawn from professional experience informed and further elaborated by the following sources of evidence and good practice which are recommended to practitioners:

- The Sainsbury Centre for Mental Health
- The Scottish Inter-collegiate Guidelines Network
- Royal College of Psychiatrists' publications
- The *British Journal of Psychiatry* and its special supplements
- *Advances in Psychiatric Treatment*
- *Evidence-based Mental Health*
- The University of York, NHS Centre for Reviews and Disseminations
- The Cochrane Database
- The American Psychiatric Association 1997 *Guidelines for the Treatment and Management of Schizophrenia.*

EARLY DETECTION AND INTERVENTION

Approximately two-thirds of patients exhibit a distinct pattern of behaviour which is an early warning signal for an onsetting psychotic episode. The so-called 'prodromal' phase lasts for up to four weeks. The most commonly reported symptoms are so-called negative or 'dysphoric'[10] and typically include:

- poor appetite;
- sleep disturbance;
- poor memory;
- depression;
- social withdrawal;
- deterioration in hygiene and grooming;
- unusual behaviour such as angry outbursts.

Each person has his or her own personalized pattern of early symptoms or 'relapse signature'. A psychotic episode is a terrifying and disabling experience. The more people have, the further they move down a spiral of reduced functioning. It is therefore crucial to prevent relapse wherever possible. Birchwood recommends a staged approach to individuals in the prodromal phase of schizophrenia. Staging reflects the intensity of symptoms stratified at three levels from those appearing at the earliest stage to those occurring immediately prior to relapse. Interventions at this stage include stress management and cognitive therapy (to challenge delusional and dysfunctional thinking), family counselling, or respite care if the family circumstances are contributing to the problem. At second or third stage there may be a temporary increase in anti-psychotic medication. Patients are also taught personal coping strategies to address their own early warning symptoms which are documented in a structured 'relapse prevention sheet' shared with the patient's carers.

PRIMARY CARE AS THE FOCAL POINT FOR EARLY DETECTION – THE NORTHUMBERLAND MODEL

Early detection is a key role for the primary care team. One approach to facilitating this has been developed by GPs and specialist mental health professionals in Northumberland. The Partnership Project[11] provides a protocol to guide the GP in identifying patients at risk and then a series of assessment schedules which score an individual's needs profile against the likelihood of his or her behaviour pattern being the early warning signs of schizophrenia. Patients who score high risk are referred to the specialists in the secondary sector, usually the community mental health team (CMHT), for more specialist and detailed assessment. Any necessary treatment programme can then be initiated.

MANAGEMENT DURING THE ACUTE OR 'PSYCHOTIC' PHASE

Not all acute episodes can be prevented, of course, and when they occur three broad symptom categories are now recognized to confirm a diagnosis of schizophrenia. The first comprises *the positive or florid symptoms*. These include:

- hallucinations;
- delusions;
- serious thought disorder such as intense paranoia.

Delusions are often bizarre and hallucinations can be aural such as a voice keeping up a running commentary on the person's behaviour or thoughts, or sometimes two or more voices conversing with each other.[12] The second category is *the negative or deficit symptoms*. These are similar to the prodromal symptoms but more intense in their effect and include:

- withdrawal;
- lack of emotional expressiveness and experience;
- reduction in social speech;
- lack of responsiveness;
- neglect of self-care.

Third, patients experience *impairment of cognitive functions* such as memory and intellectual functioning. Literally, the mind does not function properly. These symptoms deteriorate further over time. It is therefore recognized that effective and rapid management of negative symptoms and cognitive impairment is crucial to longer term prognosis and a patient's likely use of service over time.

The first point of referral is usually the CMHT which includes a consultant psychiatrist member. Management should be 'holistic', reflecting a profound paradigm change over the last decade or so. During the 1960s a dichotomy had opened up between two schools of schizophrenia management. The 'medical' model relied largely on medication and physical forms of treatment such as electroconvulsive therapy (ECT). The 'family' model, closely associated with the radical psychiatrist Ronald Laing, sought solutions in dysfunctional inter-family dynamics and their destructive impact on the inner self. Perhaps ironically, the evidence which has emerged more recently is demonstrating the strength of both approaches and that the administration of medication and psychosocial interventions, including working with families, *used in combination* produce the most favourable clinical outcomes.[13]

As with most disease management approaches, patient compliance is critical to success. However, the medications which have been most widely used until recently, known as the 'typical neuroleptics', have unpleasant side effects at clinically effective dosages. Compliance has always been a problem with these drugs. Most psychiatrists have therefore welcomed the development of a new generation of 'atypical' drugs for the management of schizophrenia over the last ten years or so. These have a range of advantages:

- they have a much lower side-effect profile and are consequently preferred by patients and carers;[14]
- atypicals are effective on the negative symptoms of schizophrenia, unlike the older drugs which, according to Carpenter, may worsen them;[15]

- the majority of psychiatrists prefer to use the atypicals for this reason.[16]

Lieberman, an American psychiatrist with international standing in this sphere, summarizes the case as follows:

> After more than 40 years' experience with typical anti-psychotics, their therapeutic limitations have become painfully apparent to clinicians and patients alike. This is because typical anti-psychotic drugs are not effective in all patients. Between 30 per cent and 50 per cent of patients with chronic schizophrenia are either unresponsive or only partially responsive (defined as substantial reduction or remission of positive symptoms) to their anti-psychotic drugs. In addition, anti-psychotics are ineffective against other dimensions of schizophrenic pathology, namely the negative symptoms of the deficit state and neuro-cognitive deficits. Lastly, typical anti-psychotic drugs have an extensive side-effect profile, with the majority of patients experiencing one or more of the three acute extra-pyramidal syndromes.[17]

The problem for the NHS is the cost of the more effective new drugs, which can be ten times that of the older drugs over a medium- to long-term period. According to the American Psychiatric Association, people who have had one episode of psychosis should stay on medication for a minimum of one year. This increases to five years or more for people with more than one episode.[18] Of course, it is acceptable in disease management programmes for the cost of medication to increase provided the overall programme cost reduces. For example, the NHS faces this issue in relation to the wide-scale use of statins in primary care to reduce the risk of ischaemic heart disease. Hence higher drug costs in the management of schizophrenia can therefore be expected, leading some analysts such as the York University Effective Healthcare Group to advise caution.[19]

In defence of their prices, the pharmaceutical companies marketing these new drugs argue that, by increasing patient compliance, relapse rates are reduced and thus hospital costs. Indeed, there is already some evidence emerging that this may be the case. Atcheson and Kerwin reviewed costs for difficult-to-treat patients mostly hospitalized under forensic psychiatrists; this showed a reduction in costs on chlozapine – the first atypical – to all services including social services, from £36,000 to £32,800. The main shift was from in-patient care (falling from a mean of 130 to 87 days) to the cost of the chlozapine clinic.[20] Evidence from the US is also emerging that the overall costs to the healthcare system for schizophrenics on the atypical olanzapine falls due to reduced utilization of specialist in-patient and outpatient services. Moreover, patients are twice as likely to return to work than those on the older drugs, thus generating further savings in social security costs. The savings more than compensated for the extra cost of the drug.[21]

THE ROLE OF HOSPITAL ADMISSION

There is now a fierce debate among psychiatrists about the value of admitting patients with schizophrenia to hospital if they are not a danger to themselves or those around them – the overwhelming majority, of course. On balance the consensus is reflected in the *American Psychiatric Association Practice Guideline*,[22] to the effect that admission is appropriate for the first episode in order to assess patients, monitor their functioning on medication and get them through to greater stability – especially if the carers and family cannot tolerate the stress and a period of respite would be beneficial. With subsequent episodes, however, the evidence for the efficacy of hospitalization is far less firm and respite can be provided by day-care services. Hence the NSF is promoting initiatives to prevent readmissions in crisis situations.[23]

UTILIZATION MANAGEMENT THROUGH ALTERNATIVES TO ADMISSION – THE NORTH BIRMINGHAM MODEL

In the UK, patients in the acute phase of illness have generally been admitted to hospital, usually staying for up to six weeks. It is now increasingly being recognized that admission rates to hospital and bed utilization can be reduced by a 24-hour emergency response service based in the community. These services seek to manage any crisis in the patient's normal environment. One model, the Psychiatric Emergency Team in Birmingham, has been evaluated recently by the Sainsbury Centre. The work of this team has been demonstrated to reduce substantially both admission rates (by 25 per cent) and the use of hospital beds (by 40 per cent) in its client group compared to a control group.[24] Not surprisingly, crisis response services are now recommended by the Department of Health as core components of an integrated mental health service. Critical success factors listed by the Sainsbury Centre include the following.

- The service should be targeted at people in severe psychiatric emergency.
- It needs to be well known to users, carers, GPs and social workers who otherwise manage emergency situations.
- It must be available out of hours since many emergency situations leading to current admission occur after five o'clock or at week-ends.
- The service must be multidisciplinary, have the dedicated staff time and skill set including effective interventions and relapse prevention.[25]

THE STABLE PHASE

Once a client has become stable, the most important aim is to prevent recurrence of further episodes of acute psychosis. Each episode takes the patient further down a spiral of disability, aggravating the condition, worsening prognosis, and increasing hospital use and costs to the services. First, the CMHT has a major role in working with the patient and carers to try and identify the relapse 'signature' and design a strategy for early intervention which is shared with the primary care team.

Second, non-compliance with medication is the major cause of relapse.[26] Indeed, the Royal College of Psychiatrists found that lack of compliance was a major factor leading to homicides and suicides by people with mental health problems.[27] It therefore becomes important clinically to engage with the patient to discuss treatment options, including the range of drugs available, so that he or she participates in the decision on the final choice. Patients also need regular monitoring for compliance. A number of factors have been associated with poor medium-term compliance with medication and can therefore place people at relatively high risk of being or becoming non-compliant:

• a protracted period taking the drug, particularly if they have remained symptom-free, which can lead patients to conclude that they no longer need take the drug;
• side effects which they may not volunteer to their GP or other healthcare professional;
• increased consultation rate with the GP for non-specific medical conditions.

THE IMPORTANCE OF PSYCHOSOCIAL INTERVENTIONS

Third, the next major category of causes of relapse and readmission include lack of knowledge in patients and carers and the presence in the family of high levels of 'expressed emotion'.[28] Expressed emotion or EE is a term for a range of dysfunctional responses to the schizophrenic by other family members. These can include poor communication skills, tendency to blame the individual, to over-react and over-protect. Treating high EE alone can reduce relapse rates with medication from 50 per cent on medication alone to 10–20 per cent. Hence psychosocial interventions are at least as effective in reducing relapse rates and, used in combination with medication compliance strategies, will offer maximum scope for preventing further psychotic episodes.[29]

Psychosocial interventions begin with education. As with most disease management programmes, improving the knowledge base of patients and carers is critical to successful clinical outcomes. Both therefore need to understand:

• the nature and prognosis of the condition;
• how to handle the stresses and pressures which it creates within families;
• what to expect from treatment including medication side effects, and that alternatives are available should side effects prove difficult to tolerate;

- the early warning signs of impending breakdown (i.e. the relapse signature) and how and where to access services at this point;
- how and when to access help and support.

Family management is the next category. Techniques used include:[30]

- a positive, flexible and patient response to family carers;
- improving problem-solving skills;
- stress management;
- emotional counselling;
- improving the family's ability to communicate.

This is highly skilled work and is therefore delivered by a professional mental health worker from the CMHT. Research indicates that the following factors render CMHT members most effective:

- manageable caseloads of about 30–40 per team member;
- up to six months' persistence in engaging a patient and family;
- continuity of care with a single person;
- direct service provision (the staff should provide the services required directly);
- team working to support individuals;
- training in distinguishing negative symptoms from negative personality traits;
- ability to identify at least aspects of the patient which can be viewed positively.[31]

This evidence is leading people to challenge current professional boundaries radically, as we describe later in the chapter.

MANAGEMENT IN PRIMARY CARE

Patients who respond well to treatment should be transferred to the management of their GP and primary care team and receive their mental health care in a normal environment. However, research indicates that there is substantial scope for improving GPs' management of people with schizophrenia and, in order to achieve this, the communication and liaison between the secondary and primary sectors. For example, Burns and Kendrick[32] found that although schizophrenic patients were in regular contact with their GPs (at least once every six months), less than half had a documented description of their mental state which was six months old or less. Similarly, Bindman[33] found that although psychotic patients consulted regularly, it was mostly for physical problems or renewal prescription of drugs. Few consulted for psychological problems and there was little routine monitoring of mental health. GPs expressed a lack of confidence in mental health management, causing reluctance to ask patients questions. GPs and the secondary services including CMHTs and psychiatrists did not communicate effectively. Consequently GPs felt uninvolved in the psychiatric care of patients with severe mental illness. Of course, as Kendrick points out, GPs have only an average of eight minutes per consultation and inevitably are largely reactive in approach: 'the usual assumption in primary care (is) that if a person does not return, it means they are well'.[34] One of the biggest service deficiencies identified was specialist professional time, particularly from the community psychiatric nurse.

In order to ensure a high-quality primary care service integrated with secondary care, the following components need to be in place:

- GPs and practice nurses competent to carry out mental health assessments, including the early detection screening;
- liaison attachments between specialist service – say a CMHT member or attached psychiatric nurse – and practices;
- increased training in mental health management for primary care teams;
- schizophrenia disease management clinics in general practice;
- shared-care guidelines and protocols reviewed by each primary care team and tailored to local working practices;
- a mental health register in each practice;
- not least, more education for patients in using primary care more effectively.

SOCIAL CARE AND REHABILITATION

As we have emphasized throughout, patients treated with a combination of anti-psychotics, social skills training and family therapy show a better outcome in terms of relapse rates than those treated with either anti-psychotics or psychosocial interventions alone. During the stable phase of the condition, therefore, it is also important to provide constructive daytime activity and minimize stress levels in day-to-day living. With regard to the latter, there is a common anecdote that one of the major causes of crisis in the home environment is when a person's sickness benefit cheque fails to arrive! Ensuring clients have their full benefits and special needs housing entitlements is one vital need that social care agencies are well placed to meet. Providing meaningful daytime activity is also crucial to successful management during the stable phase, particularly where clients and their carers need 'respite' from each other as in the case of families where there is high expressed emotion.

Moreover, repeated episodes of schizophrenia damage a person's ability to function in daily life, relationships, social situations and, not least, the employment market. For these patients, sometimes called revolving door or 'career' schizophrenics, social skills training – sometimes called 're-enablement' – can break the vicious circle of relapse and further disability. Social rehabilitation enables clients to acquire or reacquire the practical and social skills of daily life, restores confidence, and can also modify the emotional climate surrounding the patient. It is a slow, painstaking process to reverse the damage sometimes of many years. However, in order to create an integrated treatment network, rehabilitation is a core role usually led and provided by social care agencies. Case management is another.

CASE MANAGEMENT AND ASSERTIVE COMMUNITY TREATMENT (ACT)

In the last chapter, Sherry Aliotta describes the case management approach in relation to the at-risk elderly group with general health needs which is still relatively unknown in the UK. The approach is becoming much more mainstream in British mental health services. It is a core managed care intervention and indeed was developed in the home of HMOs, California. The original US model dates back to the 1970s. As Burns recalls, Stein and Test's original study[35] and its subsequent replication 'demonstrated such impressive reductions in hospitalisation and costs that the service model spread rapidly and it is probably the world's most thoroughly researched mental health programme'.[36]

Terminology can be confusing. In the mental health sector at least, there has been an emphasis on distinguishing case management and assertive community treatment (ACT).[37] Both aim to maintain contact with clients and reduce hospital utilization – frequency and duration. The case management approach includes the following components:

- it assesses needs;
- it develops a care plan;
- it arranges for services to be in place to implement the plan;
- it monitors outcomes.

ACT goes further in that it also:

- provides rather than arranges interventions including emergency treatment;
- practises assertive outreach by seeking out the clients who would not otherwise self-refer or are difficult to engage;
- places great emphasis on medication compliance (also a core component of the at-risk elderly model);
- provides practical help in areas such as finances, social security, housing, and neighbour relations.

The Wandsworth 'ACT' team

Burns has set out the success factors for an ACT service based on an early pilot scheme in Wandsworth in inner London. First, it is expensive and must be targeted at the high-need, high-utilizing 'revolving-door' clients who are also difficult to engage. Criteria for entry into assertive outreach will therefore combine high utilization of in-patient services and a high risk and needs profile. Eighty per cent of patients coming into the Wandsworth service described by Burns were schizophrenics.[38] Medication compliance is crucial and over 70 per cent of clients in the Wandsworth service were on the newer atypical anti-psychotics. Contact rate with each patient is as high as two per week, hence caseloads for staff are as low as ten to fifteen. Clients will stay on the programme until they have been stable for the medium term – up to two years in fact. Patients discharged after two years of non-admission to hospital will be phased off the service and transferred back to the CMHT or even to the GP for their ongoing care. The National Service Framework and NHS Plan are requiring these services to be set up in every district.

The future workforce in mental health

The skill sets required by community mental health and ACT team members span health and social care. Currently most service models bring together staff with narrowly defined nursing, social work and psychiatry backgrounds. However, most of these staff groups are in short supply, particularly in areas of high need such as inner London. This issue is bringing to the top of the NHS agenda proposals on how to staff the NHS more appropriately to client needs rather than using the traditional professional demarcations. As the Department of Health recently put it:

> The traditional, professionally affiliated mental health workforce is experiencing recruitment difficulties in most areas. The disadvantages of a strict adherence to traditional professional boundaries are becoming ever more apparent as mental healthcare advances ... Increasingly, workforce planning will be based around the competencies required to deliver services rather than around numbers of professional staff.[39]

Described more fully by Margaret Conroy in Chapter 11, the national Future Healthcare Workforce Project[40] has proposed the development of new professional and support worker roles which are designed to meet a wider spectrum of client need and accordingly span the current professional boundaries. The new professional roles, known as the 'mental health practitioner', were designed by teams of professional staff in the South West Region, specifically in Salisbury and Dorset. The case for this change is as powerful in mental health as in any other service area. For the purposes of illustration we focused on the health practitioner role and support roles in community mental health teams. The Future Healthcare Workforce Phase II Report also sets out new professional roles for in-patient services,[41] which Margaret sets out in her chapter.

THE MENTAL HEALTH PRACTITIONER ROLE IN THE COMMUNITY MENTAL HEALTH TEAM

The case for a health practitioner role in community mental health derives from the evidence base on the effectiveness of community mental health team members and the need to address current problems with existing professional role demarcations and training. Research into the effectiveness of members of community teams has shown that people with schizophrenia have the following needs:[42]

- they should have a relationship of six months or more with a single core worker to optimize their trust and engagement with the service;
- they should have a 'spectrum of needs' which span the traditional healthcare disciplines;
- people with psychosis as their primary diagnosis are liable to be on long-term medication of a year or more;
- they need a mental health worker who is knowledgeable about the impact of major drug therapy and the range of alternatives if clients suffer major side effects;
- at the same time, a therapeutic programme should encompass family work, social support and psychological techniques, occupational therapy and social work;
- every client should have a key worker under the national Care Programme Approach;
- there is a need for close liaison between the mental health team worker and primary care.

Findings from the Future Workforce Project and also from research by the Sainsbury Centre[43] have identified a number of problems with the current professional role demarcations. First, narrow roles inhibit continuity of care and cover when staff from specific disciplines are off duty. Second, different disciplines gravitate to similar workload. Third, there is confusion over roles for staff and patients alike, and staff feel they are not using their full range of skills, with community psychiatric nurses complaining of low status and low morale. Multidisciplinary working is inefficient in that it involves substantial time devoted to coordination and allocation meetings which can take an entire day per week or one-fifth of the working time for team members. Current training is not sufficiently oriented towards the needs of the service. As the Sainsbury Centre puts it, 'the dominating influence of the current training agenda continues to be the needs of each professional group to define autonomously its own role and boundary'.[44] The evidence base on team-member effectiveness and these findings leads inexorably to the conclusion that moving to a core practitioner role designed around the needs of the client is the only way of satisfactorily addressing current deficiencies that a wide range of expertise has so clearly identified.

THE COMMUNITY MENTAL HEALTH PRACTITIONER ROLE
IN THE SALISBURY PROJECT

The Salisbury Project was based in a large community mental health team. It was overseen by a Steering Group which included user representation. The objectives were to develop a Core Professional Practitioner Role in mental health which addresses the needs of clients and spans traditional professional roles by encompassing *80 per cent of the activity of the community mental health team including the key worker role* under the care programme approach. The group also went on to develop a set of occupational standards for the core professional competencies required to train these new professionals. These have subsequently been field tested with a second team in the South West Region. Accordingly, the following core functions were identified and incorporated in a single professional role:

- all client assessment work including case description, but excluding diagnosis which would remain a medical function;
- care planning and the Key Worker role under CPA including the co-ordination of all services to implement the care plan;
- the lead therapist with clients including prescribing and administering medication, psychosocial interventions and any decision to admit to hospital;
- provision of advice and support to GPs on management of mental health problems including medication;
- the full range of psychiatric nursing skills including observation, support, motivation, role modelling, conflict resolution, risk and behaviour management;
- operational knowledge of the Mental Health Act, Mental Health Act Commission Code of Conduct, and clients' rights as well as social security benefits, special needs housing and social services care management processes.

The project also identified an anomaly in current practice with regard to procedures under the Mental Health Act (MHA). Currently it is often the psychiatric nurses who prepare all the information on the basis of which a decision to admit patients under the MHA is taken by medical and social work staff. To resolve this situation, it was also proposed that in the future the core professional would have this authority for involuntary admission and supervision orders. This proposal has been carried forward into the current review of the 1983 Mental Health Act.[45]

THE ROLE OF SUPPORT WORKERS IN COMMUNITY MENTAL
HEALTH TEAMS – THE SAINSBURY FINDINGS

The development of the support worker role was not a central objective of the Salisbury Project as such. However, the Sainsbury Centre has recently examined this issue[46] by conducting a semi-structured survey of a selected sample of professional staff, managers and service users alike. In relation to support roles at least, the Working Party which produced the report was convinced of the need to span current professional boundaries. What is particularly significant about its findings, however, is the range of functions and the extent to which they overlap with activities of professionally trained staff, particularly community psychiatric nurses and social workers.

The support worker role

Support workers in teams were working predominantly with people with serious mental health problems. The following list of functions were those in which 60 per cent or more of support workers in community teams were actively involved and considered appropriate by those in the survey.

The role of the support worker in a CMHT:

Mental health management
* monitoring medication compliance;
* monitoring effects of medication including side effects;
* communication with prescribing agent (mostly doctors);
* judging risk;
* communicating with GP;
* encouraging positive coping;
* monitoring and reporting general health issues.

Social and emotional support
* establishing and sustaining social networks;
* helping users communicate with family.

Daily living skills, day care and support with practical tasks
* finding suitable accommodation;
* daytime activities and leisure;
* basic literacy and numeracy;
* money management, paying bills and rent;
* sorting out benefits;
* daily living – such as shopping, cooking and cleaning.

In the survey, only 20 per cent of support workers were available out of hours. However, given the 24-hour needs of people with serious and enduring mental health problems, this is a natural extension of their contribution to the service.

Value to the client or user

What is most striking about the Sainsbury Centre's findings is the value ascribed to support workers by clients and their families. In terms of the therapeutic alliance between worker and client, the users rated support workers to be either of equal or of more value than professional key workers in terms of availability, understanding their needs and someone to trust. Specifically trained for the role, the support has a key function in helping people with severe and enduring mental health problems maintain themselves in the community and through sensitive monitoring helping to avoid the kind of breakdowns and crises which otherwise give rise to hospitalization. As one user put it: 'She (the support worker) is a stepping stone. I've always ended up in hospital before which I hate, drugged up and bored and surrounded by tobacco smoke.'

A key role in the future service

Trained support workers are valued in providing a unique service different from, but complementary to, professionals. However, the degree of overlap between their functions and those of professional staff indicates the scope for shifting the skill mix in community mental health teams. By developing and extending this role, community teams can enhance the quality and efficiency of their service and, not least, address the supply issues for professionally qualified staff.

NOTES AND REFERENCES

1 A. Scull (1977) *Decarceration*. New Jersey, NJ: Prentice-Hall.
2 L.L. Stein and M.A. Test (1980) Alternatives to mental hospital treatment. Conceptual model, treatment programme and clinical evaluation, *Archives of General Psychiatry*, 37: 392–7.
3 P. Boland (1994) Foreword to S.A. Shueman, W.G. Troy and S.L. Mayhugh (eds) *Managed Behavioural Healthcare*. Springfield, IL: C.T. Thomas.
4 Department of Health (1999) *A National Service Framework for Mental Health*. London: Department of Health.
5 Department of Health, op. cit.
6 Department of Health (1998/1999) *Bed Availability and Occupancy, 1998/99 and Ordinary and Day Case Admissions, 1997/98*. Leeds: Department of Health.
7 M. Goddard *et al.* (2000) Avoidable use of beds and cost-effectiveness of care in alternative locations, Annexe E to *Shaping the Future NHS: Long-term Planning for Hospital and Related Services, Consultation Documents on the Findings of the National Beds Inquiry – Supporting Analysis*. DoH website.
8 G. Strathdee (1997) Deploying a community mental health team for the effective care of individuals with schizophrenia, *Advances in Psychiatric Treatment*, 1: 199–206.
9 The Sainsbury Centre (1998) *Acute Problems: A Survey of the Quality of Care in Acute Psychiatric Wards*, p. 39. London: The Sainsbury Centre.
10 M. Birchwood *et al.* (2000) Schizophrenia: early warning signs, *Advances in Psychiatric Treatment*, 6: 93–101.
11 Northumberland Mental Health NHS Trust (2000) *Partnership Project: Primary Care Patient Pack*. Morpeth: Northumberland Mental Health NHS Trust.

12 American Psychiatry Association (1997) Practice Guideline for the Treatment of Patients with Schizophrenia. Washington: APA.

13 J. Leff (1998) Needs of the families of people with schizophrenia, *Advances in Psychiatric Treatment*, 4: 277–84.

14 Hence their wider use is being promoted by user groups such as the National Schizophrenia Fellowship.

15 W.T. Carpenter (1996) The treatment of negative symptoms: pharmacological and methodological issues, *British Journal of Psychiatry*, 68 (29): 17–22.

16 D. Taylor *et al.* (1999) *A Survey of Psychiatrists and Health Authorities to Determine the Factors Influencing the Prescribing and Funding of Atypical Antipsychotics.* London: Maudsley Hospital.

17 J.A. Lieberman and W.W. Fleischhacker (1996) Current issues in the development of atypical antipsychotic drugs, *British Journal of Psychiatry*, 168 (29): 7–8.

18 American Psychiatric Association, op. cit.

19 University of York: NHS Centre for Reviews and Disseminations (1999) Drug treatment for schizophrenia, *Effective Healthcare*, 5 (6).

20 K.J. Atcheson and R. Kerwin (1997) Cost-effectiveness of chlozapine, *British Journal of Psychiatry*, 171: 125–30.

21 G.D. Tollefson and A.J. Kuntz (1999) Review of recent clinical studies with olanzapine, *British Journal of Psychiatry*, 174 (37): 30–5.

22 American Psychiatric Association, op. cit.

23 Department of Health (1999), op. cit.

24 The Sainsbury Centre for Mental Health (1998) *Open All Hours: 24-hour Response for People with Mental Health Emergencies*, pp. 51–4. London: Sainsbury Centre.

25 Ibid, pp. 48–9.

26 U. Meise and W.W. Fleischhacker (2000) Perspectives on Treatment Needs in Schizophrenia, *British Journal of Psychiatry* 68 (29): 9–13; Scottish Intercollegiate Guidelines Network (1998) *Psychosocial Interventions in the Management of Schizophrenia: A National Clinical Guideline*, October; University of York: NHS Centre for Reviews and Disseminations (2000) Psycho-social interventions for schizophrenia, *Effective Health Care*, 6 (3).

27 Royal College of Psychiatrists (1996) *Report of a Confidential Inquiry into Homicides and Suicides by Mentally Ill People.* London: Royal College of Psychiatrists.

28 J. Leff *et al.* (1996) Expressed emotion and maintenance neuroleptics in schizophrenic relapse, *Psychological Medicine*, 13: 799–806.

29 Leff, op. cit.

30 E. Kuipers (1998) The management of difficult to treat patients with schizophrenia using non-drug therapies, *British Journal of Psychiatry*, 169 (31): 41–51.

31 Ibid.

32 T. Burns and T. Kendrick (1997) The primary care of patients with schizophrenia: a search for good practice, *British Journal of General Practice*, 47 (August): 515–20.

33 J. Bindman *et al.* (1997) Integration between primary and secondary services in the care of the severely mentally ill: patients' and general practitioners' views, *British Journal of Psychiatry*, 171: 169–74.

34 T. Kendrick (1998) Management of people with schizophrenia in primary care, *Advances in Psychiatric Treatment*, 4: 46–51.

35 Stein and Test, op. cit.

36 T. Burns and L. Guest (1999) Running an assertive out-reach team, *Advances in Psychiatric Treatment* 5: 340–56.

37 UK 700 (1999) Group comparison of intensive and standard case management for patients with psychosis: rationale of the trial, *British Journal of Psychiatry*, 174: 74–9.

38 Burns and Guest, op. cit.

39 Department of Health (2000) *Mental Health National Service Framework Workforce: Planning, Education and Training Underpinning Programme*, Annexe B, p. 40. London: Department of Health.

40 M. Conroy and D.A. Cochrane (1996) *The Future Healthcare Workforce Project, Phase I Report*. Manchester: University of Manchester.

41 M. Conroy and D.A. Cochrane (1999) *The Future Healthcare Workforce Project, Phase II Report*, pp. 88–93. Bournemouth: University of Bournemouth, Institute of Health and Community Studies.

42 Bindman *et al.*, op.cit.; Kuipers, op. cit.

43 Sainsbury Centre (1997) *Pulling Together: The Future Role and Training of Mental Health Staff*. London: Sainsbury Centre.

44 Ibid.

45 UK government White Paper (2000) *Reform of the Mental Health Act 1983. Proposals for Consultation*, Cmnd 4480, p. 23. London: The Stationery Office.

46 A. Murray (1997) *More than Just a Friend: The Role of Support Workers in Community Mental Health Services*. London: Sainsbury Centre.

Part three

DEVELOPING THE MANAGED CARE AGENDA

10

BENCHMARKING IN HEALTHCARE PERFORMANCE MANAGEMENT

David Cochrane

As set out in Chapter 1 the managed care sector has led the American healthcare industry in the development and implementation of performance standards. Some of this process has been generated from within the managed care sector itself, but much of it has been required through both federal and state regulatory legislation as managed care organizations have developed increasing business with Medicare and Medicaid programmes, and by the organization of large employers through the HEDIS process. For those interested in the specifics of the American experience, Coulter has documented the process and set out the major areas in which managed care organizations are now routinely monitored.[1]

This experience is being mirrored in the UK with the NHS Performance Assessment Framework[2] which is integral to the NHS Quality Strategy.[3] The performance areas on which the NHS is to report reflect the six major objectives set out in the 1997 White Paper[4] which are:

- health improvement;
- fair access and resource deployment;
- effective delivery of appropriate care;
- patient and carer experience;
- efficiency;
- health outcomes.

A key mechanism in the delivery of this process is benchmarking or, as the White Paper put it,[5]

> The new performance framework will encourage greater benchmarking of performance in different areas, and the publication of comparative information will allow people to share performance and share best practice. The Government will use these measures for a systematic drive to challenge and reduce variations in all aspects of performance across the NHS.

In June 1999, circular HSC 1999/139 announced the publication of the first set of performance indicators under these criteria.[6] The circular requires health authorities, Primary Care Groups and NHS Trusts to:

- review the performance of local services across the six areas of performance set out in the Performance Assessment Framework;
- compare local performance with that of similar health authorities and Trusts;
- share information about achieving good results for patients with other organizations and take forward work on benchmarking.

The Department of Health has already begun to issue guidance and worked examples of standard performance measures across some of these six fields, notably quality, health improvement indicators and the Reference Costs issued in January 2000. Meanwhile, through the good offices of the Audit Commission, NHS services are increasingly subject to benchmarking by local district audit studies. Understanding the benchmarking process could not be more timely for the NHS. It is therefore not the aim of the chapter to identify specific measures of performance but rather to provide a practical guide on how to identify relevant measures and use the process of benchmarking to assess and improve performance. This includes some worked examples and a step-by-step process for running a benchmarking process within healthcare organizations. We then go on to list some of the commonly expressed concerns and discuss how these can be addressed.

A BRIEF HISTORY OF BENCHMARKING

Benchmarking was first developed by Rank Xerox in the late 1970s. The company introduced and came to lead the world in the manufacture and sale of reprographic machines. Then during the 1970s Xerox executives watched the company's market share drop dramatically in the face of cheaper, more reliable machines produced largely by Japanese competitors. Rather than simply panic, Rank Xerox identified those companies which were beginning to outstrip it in market share, studied both their manufacturing and marketing processes and re-engineered its own. The resultant turnaround in the company's fortunes established benchmarking as a central process for turning strategic business objectives into reality in the corporate sector.

During the last ten years, benchmarking has emerged from the corporate sector as 'one of the most powerful techniques for monitoring and improving organizational performance'.[7] Achieving best performance becomes a constant business objective. Since performance is constantly moving forward, benchmarking creates a permanent dynamic and culture for positive change within the organization.

THE BENEFITS OF BENCHMARKING

All successful large organizations employ benchmarking. It is a research and learning process which spans industries and service sectors and taps the collective knowledge base. It uses the principle that the collective heads of two or more organizations are bound to be better than one. In this way benchmarking can promote:

- an *open organization* which shares experience and expertise within its own departments and with other similar organizations and also welcomes constructive criticism;
- a *dynamic-learning organization* which values and actively seeks out experience and influence from the outside, and facilitates the flow and uptake of new ideas and practices between departments;
- an *informed organization* which takes decisions on the basis of systematic analysis of relevant evidence;
- an *improving organization* which is never complacent about its current performance and which has incorporated the constant drive for improvement within its organizational culture.

Accordingly, we can contrast organizations which do not use benchmarking with those who do.

Without benchmarking	*With benchmarking*
Internal focus	Best practice focus
Resistant to external ideas	Open to ideas and learning
Decisions on 'gut feel'	Evidence-based decision making
Agents of conservatism	Modernizing

BENCHMARKING

In terms of organizational performance, a benchmark is a reference point for business excellence against which others can be measured and compared. In practice, it is the combination of two elements. First, it involves quantitative measurement of performance in a range of comparator organizations or departments. This data gathering and analysis is often called *metrics*. Quantitative analysis enriches any planning and decision-making process in two ways:

- it informs decision making on issues which managers have identified, making the process more evidence-based;
- it identifies key issues which would not otherwise have arisen had the analysis not been undertaken.

However, the capture and analysis of data is of little value unless it leads to management action. Hence benchmarking also involves studying processes and practices in those organizations and departments highlighted by the metrics analysis and above all *learning from them*. The process is well illustrated with a golfing parable.

> Mr Slice, a surgeon, had been a member at his golf club for ten years and never once made par at the fifth hole, a sharp dog-leg to the right. Problems with his grip caused him to fade the ball to the right off every tee-shot and that meant that he invariably finished up deep amongst the fir trees to the left of the fourth fairway. So one day his frustration grew to such a pitch that he decided to do something about it. He spent the next two weeks collecting score-cards from his fellow members at the door of the nineteenth hole. He inputted 150 scores onto the database of his son's personal computer and ran an analysis of those players who consistently scored four or less on the fifth hole. The analysis showed that in ten rounds of golf, a Dr Hook – a GP – had consistently made or broken par on this hole. So Mr Slice sought out Dr Hook in the clubhouse and arranged to play a round with him. During that game, Mr Slice took the opportunity to study Dr Hook's swing and noted down his grip of the club which seemed to help Dr Hook pull the ball round to the left. Mr Slice then took to the practice ground and practised his own swing – incorporating his learning – until he began to hit the ball straight off the tee. Two months after his round with Dr Hook, Mr Slice made his first par four on the fifth hole.

Mr Slice followed a logical process:

- he identified a crucial area of poor performance;
- he found a population of relevant comparators;
- he identified a reliable, quantifiable measure of best practice;
- he collected data on that measure from his comparators;
- he identified the source of best practice by comparative analysis through *metrics*;
- crucially, he studied the process underlying the best practice position;
- equally important, he changed his own practice in the light of that learning.

Hence, benchmarking is more than just a numbers exercise. Setting goals comparable with the best in the class without understanding the underlying processes can be a pointless exercise. Understanding how the best results are achieved is much more important.

TYPES OF BENCHMARKING

Boxwell[8] identifies four types: competitive, cooperative, collaborative and internal.

Competitive benchmarking

This takes place when organizations or their constituent departments do not wish to be studied and therefore do not cooperate with the data collection exercise. In the NHS, Trusts or their constituent departments resist sharing their data, usually for one of two reasons:

- They know they are resource-rich and do not wish to have this made transparent to other stakeholders – such as the district health authority, the Regional Office, corporate management or other departments and service areas.
- They are tight for resources but have been repeatedly targeted for cost-reduction exercises so fear that the current study will only leave them in a still worse position.

Since this was a tendency very much fostered by the internal market, this approach should now be passing into the organizational history of the NHS.

Cooperative benchmarking

In this model, organizations targeted by others as examples of good practice willingly supply data but do not participate in the study or share the results. Usually the organization providing the data will have experienced the value of benchmarking. Again under the internal market, NHS Trusts were more willing to cooperate with more distant Trusts who were not direct competitors but less inclined to share staffing data with neighbouring Trusts for fear this information which is key to their cost structure would filter back to their common purchaser authorities. Although at first glance this seems like a low-risk strategy, in reality staffing problems and difficulties are often determined by local labour market forces. Hence Trusts who refuse to collaborate at local level may be denying themselves access to best practice information which is far more relevant to their own organizational objectives.

Collaborative or 'partnership' benchmarking

This is the most mature model of benchmarking in which organizations with common issues and challenges agree joint objectives for a study and share the results of data collection and analysis. Each of the participants will have valuable practices to share which are the currency for the collaboration. Often a third party agency may act as coordinator, collecting and analysing the data and providing feedback to the participants. Organizations may subscribe to 'benchmarking clubs' where commonly a consulting firm charges a moderate fee to collect data, undertake comparative analysis and provide the results. Apart from gaining access to common data sets, participants are by definition those who value the process of sharing common learning. However, since benchmarking clubs are a self-selecting group, there is no guarantee that all relevant organizations are included.

Given that the NHS now has a duty for partnership under the 1999 NHS Act, the collaborative model of workforce benchmarking can best promote the NHS modernization agenda but it requires careful construction. First, since the key mechanism for ensuring partnership in the NHS is the Health Improvement Programme (HIMP), it is becoming essential for NHS providers to collaborate at local level against the service objectives and priorities set out in the HIMP. Furthermore, the health authority's constituent Primary Care Groups are major players in the demand and supply of staff groups common to all other NHS providers and GPs. All this clearly implies that the local health authority and PCGs/PCTs should participate as key stakeholders alongside NHS Trusts in local workforce benchmarking exercises.

Internal benchmarking

Organizations should also be mindful that benchmarking is not restricted to external comparison and that internal benchmarks can be an equally powerful driver for positive change. Internal benchmarking involves analysis of comparative performance between similar departments within organizations. Within hospital-based providers, useful internal comparisons are undertaken between service-based units or directorates, and medical specialties. Within community-based services, it is useful to examine locality-based benchmarks. Within primary care, comparisons can be studied at practice or PCG/PCT level.

THE PROCESS STAGE BY STAGE

Figure 10.1 sets out a step-by-step approach to benchmarking in workforce planning. This is subdivided into the study design, the analysis and the action phases. Each phase is covered in turn in this and the subsequent sections.

THE STUDY DESIGN PHASE – DEVELOPING BENCHMARKS AND SELECTING VALID COMPARATORS

Step 1 – identifying areas to benchmark

The first stage is to identify those areas for which benchmarking data is required. There are a number of key questions which arise at this stage:

- Is the topic area consistent with the strategic vision and key business objectives of the organization?
- Is the process structured by the business objectives of the organization?
- Is it significant for efficiency and resource use?

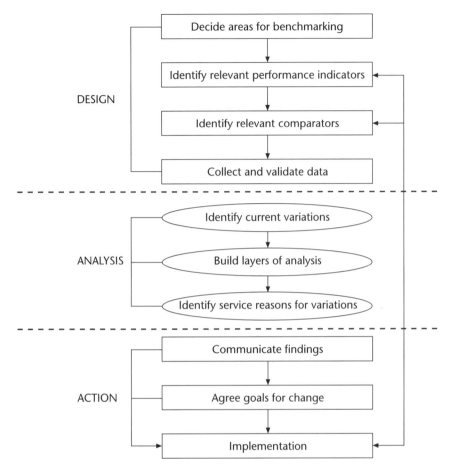

Figure 10.1   Principles of good practice – step by step

- Will it impact on patient care in terms of both the outcomes of care and the patient's experience?
- Are there specific resource problems developing in the organization (these may include budget overspends or service supply problems)?
- Is the time and energy invested in the benchmarking likely to generate dividends in terms of positive changes to current plans and strategies? Where benchmarking studies fail, they do so not because the data cannot be collected and analysed, but rather because key managers do not use the information generated to change practice.

Within healthcare, the following key areas meet these criteria:

- the range and configuration of services;
- service availability and utilization data such as location, waiting times, admission rates, lengths of stay in hospital;

- unit costs, including workforce costs in turn determined by factors such as levels of staff, the profile in terms of skill and grade mix and the balance between staff groups;
- patient-care process and staffing skills;
- outcome measures;
- health gain indicators;
- indicators of patient satisfaction.

Step 2 – defining relevant performance measures

There are several golden rules to defining benchmarks in healthcare.

They should be based on easily-accessed data sources
Our first requirement is not to over-burden the process with complex data collection exercises which require several months or even years to complete. However sophisticated we would like to get, it is vital to sustain the momentum and interest in any project.

The measures should be meaningful to key stakeholders
– staff and managers
Performance measures should be common currency within the NHS. Remember our central objectives of openness, communication, need to challenge existing practices and shared learning. To facilitate these objectives it is vital that performance measures can be understood by all participants in the process. Measures which are meaningful only to NHS managers may remain remote for service users and the public at large. This will militate against communication, and the accountability process. That is not to say that within clinical departments a more detailed set of indicators cannot be maintained, provided they map back to the core measures used corporately.

Key stakeholders

NHS organizations
- chairs and chief executives;
- executive and non-executive directors;
- lead professional managers;
- contracting and quality managers;
- business managers;
- locality managers in community and mental health trusts;
- managers at service level such as A & E, theatres and ward sisters.

Other stakeholders
- service users and their representatives;
- local authority and other health-related service providers;
- the press;
- the research community.

They should be agreed and supported by key stakeholders
It is essential to develop a list of agreed indicators through a collaborative process. One method is to conduct a workshop with service-level staff and managers. The project coordinators present the aims of the exercise and a set of proposed indicators. These can then be challenged, amended, augmented and refined. Not only does this foster ownership, it taps the specialist knowledge of clinical staff, thus greatly improving the sensitivity and scope of performance indicators and thus the authority of the exercise.

They should allow both internal and external comparative analysis
Clearly, comparative analysis involves comparing like with like. Hence the core performance measures need to be standard between departments or localities, within providers and between them.

Hitherto, this requirement often precluded measures of quality. However, as the National Performance Assessment Framework develops standardized measures of quality in terms of outcomes and patient satisfaction, it should become increasingly possible to benchmark providers on quality indicators.[9]

They should span all key indicators within each field of the
Performance Assessment Framework
Recommendations arising from the benchmarking exercise will have implications for the patient's experience, for cost, quality, staff morale. It is crucial therefore to encompass the full range of indicators that can be quantified, measured and standardized.

Examples of significant indicators in healthcare

Here are some examples of performance measures in healthcare which can be readily benchmarked:

- acute admission rates by health resource group per 1000 population;
- hospital length of stay in days by health resource group;
- waiting time for admission for elective surgery;
- percentage of elective surgery on a day basis by health authority;
- percentage of elderly people on a GP's list screened for high blood pressure and on appropriate medication;
- percentage of people with severe mental health problems who have an agreed care plan under the Care Programme Approach;
- cost of fractured neck of femur repair in patients aged over 70;
- consultation rates per GP within a Primary Care Group;
- referral rates to outpatients by GPs within a primary care group.

Building benchmarks from base data

In the field of healthcare we will often need to derive benchmarks from base data sources. Others will be generated through benchmarking clubs or direct approaches to other providers. Let us take an example from outpatients. A new outpatient department is being planned for a local health community. How can the current level of activity be critically reviewed? One way is to develop a number of indicators of the efficiency in the use of outpatient services. This can be drawn from the Department of Health publication, *Outpatients and Ward Attenders*[10] which sets out for each Trust by specialty the total number of outpatient attendances as first and subsequent attenders. From this database a number of Trusts can be selected as comparators and the following indicators calculated:

- attendance rates per 1000 population;
- ratio of first to total attendances.

A key question in this process is how to select valid comparators.

Step 3 – identifying valid comparators

Criteria for selecting organizations
No two organizations are identical. If this were a requirement of benchmarking then no commercial company or public sector provider could begin to attempt it. However, many NHS organizations are very similar overall or provide very similar services. This gives us our first guiding principle to selecting comparators:

- *Selection should be service based.* In this way a standard district general hospital may not be a valid comparator for a large teaching hospital.
- *Selected comparators should serve similar populations.* However, providers from more affluent areas should not rule out comparators whose served populations have higher indicators of morbidity such as deprivation scores. Providers in these areas may be managing their more challenging caseloads perfectly well with more efficient resource deployment.
- *Comparator organizations or health communities should be of similar size and provide or offer a similar range of service.* That said, restricting membership of benchmarking clubs to large teaching hospitals or health authorities with urban, deprived populations may be simply reinforcing the group's suboptimal practices. Not least, providers with a historically smaller resource base, for example, will sometimes have developed more efficient service delivery processes which maintain excellent quality within a lower cost.
- *Internal comparators should be limited to similar services.* For example, acute Trusts will compare resourcing in mainstream services internally but should benchmark their specialist services against those of other Trusts. Within the same community Trust, there are often great similarities between the populations of the localities served, providing ideal opportunity to assess equity in resource deployment. Where there are significant differences in needs profiles, internal benchmarking will demonstrate whether there is a correlation between population needs and resource deployment. Often there is not!

Step 4 – gathering the data

Standard proformas for data gathering should be designed and agreed with participants
Some of the data required will already be readily available within the organization but usually located in various functional departments. Staffing and finance data will be available on personnel and budgetary systems. Patient activity data will be found in business planning or contracting directorates. National data sources will be useful to provide data on comparators. Some data items, such as activity in specific GP practices, are likely to require special exercises such as short-term surveys.

Put strict time boundaries around the data gathering exercise
Protracted periods of data collection can cause the project to lose focus and momentum and, not least, the results of the benchmarking analysis when finally available will be vulnerable to criticism that the data is no longer current. *As a general rule, it should take no more than six to eight weeks to gather the data.*

Minimize the irritation factors
Data is rarely formatted as you need and request it. It can therefore mean a lot of work for those providing it. So make the task as least onerous as possible:

- draw on existing standard returns as much as possible;
- ensure that the people you are approaching were not recently asked for the same data in some other exercise;
- incorporate those providing the data in the design of reports so that they can get something back in return for their efforts;
- be diplomatic and courteous but purposeful – do not be short-changed on key aspects of data.

Validate the data with stakeholders
Once the data is collected, *and before undertaking any analysis*, it is important to ensure all participants are signed up to its accuracy. Remember that questioning the accuracy of data is the first defence of the opponent of benchmarking. Moreover, a great deal of time and energy can be wasted discussing the findings from a benchmarking analysis – however beautifully reported – which is based on disputed data.

Be realistic about your expectations
You will never get 100 per cent of the data you require. If you get 90 per cent you are doing very well. Remember, data gathering can become addictive and obsessive. Do not exhaust your team and your collaborators trying to find the remaining 5 per cent or 10 per cent.

THE ANALYSIS PHASE – INTERPRETING BENCHMARKS

Step 5 – analysis and scope for change

The critical question underlying the analysis is what constitutes best practice? How does that inform our choice of benchmark values in the selected performance measures? In practice it is advisable to use a range of benchmarks drawn from each of three sources:

- statistical averages and percentiles;
- results of special studies;
- local professional and managerial consensus.

Using statistical averages and upper percentiles

The sample average
This is usually taken as the mean average. We simply add up the values from each service in the sample and divide by the number of services. This is most useful in large data sets. A national or regional average figure is often criticized as the lowest common denominator and insensitive to local needs. However, it can be a useful starting point because large samples tend to cancel over- and under-provision and reflect a wide range of professional and managerial views on effective and affordable service profiles. At the very least, the mean provides a useful measure by which to identify significant outliers with values substantially higher or lower than the mean. If using small samples, it is advisable not to include substantial outliers from the calculation of the mean average.

The median range
Taking this approach assumes there is safety in numbers. This is defined as the range which incorporates the largest cluster of values. We select a narrow range of values within which the largest group of providers fall. Hence we can take a benchmark as the range within which 25, 50 or 75 per cent of the sample fall – depending on how widely spread the distribution is. A useful elaboration of this is to mean the provider values in the median range to give a single benchmark figure.

The mode value
This is the one single value scored by the highest number of providers. This measure is only a useful indicator in very large data sets.

   Whether we select the mean or the median average depends on how skewed the distribution is – in other words, the extent to which the distribution of the values differs from the balanced bell curve of an even or *normal* distribution. In a normal distribution the mean, the mode and the median range will coincide. This is illustrated in Figure 10.2.

Using mean averages in a skewed distribution can be very misleading. For example, although we use the average wage as benchmark for our own earnings, this overlooks the fact that two-thirds of employees earn less than the mean average! In the case of a skewed distribution, therefore, the upper or lower quartiles may be a more valid benchmark.

Lower and upper percentiles
Since we are looking for best practice a useful measure to take as our benchmark is a value which indicates best performance. For example, we may be assuming that the lower the staffing levels or higher the proportion of support staff the more cost-efficient the provider. Hence we can fix our benchmark as the provider at the lower end of the distribution on levels of staff but at the upper end of the distribution of percentage of support workers. It is usual practice to take the 25th or 75th percentiles, being the value at or below which 25 or 75 per cent of the sample falls.

Statistically derived benchmarks demonstrate financial comparability of staffing levels and profile but used alone are likely to generate concerns among staff that quality issues are not being adequately addressed.

(a) A normal distribution showing averages, best and worst performing 'quartiles'

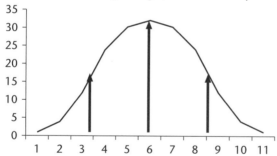

(b) A skewed distribution showing the mean average

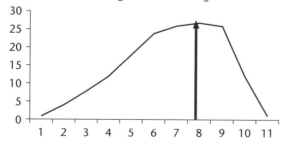

Figure 10.2   Normal and skewed distributions

Standards set by special research studies

Sometimes services under review will have been subject to special study to define the standards required for specific services. These can be particularly helpful where quality and cost-effectiveness have been considered together. Provided they are used in combination with statistically derived benchmarks, the interests and concerns of all stakeholders are addressed. The research-based standard reassures staff on quality issues whereas the statistical benchmarking can demonstrate comparability on cost parameters and satisfy managers with responsibility for resource use.

Empowering local staff to derive the benchmarks

A third approach is to facilitate discussion with local service-level staff to draw on their assessment of the appropriateness of performance measures. Required levels of staff are derived by asking the staff directly in a facilitated workshop. Facilitation is necessary, however, to ensure that quality and efficiency are considered as 'both sides of the same coin' as the NHS Quality Strategy requires. Cost comparability is ensured by using this approach alongside statistically derived benchmarks.

Combining approaches

Ideally the benchmarking process should use a combination of all three approaches as shown in Figure 10.3. If this is done, the finding is usually that all three approaches support one another. Or at least the margin of variation between them tends to be small, thus allowing benchmarks to be developed which promote cost-effectiveness within quality parameters acceptable to the staff delivering the service.

Draw a boundary around the analysis stage

Whichever methodologies you employ, never lose sight of the main purpose which is to inform and facilitate decision making and improvements in practice. Analysis of data can throw up more and more issues and the process can become an end in itself. Set a deadline for report back to prevent this *analysis paralysis*.

The inter-quartile range
A useful way of eliminating outliers from a database is to take the values in the range between the 25th and 75th percentile and calculate an average of these values. This is an approach followed in the NHS Reference Costs, for example.

Step 6 – building layers of analysis

Using benchmarks has been likened to peeling the layers of an onion. There are three useful techniques:

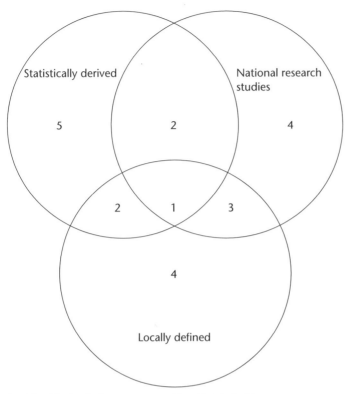

1   The ideal solution – supported by all stakeholders
2   The next best – should command a consensus of stakeholders
3,4 Professional staff agree but resource managers remain concerned
5   Resource managers satisfied but professional staff concerned

Figure 10.3   Combining approaches to benchmarking

- single indicators;
- two or more related indicators;
- profiling.

Analysis of single indicators

Using bar charts
Vertical and horizontal histograms are useful for single indicators such as productivity measures. Figure 10.4 shows the productivity of cardiologists and surgeons as whole time equivalent (WTE) per 10,000 finished consultant episodes across four hospitals in a consortium compared to the sample mean and the English average.

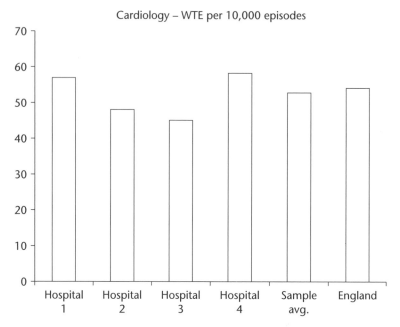

Figure 10.4   Using bar charts

Analysis of two or more related indicators

Scatter diagrams
A scatter diagram such as Figure 10.5 can be used to plot two related indicators at once. For example, it is argued that the shorter the length of stay on acute wards, the higher the workload for nursing and thus the higher the levels of nurses required per occupied bed. Ward nursing productivity is therefore plotted against patient throughput since the higher the throughput, the shorter the length of stay. The benchmark can be derived in two ways. First, we can take an average of the dense cluster of values – shown encircled in the diagram. Alternatively we can undertake a regression analysis and find the best fit relationship between patient throughput and bed availability productivity. In this way we can both audit current staffing levels and identify a planning benchmark which corresponds to the throughput in the providers under review as it changes over time.

Tabular format
If using tables, make them clear and informative. The following benchmarks show productivity of occupational therapists.

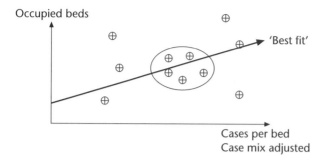

Figure 10.5 Using scatter diagrams

Table 10.1 Productivity of community occupational therapists

Measure	Current performance value	Best practice		Variance		Sample ranking
		Trust	Value	Net	%	
WTE per 1000 contacts	0.2	A	0.4	0.2	50	12
Contacts per week	20	B	30	10	33	8
% helpers	30	C	30	0	0	1
% Grade I and above	40	D	30	10	33	5

Profiling

A profile is a range of indicators which span several fields of perform-ance. Table 10.2 is a profile of mental health services within a health authority. It shows indicators across population need, service utilization, expenditure and staffing. Against each measure there is a ranking show-ing the performance of the health authority ranked against another 11 who participated in the exercise.

This health authority ranks as one of the most deprived in the country and has indicators of high mental health need, but its mental health expenditure is only at the midpoint or average for the sample. As a result, 95 per cent of expenditure was in hospital services to cope with demand for admissions. The profile indicates that this health authority needs to increase its mental health expenditure in community services to develop a more balanced service profile. Nurse staffing in the hospitals is relatively high, indicating that there may be scope for transferring resources from the hospital sector to community services.

Table 10.2 Mental health performance profile

Indicator	Value	Ranking
Size of population	585,900	3
Jarman deprivation score	60	1
Suicide rate	2.4 per 1000	4
% homeless	3.9%	2
Unemployment rate	12%	1
% population from ethnic minorities	39%	1
Service provision and utilization		
Admission rate per 1000 population	4.4	6
Acute beds per 1000 population	0.4	8
Throughput per bed	12.1	2
Community psychiatric nurse contacts per 1000	86	3
Expenditure		
Mental health expenditure per 1000 population	6.32m	7
Mental health as % of DHA total	13.2%	9
% spend on community services	5%	8
Staffing		
Consultants per 100,000 population	5.33	5
Nurses per patient in hospital	1.75	3

Step 7 – identifying service reasons for variations

Where there are significant variations from expenditure benchmarks, we must first identify any underlying service explanation. For example, where costs in a service are untypically high this may be due to:

- more complex case mix;
- faster turnover of patients which increases acuity;
- improved and demonstrable outcomes for patients;
- elements of workload not captured by the benchmark – in which case additional benchmarks should be used.

Where variations cannot be explained in these terms, there is a clear indication of inefficient resource deployment and the case to move the benchmark is demonstrated.

Comparative analysis versus standards or yardsticks

A clear distinction needs to be drawn between comparative analysis and standard setting. In a comparative analysis in benchmarking the objective is to compare performance on similar indicators, to identify variations and stimulate discussion. The aim of standard setting is to fix a value for the benchmark as a yardstick against which to adjust current performance and/or plan the future. Comparative analysis is *normative and shows where the provider stands in relation to others*. Standard setting is *prescriptive and tells us what performance levels are required* to deliver quality and efficiency. This distinction should always be emphasized to stakeholders when comparative analyses are fed back to them, in order to prevent unhelpful confusion.

THE ACTION PHASE – INTERPRETATION AND INFORMING DECISION MAKING

Step 8 – communicating the analysis

The next stage is to feed back and discuss the analysis with participants. There are a number of golden rules in reporting:

- *Before writing the report, feed back your analysis informally* and check all the assumptions and data accuracy. Any major findings will then come as less of a surprise or shock to your audience. Avoid circulating preliminary findings on hard copy. Bar charts and pie charts are powerful tools in the wrong hands, especially if their content has not been fully confirmed.
- *Use clear presentation techniques* employing graphics which make the key points explicit.
- *Target your reporting to your various audiences*. Agree up front which data will be fed back to which organizations. This is critical in collaborative exercises which involve NHS Trusts, health authorities and social services. This can be achieved by preparing a specific report for each organization and overviews for the others with sensitive data anonymized.
- *Expect a bumpy ride from some participants*. No matter how carefully you prepare the ground, you cannot expect every participant to welcome the findings, particularly where they are shown to be of relatively poor quality or inefficient in resource use.
- *'How?' is more important than 'how much?'* Don't just present data; interpret it. The most useful aspects of your report are your interpretations of the data and the action points it implies. This does not have to be in the form of definitive statements in all cases but can list options for change which arise from the analysis.

Step 9 – setting goals in the light of the benchmark analysis

You have completed your data acquisition and analysis and put together a nice report . . . Unless you do something at this point, you have performed a great intellectual exercise with little or no added value.[11]

The objective of the feedback and discussion is to set targets for moving current practice towards the benchmarks. Targets should include the levels to be achieved and the timescales for implementation. If the benchmark is being used to plan services for three to five years ahead, the value may need to be adjusted to reflect changes in the nature of workload over that time such as:

- shorter lengths of hospital stay which may increase acuity;
- improvements in anaesthesia and surgical techniques which may reduce post-surgical acuity;
- more complex cases in primary care due to devolution from the hospital sector.

Step 10 – implementation and monitoring

Implementation should be phased over a workable timescale – say two financial years. Sometimes practices can be adjusted relatively quickly. This is often necessary where resolving financial difficulties such as projected short-term overspends is a prime objective. In some instances the benchmarking analysis may confirm local knowledge, and consensus on implementation can proceed smoothly.

In other cases, changes will require careful planning and staff and managers need more convincing. Benchmarking in the commercial world is often a precursor of process re-engineering informed by study of processes in the company selected as the benchmark. Similarly, in NHS providers more detailed work is often needed to turn agreed targets into practice. For example, significant changes to staffing skill mix can require a detailed analysis of current activity and facilitation over what element of current professional workload could be devolved through to support staff with specific competence-based training. Such exercises pay dividends in the longer term for not only do they produce more cost-efficient staffing profiles, but they generate wide ownership of the benchmark by addressing any staff concerns over quality. Given that these projects take six months to complete, full implementation of the targets may need to await the completion of this work.

Guidance on implementation planning

Be realistic on content and phasing
Implementation plans which are over-ambitious will not be achieved and will delegitimize the process. Major changes in service delivery cannot be achieved overnight without considerable disruption. Plan changes over two to three years at least.

Plan action around area identified for improvement
Develop a chart linking benchmark targets to implementation action points (Table 10.3).

Table 10.3   Community occupational therapy – targets and implementation

Target	Implementation
Increase contacts per week for qualified staff *and* maintain current skill mix	• Rationalize paperwork • Extend support roles • Reduce travel time by reorganizing locality structure

Manage the politics

Politics is defined as 'the management of vested interests'. All organizations generate politics. These should be addressed to keep the most deleterious effects in check. Time should not be wasted and best practice should not be buried by inflated egos and sectional interests. To minimize the impact:

• Decide at the outset who should be consulted – including all groups affected by change.
• Identify likely concerns early in the project or when the analysis has identified key issues and decide how they can be addressed.
• Do not require unanimity or allow the consultation process to turn into a vetoing process. Proceed on a majority verdict.
• If you have 90 per cent support and 10 per cent opposition, do not amplify the 10 per cent by over-reaction.
• Produce a high-quality analysis and report. Clinical staff in the NHS respond to and respect empirical analysis. The better the benchmarking product, the less the political flack.

Addressing commonly expressed concerns

Although benchmarking is now being promoted by ministers as a key technique for implementing NHS modernization, we still need to ensure consensus at local level in using the approach. We can mitigate some concerns at the outset of any project by briefing all key stakeholders and involving them in the design of the study, including the choice of comparators. Nevertheless, and however carefully we prepare the ground, the results of the quantitative analysis may generate criticisms. In our experience, this is more likely to arise where the current staffing is significantly higher than the benchmarks. In cases where it is equivalent or lower, the benchmarks are usually accepted readily.

In this final section, therefore, we look at some of the more common concerns and how to discuss them with staff who raise them.

'My service is different'
The most common objection to benchmarking is claimed differences in the services being compared. Of course, no two NHS providers are identical. They have different service configurations, are different sizes and serve a wide range of population profiles. Indeed, if it was a requirement of benchmarking that two comparator organizations should be identical, then no commercial company would invest resources in it. The services and comparators clearly need to be carefully chosen, however. For example, the performance of psychiatric services in inner London, with its high morbidity rates, should not be compared with those of a semi-rural mental health trust. Moreover, many organizations are very similar overall or provide very similar services. Indeed, as the NHS strives to achieve equity in service quality, delivery and resource deployment, the only legitimate varying factor is the differing needs profile of the population served. And let's be honest – how many NHS providers have been resourced from a baseline which reflects the needs of the local population as the primary consideration?

However, just as we need to make all reasonable efforts to ensure comparability, we need to bear in mind that the NHS has a clear principle of equity in resource distribution. In addition, resource inefficiently used in one service is a service underfunded or simply not provided elsewhere. This places an onus on service managers with a higher resource base to demonstrate their need for it on valid criteria. A useful approach therefore is to ask those raising concerns about comparability to provide the evidence on how and to what extent their service is actually different.

'The lowest common denominator'
Using sample, national or regional averages as benchmarks often generates the criticism that we are rendering staffing levels down to the lowest common denominator. First, and as we have seen, much depends on the average chosen. Equally, smaller sample averages cannot simply be dismissed as invalid provided the comparators themselves are well chosen. Criticism of using averages can be mitigated by omitting outliers from the analysis or using an inter-quartile range. The criticism can often arise when a comparative analysis is fed back to stakeholders without emphasizing that the objective is to stimulate discussion about variations and not to use the comparators as standards for adjusting or planning resource deployment in their departments.

'Another exercise in feeding the beast?'
You will commonly be challenged that these exercises simply generate work for no useful purpose. Indeed, it has been a common experience for service managers in the NHS to supply information upwards without getting any helpful feedback. To mitigate this concern:

- provide feedback to participants in data collection in a timescale and format they consider helpful;
- facilitate the process of data collection;
- ensure that it is timed not to clash with other peaks in workload.

Sharing sensitivity to these concerns will greatly enhance the benefits from the exercise and ensure that benchmarking is truly a collaborative exercise.

NOTES AND REFERENCES

1 C.H. Coulter (1993) Developing and implementing performance standards, *Managed Care Quarterly*, 1 (1): pp. 8–15.
2 Department of Health (1998) *A First Class Service: Quality in the NHS*. London: Department of Health.
3 Department of Health (1999) *The NHS Performance Assessment Framework. Attachment C: Developing Benchmarking*. London: Department of Health.
4 Department of Health (1997) *The NHS: Modern, Dependable*. London: Department of Health.
5 Ibid.
6 Department of Health (1999) *Improving Quality and Performance in the NHS*, HSC 1999/139, pp. 10–20. London: Department of Health.
7 R.J. Boxwell (1994) *Benchmarking for Competitive Advantage*. New York: McGraw Hill.
8 Ibid.
9 NHS Executive (1999) *Performance Assessment Framework, Quality and Performance in the NHS: Clinical Indicators*. London: National Health Service Executive.
10 Department of Health (1999) *Outpatients and Ward Attenders 1998/99*. London: Department of Health.
11 Boxwell, op. cit.

FURTHER READING

J. Brockman (1997) *Quality Management and Benchmarking*. New Providence, NJ: Bowker.
J. Bullivant (1994) *Benchmarking for Continuous Improvement in the Public Sector*. London: Longman.
S. Codling (1993) *Benchmarking*. Aldershot: Gower.
NHS Executive (2000) *NHS Reference Costs*. Department of Health website, http://www.doh.gov.uk.

MODERNIZING THE HEALTHCARE WORKFORCE

Margaret Conroy

INTRODUCTION

A key component of any integrated delivery system is to ensure that services are delivered by the right numbers of staff with the appropriate competencies. Highly trained and expensive professional staff should not be performing tasks which can be performed equally well by support workers with appropriate training. Similarly, integrated care requires an adequate supply of competent staff whose skills are designed around the needs of patients and not the often rigid professional demarcations which have been characteristic of the NHS workforce for most of the last 50 years. There are therefore major issues to be addressed right across the human resource agenda if the modernization agenda is to become a reality in the NHS. The government and professions have publicly expressed concerns about a shortage of professional staff slowing the momentum of healthcare reform. The major challenges and opportunities have also been highlighted recently in the government's recognition of the need to integrate health service and workforce planning, and can be encapsulated in two main areas:

- the development of workforce plans which are based on patient need and are integrated with service and financial plans;
- the design of a flexible workforce with enhanced roles to improve the quality and efficiency of patient care.

WORKFORCE PLANNING – THE NATIONAL CONTEXT

The NHS workforce numbers close to 1 million people whose salaries and benefits account for approximately 70 per cent of the total cost of the service. The NHS is a labour-intensive organization and the provision of a quality service is absolutely dependent on the supply of a competent workforce. These two statements seem at odds with the lack of a systematic approach to workforce planning in the NHS. They should arguably place workforce planning at the top of any management agenda. Despite this, workforce planning is still a relatively neglected field and there is enormous scope for improvement.

How does this fit with the national context? The government has embarked on a programme of continuous improvement to modernize the NHS over the next ten years. The NHS Plan[1] sets out a challenging agenda for 'modernising and rebuilding the health service'. But if this challenging agenda is to be met there are major issues to be addressed with regard to both the demand and supply of the workforce.

The quality of workforce plans will be a key determinant of the ability of the NHS to deliver the agenda spelled out in the NHS Plan. Why is workforce planning so strategically important? The simple answer is that the NHS needs to ensure that staffing is consistent with service plans and developments. The NHS needs to take a quantum leap forward in the quality of workforce plans and to ensure that:

- workforce numbers and profiles are planned to deliver the twin aims of quality and cost-effectiveness;
- service plans are not constrained by an inability to deliver a suitably qualified, flexible and affordable workforce;
- work roles are developed to reflect patient need and the objective of improved quality and convenience.

One of the biggest challenges facing the NHS is to design the workforce for the future service and to ensure that plans are in place for the provision of appropriate numbers of these staff. The scale of the problem is illustrated by the current supply problems facing the service with serious recruitment and retention problems across all staff groups. In London, for example, 20 per cent of qualified nursing posts are unfilled and in some boroughs 30 per cent of GPs will have reached retiring age in five years' time and say they intend to go!

NATIONAL RECOMMENDATIONS

The 2000 consultation document on workforce planning[2] sets out the reasons why the current workforce planning processes need to be improved 'in order to deliver the workforce which the modernised NHS requires'. In particular, the document notes that current workforce planning arrangements are deficient since they are not:

- built around service needs and the skills required to deliver them;
- well integrated with service and financial planning;
- holistic in their approach, looking across primary, secondary and tertiary care or across staff groups;

- responsive to service changes and developments;
- supportive of multidisciplinary training, education and working.

DEVELOPING THE WORKFORCE PLAN – A PRACTICAL APPROACH

The national consultation document sets out a clear framework for the development of workforce plans. The rest of this chapter outlines a proposed approach: a step-by-step description of the process involved in the development of a workforce plan. This draws on pilot work undertaken by the NHS Executive South West Regional Office in collaboration with NHS trusts and primary care groups.[3] The process is designed to ensure that workforce plans:

- are 'needs-based': based on the service need and the workforce and skills required;
- are fully integrated with service and financial plans;
- take full account of service changes and developments.

BEST PRACTICE IN WORKFORCE PLANNING

There seems to be a perception, even now, that workforce planning is just a 'numbers game' tucked away in isolation from top management and the business and financial planning processes. This is far from the truth, and the reality is that workforce plans need to be consistent with the strategic direction of the organization and will, inevitably, result in some unpopular decisions. It is essential to ensure that the organization is 'ready', that the appropriate structures are in place to deliver the plan and that some principles of good practice are adhered to. Table 11.1 on page 206 outlines a number of principles of good practice which emerged from the South West regional work programme.

THE COMPONENTS OF THE WORKFORCE PLAN

The step-by-step process involved in the development of a workforce plan is described here. This process has been designed to ensure that the workforce plan is developed as an integral part of the business planning process. The service plan forms the basis for the workforce plan and the main components of the plan are the demand forecast, the costs and the supply plan. One important point needs particular emphasis – the process is iterative. The demand forecast may indicate, for example, that the location or mode of delivery of services is driving up the staffing cost. In this case there will be a need to revisit the service strategy. Alternatively, the supply plan may demonstrate that the demand forecast for the workforce cannot be achieved, leading to the need to review both the service strategy and the demand forecast.

THE STAGES OF THE WORKFORCE PLANNING PROCESS

The components of the workforce plan can be subdivided into four main planning stages which are then divided further into a number of planning steps.

- The strategic vision.
- What staff have we got now?
- What staff do we need?
- How do we ensure we secure them?

The strategic vision

This is a vital stage of the planning process. It gives the organization the opportunity to review the strategic direction of services and to develop scenarios for the future workforce before getting into the detail of the planning process. It prompts the organization to consider more innovative approaches to the future workforce. Would quality and efficiency be improved by a redesign of work roles, for example? How does the organization ensure that the majority of staffing time is focused on direct care rather than on coordination or paperwork? What action could be taken to address supply problems? The broad vision developed at this stage provides a framework for the planning process.

What staff have we got now?

The aim of this stage is to present a clear inventory and audit of the current workforce in relation to the workload. This stage provides the baseline for the development of the plan.

Step 1   Inventory of the current service and workforce
The process starts with the collation of a comprehensive inventory on the current situation (service and workforce). The data set is not confined to staffing levels and the workforce profile but includes additional information such as supply indicators, absence levels and the use of bank, agency and overtime. The information from this initial planning stage provides the baseline for the workforce plan and gives an early indication of issues which will have an impact on the demand and supply of staff, e.g. high absence levels, wastage rates, or an inappropriate use of agency staff or overtime.

Step 2   Workload measures and productivity ratios
This section of the work programme develops the links between the workforce and workload. It involves:

- the identification of the workload measures to be used in the planning process;
- the generation of productivity ratios.

Typical workload measures used in staff productivity measures might include:

- number of GP consultations;
- patients on the ward for in-patient nurses;
- numbers of X-ray procedures for radiography staff;
- patient contacts for community nurses.

Step 3   Audit of current situation: 'what workforce do we need to deliver our current services?'
The current workforce is audited on productivity ratios, the workforce profile (such as the staff group mix or proportion of professionally qualified staff and grade mix) and current work roles. Audit techniques include benchmarking (see Chapter 10) against a range of similar services within similar providers or comparison with national standards where these exist. The NHS Executive South West has also produced a helpful guide to benchmarking in workforce planning.[4]
Where they do not exist, the staff can be asked to identify their needs against average workload flowing through the service over a 24-hour period. The aim of the audit is to identify the optimum workforce for the current services and set this against actual staffing to highlight scope for change in the existing workforce. It also sets the agreed parameters for the workforce plan in terms of productivity measures, staffing ratios and agreed skill mix.

What staff do we need? The demand forecast

The aim of this stage is to project forward the workforce required to meet planned service configuration and activity levels. A range of scenarios is modelled and their feasibility tested against budgetary and workforce supply constraints.

Step 4   The workforce implications of the service strategy
The service strategy (including activity levels, location of service and mode of delivery) is reviewed and the impact on workforce numbers and profile identified.

Step 5   The demand forecast: 'what workforce do we need for future services?'
The demand forecast takes a 'needs-based' approach to the identification of the workforce required in the future and is based on the productivity ratios and workforce profile agreed in the audit. 'What if' modelling is used to explore a range of options and to identify the best fit between

the workforce and the workload. The variation between the current work-force and the demand forecast is identified to inform the supply plan. A number of systems are available to support this process including the decision-support model available in the South West Region.

Step 6   Costs
The costs of the demand forecast are compared with the current workforce.

How do we ensure we get them? The supply plan

The aim of this stage is to develop a supply plan so as to ensure that the right numbers and mix of staff will be available for future services.

Step 7   A review of the current supply situation
The flows of staff into and out of the organization (recruitment and retention rates) and also training commissions. This identifies the issues to be addressed (for example, are wastage rates too high?) to ensure that there is an adequate supply of staff in the future.

Step 8   The supply plan: 'how do we ensure that the right numbers and mix of staff will be available?'
This stage identifies the variance between the current and the future demand for staff and reviews the options available for closing this gap – whether it be an over- or under-supply.

Step 9   The implementation plan
This should identify all of the action required to ensure that workforce demand and supply are balanced.

Principles of good practice to deliver the workforce plan are summarized in Table 11.1.

REDRAWING PROFESSIONAL BOUNDARIES TO DELIVER THE FUTURE STAFF

The NHS Plan gives a clear message on the need for radical change in the way work roles are designed and the importance of a patient-focused approach – designing services and jobs from the patient's perspective. The Plan highlights the current demarcations in the workforce and recom-mends the design of enhanced, flexible roles: 'Unnecessary boundaries exist between the professions which hold staff back from fulfilling their true potential.' Similarly the consultation document on the review of workforce planning[5] points to the need for the NHS workforce to be '. . . transformed in order to provide the sort of care which will be needed in the future'. The document highlights the need for 'flexible working to

Table 11.1   The workforce planning process: principles of
good practice

- **Strategic direction:** ensure that the workforce plan is consistent with the strategic direction of the organization.
- **Integrate with financial and service plans** and demonstrate the links between the workforce and the workload.
- **Challenge the culture:** NHS organizations have both the right and the responsibility to review workforce plans for all staff groups. There should be no 'no-go' areas.
- **Involve key personnel:** including clinical leaders and senior managers.
- **Total workforce:** include all staff groups, including management and headquarters staffing.
- **Create a questioning and challenging environment:** be 'up-front' about challenging accepted wisdom and professional/occupational norms. Sell the legitimacy of this approach to managers and staff.
- **Accurate database:** ensure that the data are accurate and that they have been validated by all those involved in the development of the plan.
- **Identify priorities:** use the workforce planning process to set the agenda for project work to review the assumptions and inform the next planning round.

---

make the best use of the range of skills and knowledge which staff have'. This is a challenging agenda for the NHS – but the good news is that the national reports are effectively empowering the service to tackle the well-documented problems associated with professional demarcations.

The past ten years has seen a myriad of local projects established to review work roles or the profile of the workforce (the balance between professionally qualified and support staff). But these projects were usually ad hoc responses to service changes and supply problems rather than a more comprehensive review of the workforce structure. The patient-focused initiatives have been effective in adopting a holistic approach to the review of the service and the workforce, and have been influential in identifying the drivers for change in work roles. But the most influential work in this field, and one which is proving to be an effective catalyst for change, is a national project entitled 'The Future Healthcare Workforce'.[6] Since we lead this project, this chapter naturally draws on this timely work.

HEALTH PROCESS RE-ENGINEERING OR 'PATIENT-FOCUSED' CARE

Patient-focused (or centred) care is a process re-engineering approach designed for healthcare providers which was introduced to the UK at the end of the 1980s from the US, initially in Kingston Hospital and subsequently at sites such as Central Middlesex Hospital and Leicester Royal

Infirmary. Although the patient-focused projects were in acute hospitals, the concept has since been extended to mental health and community services.

One of the main thrusts of the health process re-engineering approach is to achieve a significant increase in the proportion of healthcare funding which is spent on direct care. Patient-focused sites demonstrated that there was scope for redirecting resources from 'unproductive' activities (such as unnecessary paperwork, coordination, meetings and communications between staff). By way of illustration it was common to find that only 35–40 per cent of qualified nursing time on acute wards was actually spent on direct patient care.

The process re-engineering projects also adopted a radical approach to the design of job roles and offered a clear indication of the direction of change in the UK workforce in the future. Analysis in patient-focused hospitals found that a patient on an acute ward for a stay of four to five days would be cared for by nearly 50 staff ('the procession of faces'). This fragmentation of the workforce and the obvious implications for the care process and the continuity and personalization of care are at the heart of job design. The improvements in quality and efficiency are achieved through:

- a customer focus – putting the customer at the forefront of service design;
- decentralization of decision making and services to subunits and work teams;
- a focus on the process of service delivery rather than on individual tasks;
- a reduction in unproductive work, for example time spent on coordination;
- a flexible workforce, with enhanced roles, to improve the personalization and continuity of patient care.

For a time patient-focused sites led the field in job redesign. However, the enhancements to professional roles were, on the whole, marginal and the sites were constrained by professional boundaries from developing the structures which would be a more accurate reflection of service need. But their pioneering work has given a clear indication of the changes we can expect for the future and has highlighted the major consequences of a multiplicity of narrow roles for both quality of care and value-for-money.

THE FUTURE HEALTHCARE WORKFORCE: NATIONAL PROJECT

This national project was initiated to enable all those concerned with the health service workforce to stand back and consider the fundamental issues to be addressed if we are to ensure that the future workforce meets the needs of the service. It addresses the fundamental question: 'If we were designing the workforce today for tomorrow's health service, what would it look like?' This radical approach has resulted in innovative recommendations with regard to both job design and education and training. The findings and recommendations have been well received and supported within the service and are proving to be highly influential in plans for the future workforce – we have, therefore, drawn on the project reports extensively.

The first stage of work was published in 1996. Since then the national steering group has taken soundings on the findings and recommendations in that report and launched a further phase of work which was published in October 1999. This second phase of work was overseen by the national steering group but was undertaken primarily at local level. This work at local level confirmed the findings and recommendations in the first report and has resulted in a clear message from the steering group:

> There are some brave decisions to be made on structures and roles if we are to modernise the healthcare workforce to meet the challenges of the 'New NHS'. We are convinced that there are major benefits to be derived from a radical shift in job design . . . tinkering around the edges and piece-meal changes will not be enough.

THE PRESSURES FOR CHANGE

The first stage of work was to review the current characteristics of the workforce and identify the pressures for change in work roles. These are outlined here in terms of the fragmentation of the workforce, inflexibility in career structures, the workforce profile, the labour market problems and the accelerating pace of change in service delivery.

Fragmentation and role demarcation

The fragmentation of the workforce into a multiplicity of professions and occupations has major implications for both the quality and cost-effectiveness of services:

- the lack of continuity in the care process;
- increased delays and confusion for patients;
- time wasted on 'unproductive' activities;
- too little time spent on direct care of patients;
- inflexibilities in responding to peaks and troughs in the workload;
- lack of clarity on accountability.

Inflexible career structures

The healthcare workforce is locked into an inflexible structure, with students being recruited to single-discipline training programmes despite the acknowledged overlaps in the requirements of the various professions. This inflexibility acts as a constraint on the supply of staff, making the NHS unable to respond to labour market pressures through specially designed, shortened training programmes. The aim should be to create flexible structures and to provide real opportunities, links and ladders to meet the needs of the organization and the workforce.

Workforce profile

There is a significant body of evidence to illustrate that professionally qualified staff spend a high proportion of their time on work which does not require their level of training and expertise. It is fair to say that the NHS has been ambivalent on this issue until now but there are a number of reasons why it needs to be confronted as a matter of urgency.

- *Labour market problems*: a review of workforce data indicates that the NHS is battling to maintain numbers of professional staff which are not justified by the workload – the supply problems are, therefore, partly the result of an inaccurate demand forecast. The recruitment and training of an increased number of support workers would have a major impact on the supply problems, and the progression of some of these support staff to professional training would widen the labour market available and impact still further on the future supply of staff.
- *Workforce costs*: nobody would argue with the statement that healthcare professionals should be appropriately rewarded for their skilled input to patient services and, in the future, it is anticipated that labour market forces will drive pay levels upwards. It will be all the more important, therefore, to ensure that work roles and pay levels are linked to the needs of the service and that there is appropriate delegation to a support workforce.
- *Morale and job satisfaction*: as any human resources specialist will attest, these are notoriously difficult to measure. But it seems reasonable to make some connection between the attainment of a professional qualification and the frustration of staff who may find themselves operating at a routine level.

Service changes

The pace of change is accelerating with the need to expand services and to re-engineer the care process as stipulated in the NHS plan. The new primary care trusts will be coping with increasing demand while at the same time planning for an enhanced role in patient management. The acute sector is faced, similarly, with increasing demand and faster throughput. Other changes will emerge from the developments in technology and drug therapy which will have major implications for the pattern and location of service delivery.

DEVELOPING NEW STAFF ROLES – THE PROCESS

The structure

New staffing roles are not developed in the abstract. It is a practical approach based on the empowerment of current professional and managerial staff with expertise in care delivery. The first stage therefore is to set up multidisciplinary working groups spanning all current professional groups involved in the care process under review. Thus an acute medical group will comprise:

• consultant physician;
• junior medical staff;
• nursing staff;
• physiotherapy;
• radiography;
• pathology;
• pharmacy;
• support staff such as ward clerks and nursing assistants.

The group will need facilitation including leading and structuring discussion, keeping to work schedules and documenting discussion and output stage by stage. Facilitators often need to challenge assumptions and bring evidence and outside expertise to stimulate creative thinking and discussion.

Activity analysis

The first stage of the process is to track current patients through the system. This will begin by selecting typical cases managed in the medical unit such as stroke, respiratory and cardiac patients. The group is taken through typical working days and the current care process captured in a database which maps the activity of all staff by task, staff group and grade. This output is called the activity analysis and is usually a detailed and comprehensive activity database in column and row format.

Process analysis

The objectives of the process analysis are to identify avoidable delays for patients or other staff, duplication in functions and inefficiencies in the care process. This may include the procession of faces referred to above, inappropriate demarcations which lead to fragmentation in the care process or, commonly, different staff groups keeping their own notation and consequently asking patients similar questions several times over. In this stage, group members should also be given the opportunity to list their own 'hassle factors' or those elements of their current role. Service delays which add unnecessarily to length of stay should be identified as a priority.

Future care processes

Drawing on their own knowledge, an evidence review and input from outside expertise, the group is tasked to look forward five years to envisage how medical technology and techniques will have changed and also the type of patients they will be managing in the future. For example, to create a typical scenario, expanding intermediate and primary care management is likely to focus the acute hospital medical service on patients in the acute phase of illness who need more intense medical and nursing input. Similarly the employment of near-patient testing diagnostic equipment will reduce the need for patients to leave the ward area for tests. Hence 80–90 per cent of all the care will be managed by the ward team.

Process redesign and reviewing activities

At this stage the current list of activities is reviewed against the envisaged care processes and current problems and processes are redesigned to meet future service needs and address fragmentation, delays and inconveniences to patients. Activities are then reviewed to confirm, delete or augment accordingly.

Designing new staff roles

The final list of activities are then allocated to one of three categories:

- *specialist* activities are those which can only be carried out by professionals from a given background such as medical or nursing;
- *discretionary* activities are those which could be performed by any professionally qualified staff member;
- *core* activities are those which could be performed by any member of the group with appropriate non-professional training.

Once the group has agreed *who could do*, they then review *who should and will* and group activities into job roles. The health practitioner role is designed around the core needs of the patient care process or those activities which fall within the discretionary category. This usually encompasses 80–90 per cent of professional work. The core activities inform the design of extended support worker roles.

By way of illustration of how this work outputs radically different professional job designs, typical health practitioner roles from acute, primary and in-patient mental health care drawn from the Future Healthcare Workforce Project are set out in Tables 11.2–11.4.

Although these roles may seem futuristic they are clearly on the near horizon. Kingston Hospital is already starting to train the first health practitioners in British acute care. The need to address supply problems for GPs, particularly in London, combined with the changing clinical role of primary care is demanding a new primary care workforce. The

Table 11.2   The healthcare practitioner role: acute hospital

Assessment of the patient's condition
- Case history
- Observations

Physical examination including chest, abdominal, rectal, vaginal, central nervous system assessment

Diagnostic tests: order, undertake and interpret appropriate tests under protocol

Diagnosis and treatment plan
- Provisional diagnosis
- Develop and implement patient treatment plan
- Commence oxygen
- Prescribe and administer medication within agreed protocols
- Catheterization
- Mobilization and rehabilitation including neurol and pulmonary
- Dietary assessment and advice and the prescription of supplements
- Swallowing assessment
- Change a peg tube
- Change supra-pubic tube
- Arterial puncture
- Pass naso-gastric tube
- Resuscitation and advanced life support

Ongoing assessment and management: advanced life support and stabilization

Admission and discharge: decision to admit or discharge on the basis of a scoring system

Table 11.3   The healthcare practitioner role in primary care

The healthcare practitioners will be trained to manage their own caseload in a wide range of conditions (see below)

Role content
- Patient assessment
- Patient history
- Physical examination, such as chest, abdominal, gynaecological, joint
- Diagnosis
- Development and implementation of treatment plan

Conditions
- Asthma
- Diabetes
- Hypertension
- Hormone replacement therapy
- Family planning
- Elderly check and aches/pains in the elderly patient
- Minor acute and wound management
- Self-limiting conditions: URTI, sore throat, red eye and flu
- Paediatrics surveillance
- Immunization and vaccination
- Patient registration – medical

Table 11.4   The healthcare practitioner role in in-patient mental health services

This role is designed to encompass activities which need to be provided 24 hours per day, seven days per week and particularly during the waking hours of the client. It builds and enriches the current nursing role to include work which is also undertaken by:

- Medical staff
- Occupational therapists
- Psychologists

Role content
- Psychiatric assessment
- Participation in decision to admit
- Active participation in all clinical meetings including care programme approach
- Medication – administration, compliance and side-effect monitoring
- Blood samples
- Advising GPs on medication
- The application of psychological techniques including assessment of risk, motivational and delusional work, cognitive and behavioural therapy, family work
- Social functioning and skills training: across the whole range of social functioning, home management, personal care and activities of daily living
- Leading group work
- Monitoring and advising clients on diet

National Service Framework for mental health is challenging existing professional roles in the face of the spectrum of need which characterizes most clients. Extended support worker roles free professional staff to use their skills most productively and can assist in delivering the growth in workload which the NHS can expect over the next five years. Whether trained to National Vocational Qualification standards or holding a 'portfolio of achievement' which documents their practical competencies, support staff are also an alternative source of recruitment to professional training.

With the launch of the National Plan, the climate is now ripe for change. Not only will these new roles deliver more patient-focused care during the next ten years, they will improve job satisfaction and assist with the supply problems in the NHS which more than any other factor threaten to slow or even halt the modernization programme.

NOTES AND REFERENCES

1 Department of Health (2000) *The NHS Plan: A Plan for Investment, A Plan for Reform*, Cmnd 4818-I. London: Department of Health.

2 Department of Health (2000) *A Health Service of All the Talents: Developing the NHS Workforce,* Consultation Document. London: Department of Health.
3 NHS Executive (1999) *Workforce Planning – A Guide for Policy-Makers.* Bristol: NHS Executive South West; J. Davies (2000) The devil is in the detail, *Health Services Journal,* 1 June: 18–20.
4 Conrane Consulting (2000) *Benchmarking in Workforce Planning.* Bristol: NHS Executive. South West.
5 Department of Health, op. cit.
6 M. Conroy and D. Cochrane (1996) *The Future Healthcare Workforce Steering Group Report.* Manchester: University of Manchester; M. Conroy and D. Cochrane (1999) *The Future Healthcare Workforce – Second Steering Group Report.* Bournemouth: University of Bournemouth.

12

THE CONSUMER – LAST BUT NOT LEAST

Rita Lewis

INTRODUCTION

Comparing models of healthcare delivery in the US and the UK, and identifying where consumers, patients and the public have power to influence and control the provision of health services, requires careful analysis. In this chapter we look at the two models of service organization, funding and delivery from the perspective of the true payers – the consumers or users of the service. The mechanisms for consumer representation and empowerment in both systems are described and documented. The recent proposals in the NHS Plan demonstrate that the modernization agenda is not unmindful of the consumer. However the conclusion is that there is still a long way to go before the views of users are at the top of the average NHS Trust board or health authority meeting agenda, as they are in the corporate headquarters of the major American managed care organizations.

The political and economic contexts of the two systems are clearly different. The US has a fragmented, pluralistic healthcare system shared between indemnity, private, managed care and a residual government service. The UK has the majority of healthcare services for its citizens, provided by the government in the National Health Service funded from central taxation with indemnity insurance very much at the margins and even then largely covering private elective care.

In the US demands for patient rights, information over choices, and protection in the competitive economy developed in the 1960s. In the UK consumer movements were developing in parallel with voluntary organizations taking a dominant role in the 1960s and 1970s in presenting challenges to institutional healthcare. This movement particularly arose out of the scandals in services for people with mental health or learning disabilities. The government responded with the establishment of

Community Health Councils (CHCs) in 1973, to represent the interests of the public in the NHS. They have statutory powers to request information, to visit NHS hospitals and to monitor local health services publicly. The National Consumer Council followed in 1975, with a broader consumer focus.

THE CONSUMER IN MANAGED CARE

Although the development of healthcare services in the US and the UK has been very different, instructive comparisons can be drawn in terms of the power of the consumer in healthcare services. The managed care model operated by the higher quality health maintenance organizations (HMOs) in the US contains a dynamic which focuses services on the consumer. Healthcare plans are purchased by employers for their employees, with a specified benefits package to be provided within cost and quality standards. The major parallel with the UK's taxation-funded model are retirees who are Medicare beneficiaries, funded by the federal government also from taxation and on eligibility criteria of ten years' employment contributions. They may change at a month's notice taking their $400- to $700-per-month premiums with them. Employers review their contracts annually. Hence responsiveness to consumer views has to be meaningful and fast, and services are planned and delivered with the consumer satisfaction central to management agendas. The intensely competitive environment of healthcare services in the US has provided the essential motivation for managed care to thrive by placing the member in the driving seat. In contrast to the UK, this model has created an interdependency and set of common interests between the consumers, the government, the HMOs and healthcare professionals.

The aims of managed care are to provide comprehensive healthcare and preventive services at economic cost. The growing market share and spread of managed care has challenged the traditional dominance of indemnity insurance in the US healthcare market. Despite the poor media image of managed care, consumer surveys consistently report high satisfaction rates reflecting a service of at least comparative quality to fee-for-service (see Chapter 1).

High satisfaction rates with managed care reflect the more comprehensive range of benefits to consumers than indemnity insurance can offer for similar costs. This has been made possible by the more cost-effective utilization of physicians and facilities. Thus consumers receive more cover, with fewer and smaller co-pays than other finance schemes in American healthcare. Additional benefits provided free at the time of use can include preventive services and prescription drugs. These benefits are particularly attractive to elderly Medicare beneficiaries with limited means. Costs are contained effectively by an integrated healthcare service including preventive advice, health education and services for early detection of medical problems. The healthcare plan includes individualized and proactive co-ordination and management of effective healthcare for patients. The aim is to harmonize cost control, quality assurance and patient preferences.

Consumers have a choice of scheme either negotiated by their employers or individually. Upon enrolment, members choose from a list of personal physicians in primary care responsible for coordinating the healthcare needs of patients. They are also given a choice of hospitals and other providers which seems relatively limited compared to the open access, fee-for-service system but compared to most people's experience of the NHS constitutes wide choice. The healthcare needs of members are assessed regularly and inform the planning of resources, facilities and services. Use of resources and healthcare plans are continually monitored and changed to reflect member perceptions of their care. The development of an integrated, electronic medical record used by primary and secondary care clinicians and other networked healthcare providers has considerably improved communication between different areas of care. Other aspects of coordination are encapsulated in the contractual arrangements between the different service providers. These measures have all improved the responsiveness of services to patients.

A feature of managed care is the low utilization of in-patient services and the provision of outpatient services. Evidence-based clinical guidelines and protocols form the basis of treatment and service design ensuring minimal variations in the delivery of services to members. High-risk patients are identified and referred for proactive case management to prevent more invasive intervention through better management of chronic disease. Treatment compliance is essential to good outcomes and lower hospital use. Hence 'free' drugs are provided according to agreed formulary schedules and budget incentives, and pharmacists are a significant member of the healthcare team.

There are other quality controls which cover services provided by all providers, including doctors, hospitals, nursing homes, laboratories, pharmacies, home health agencies, radiology and physical therapies. All professionals employed or contracted are credentialized to protect both the member and the managed care organization. Checks are carried out on both employed and contracted doctors including validation of licences to practise, drug enforcement numbers, malpractice records, sanction lists and professional references, including any private practice. If the doctor's group does not comply with the managed care organization's quality standards, the contract is simply terminated. Plan members may not be in a position to judge clinical quality issues and rely on others to protect their interests. Public pressure for more accountability from professionals and organizations in healthcare has led to credentializing of doctors – a requirement of the service purchasers and providers and a professional and legal obligation to the paying public.

The consumer is also protected by the extensive regulation of managed care organizations by federal and state governments. The states require that minimum access standards are observed, including the appropriate location of offices and the provision of a comprehensive range of specialist and other services available for patients. These include rapid access to specialist opinions and elective surgery once assessed as necessary. Waiting lists are unheard of in the better HMOs. Federal government requires mandatory reviews under the National Committee for Quality Assurance (NCQA) for managed care organizations with Medicare contracts. NCQA was also founded by the managed care industry, initially to defend its position on quality under assault from medical lobbies and the indemnity insurance system.

At corporate level, customer satisfaction is as important a management objective as cost control. The competitive environment in healthcare ensures that plan holders and purchasers must be satisfied with the plans and services offered. Indeed, it is crucial to the business that any concerns and grievances are picked up and dealt with quickly. Hence patient care is extensively monitored through the functions of the 'member services' department. These departments wield enormous power within HMOs. Alongside market research studies, member services provide the lifeblood of information on member satisfaction. If the department's intelligence networks fail, the organization can lose its customer base and profitability.

Member services do more than protect profitability, however. They also act as advocates for patients and pride themselves on being easily accessible to members. Support includes a range of member education, about the organization and its services and about health matters, management and prevention of disease and conditions. Full information is provided about doctors to enable patients to make informed choices about their primary care physician and other doctors. They provide information about individual health plans, eligibility verification and disenrolment procedures. A free telephone line is provided. Members' concerns and suggestions are fed directly into the management monitoring systems and linked to the quality assurance protocols and systems. A service grievance system with a structured process and 30-day resolution objective deals with complaints and concerns. The member services department is a powerful section of any HMO. Its success and the reliability of its intelligence networks are crucial to developing and sustaining the client base.

This brief summary of the managed healthcare model in the US highlights how relative choice is built in at all stages for consumers. It demonstrates good access to the services. It provides very detailed information for consumers and the organization as well as a range of quality control systems for services and individual health professionals. It shows how detailed cost and resource management helps the service provider and recipient and the broader public, by the efficient use of resources. It demonstrates that consumerism has real power and influence at senior level in the organization. It demonstrates that the consumer, the healthcare professional, the organization and the government can work together to achieve quality healthcare services.[1]

CONSUMERS AND THE NATIONAL HEALTH SERVICE

In the UK the majority of healthcare is provided by the government via the National Health Service as a virtual monopoly provider funded through a central bureaucracy reporting to politicians. The service aims to be comprehensive, to cover all citizens from before 'the cradle to the grave'. The NHS is government-led and forms a substantial part of any political party manifesto. The adequacy or otherwise of the funding for healthcare in the UK is a frequent matter of public debate and is said to influence voting behaviour. It certainly reflects on the image of the government of the day. The NHS therefore has a very large profile in national, regional and local politics. However, since it is funded from taxation and tax thresholds also influence voting behaviour, the NHS has been under constant central government pressure to deliver more services, more cost-effectively.

Consumerism in the NHS has its legitimacy in the public and political nature of the NHS which demands accountability for public expenditure. One key theme is participation. This is emphasized by European and World Health Organization policies and programmes. In February 2000, the Committee of Ministers of the Council of Europe under recommendation No. R (2000)5 adopted the Development of Structures for Citizen and Patient Participation in the Decision-Making Process affecting Health Care, in European member states. This is supported by the Parliamentary Assembly of the Council of Europe which, in 1977, produced a report on instruments of citizen participation in representative democracy (Doc. 7781). This includes guidance to member states on citizen and patient participation within a democratic process, information about health-care and the processes of decision making, supportive policies for active participation and participation mechanisms. Also, the World Health Organization's Health 21 programme for the European region, including its documents on patients' rights and citizen participation, have been incorporated.[2]

Patient choice is another theme. In 1989, the government turned the focus of the NHS to patients by introducing competition and a market environment, and by establishing hospital Trusts and general practice fundholders. The attempt was to ensure greater patient choice of services. The result of this move was to produce a more fragmented service with greater variation in availability, access and quality of services throughout the UK. GP fundholding was seen as creating a two-tier service to patients, with those within fundholding having greater availability and access to services and those with other GP practices experiencing longer hospital waits and less access to, and choice of, services.[3]

Citizen rights is a third area of emphasis in the UK. In 1991 and 1995 the government introduced its Patient's Charters into the NHS in an attempt to set standards via national and local service guarantees and targets. These standards would be monitored by patients and could be used as a reference for evaluating the service received.[4] The first Charter included the following citizen rights:

- to receive healthcare, to be registered with a GP, to be able to change GP easily, to receive health checks, to be prescribed medication, to receive emergency care;
- the right to a consultant referral and a second opinion, to receive a proposed treatment after full explanation and to have access to health records;
- to have a choice as to whether to participate in clinical research programmes;
- to be given detailed information on health services locally including the standards to expect and whether in-patient services offered were on mixed gender wards;
- to be given a guaranteed admission for treatment within 18 months of being put onto a waiting list;
- to have any complaint about NHS service investigated within the process.

The first Charter was very basic and simply highlighted patients' rights within the service where they were not previously well known. Many patients took the Charter seriously, and when they discovered that the service was unable to deliver, there were consequent tensions – the users were disappointed and the professionals blamed the patients for being over-demanding and expecting too much from the service.

The second Patient's Charter comprised a set of standards for health authorities to put in place for the services that they purchased. They included respect for privacy, dignity, religious and cultural beliefs and ensuring that arrangements were in place for all people with disabilities to have access to services. The second Charter set new standards for out-patient, ambulance, and accident and emergency services waiting times. Targets for cancellation of operations; readmissions timescales; procedures for discharge; clean, safe environments for services; and appropriate homecare response targets were all included. Separate Charters were provided for mothers-to-be, children and young people and mental health service users.[5]

The aim was to try to establish a role for the Charters in building the needs and wants of consumers into service planning and management. However, the lack of effective patient involvement in drawing up the Charters, the lack of public awareness of Charter standards, and the service's diluted and ambivalent response to the requirements all mitigated against this mode of setting standards in service delivery. They resulted in a great deal of work for an already over-stretched service. Nevertheless, there should be service standards that are easily published for the public and Charters are a way of providing this. However, such measures are easily discredited if the service cannot deliver the standards and targets. While not all the aims of the Charters were achieved, the publication of rights and standards provided a focus for the service and the public.

The next government theme is ensuring public confidence in the NHS and thus presumably maximum votes from its users. The Labour government elected in May 1997 has been determined to make health a major policy drive. In December 1997 the Prime Minister led a major policy initiative to modernize the NHS over a ten-year period. The statement of principles on which the NHS modernization is founded are to provide fair access to high-quality services to national standards set for services. Efficiency and its drives will now include rigorous performance targets and guarantee quality of care and services, working in partnership with local authorities. The aim is to rebuild public confidence in the NHS as a public service, accountable to patients, open and shaped by public views. The internal market system was seen to have distorted and fragmented healthcare and the primary care sector needed more power. Greater public involvement in health decision making was to be the focus, with Community Health Councils initially given a prominent and improving role. A new quality strategy included the Commission for Health Improvement and the National Institute for Clinical Excellence, both set up with clinical and public involvement. Primary Care Groups and later Trusts would become major purchasers of health services for their patients. The emphasis on primary care as the key commissioners for health services was a fundamental change of emphasis from health authority purchasing.[6] Public participation and accountability for primary care would be required for the first time since 1948.

The quality strategy has put the government in a key position to determine the standards of service to be provided by the NHS and includes mechanisms to incorporate consumer views. A national patient and user experience survey is to be undertaken and the results fed into the NHS. The quality agenda is also to focus on the patient perspective such as the responsiveness to patient needs and preferences, the care skill and continuity, levels of patient involvement and information, the physical environment and the accessibility of services.[7]

The next key theme was the need to give CHCs more powers and resources. Up to this point the modernization agenda has provided a substantial public and patient focus in the process and quality of changes envisaged. This has centred around the Community Health Councils locally, regionally and nationally, in England and Wales, and Health and District Councils in Scotland and Northern Ireland respectively. Such organizations were set up under statute with membership drawn from voluntary agencies and local councils and given specific consultation and visiting powers. Their need to be strengthened to empower them more appropriately to represent the public in the NHS has been recognized. For example, in order to support complainants, sufficient appropriate patient advocacy staff are required who are independent of the NHS. CHC rights of access to scrutinize services and be consulted in decision making need to be developed. Staff and member training and formal links with Trusts and national quality bodies, such as the Commission for Health Improvement and the National Institute for Clinical Excellence, will all be required. National standards for the range and quality of services from CHCs also need to be in place.

Strengthening CHCs could address the weaknesses already identified over the years in their powers, and the range and quality of their work. When most effective, CHCs have been the focal point for their community for all people and organizations that have an interest in the NHS. Much work is undertaken by service users' groups, often supported by CHCs, and general and specific voluntary organizations in the community, in drawing attention to the health needs of specific groups and people. Much of the effectiveness of CHCs in representing patients and the public at all levels of the NHS depends not on powers, but on developing good relationships with people who are able to effect change in the NHS. Continuity and appropriate administrative support appear to be crucial in support of the volunteers who are members of CHCs.[8]

THE NHS PLAN AND THE FUTURE

In the summer of 2000 the NHS Plan[9] was published, applying to England, with all or some of the aspects taken up and supported in Scotland, Wales and Northern Ireland. The health service powers given to the four countries in the UK are significant, if they are used to the full. However, the consultation leading to the Plan was centred on professionals, academics and managers with user and voluntary organizations taking a back seat.

The public remains dissatisfied with the NHS it pays for. As the Plan is launched the major deficiencies in the NHS include variations in quality of services, long waits for access, no nationally agreed minimum service package, supply problems affecting staff, and service availability. The Plan reports on a national public consultation survey of perceptions about the NHS. This produced a long list of problems including that the needs of the patient should be paramount. This feedback highlighted the more well-known inadequacies of the NHS such as long waiting times, poor physical environments, too much bureaucracy, poor food, and fragmentation between health and local authority services. Many users also demanded better staffing resources and pay, a greater role for pharmacists, improved transport and retention of community hospitals. A range of service failures such as cancelled operations, long trolley waits, restricted service availability and poor staff attitudes featured highly.

The government has committed additional resources to the NHS to address some of these deficiencies. But as the percentage of GDP spent on healthcare approaches European averages, consumer empowerment becomes even more important. This is public money and, after all, the higher the taxation surely the greater the representation.

To be fair, the NHS Plan proposes a new agenda for the involvement of patients in the NHS. It thus constitutes a major step forward in consumer rights. Patients can expect more information locally and nationally about clinical conditions and local services. Clinical guidelines from the National Institute for Clinical Excellence presented in patient-friendly formats will be available. Patients will have smart cards incorporating their health records, and letters between clinicians will be copied for patients. More choice will be available in choosing a general practitioner, with a range of information supplied about practice services and standards. GPs will be able to refer patients to a hospital of their choice. Information will be available about how many patients have been removed from the list of any general practice.

Patients will also be protected by full mandatory reporting schemes for adverse healthcare results, and incident lessons will be learnt and shared. Professional regulatory bodies will be reformed, increasing public participation and membership and developing more public accountability. A UK Council of Health Regulators will coordinate common approaches and policies and act as a forum for common issues.

Ironically, after over 25 years of fighting the good fight, Community Health Councils will be replaced by Patient Advocacy and Liaison Services (PALS) in each larger hospital within Trusts. It is as if the intrinsic weaknesses of CHCs have rendered them dispensable. The new mechanisms will provide a service to patients from within provider organizations dealing with queries and, with the Citizen's Advice Bureaux, support for complainants. Patients will also have direct access to Chief Executives of Trusts and be able to negotiate immediate solutions. Further redress will be available for cancelled operations and a more independent complaints process. Patients' views will be surveyed by all Trusts through an 'exit survey' provided to patients leaving hospitals. All NHS services and homes in the community will provide a patient prospectus and an annual account of patient views and action taken, and patient ratings. Each Trust is to set up Patient Forums for patient views. and to be represented at Board level. These Forums will be supported by the Advocacy Service. Patients and citizens will be represented on Local Advisory Forums in the health district as a 'sounding board' for health priorities. Local authorities will be given powers to scrutinize health service plans and service changes as part of Independent Reconfiguration Panels which will include lay membership.

COMPARISON OF MANAGED CARE AND THE NHS IN TERMS OF CONSUMER POWER

Both models aim to empower consumers so that their views may be incorporated into the service. Although the PALS proposals are a great step forward, they run the risk that placing safeguards for consumers with the providers will leave questions open about the independence of this service and influence and sanctions it can bring to bear on management. First, in the US the patients' advocates are part of the purchaser function and independent from service provision. Moreover, unlike American HMOs, British Trusts do not face commercial pressures to preserve market share. Hence the view of their PALS will be readily deprioritized in management agendas in relation to other pressures on Trust Boards – notably cost control and the demands of professionals and politicians.

The managed care model has a central focus on satisfying the members and plan purchasers, as the very survival of the organization depends on meeting their needs. Competition is such that others in the managed care market hover like vultures for disaffected members. In contrast the monopoly provision of healthcare in the UK and the centralized funding mechanism limit the potential for patient empowerment and restrict choice and access. Individual services are available only to the extent that resources allow. Treatments for some conditions are now not available at all on the NHS, whereas others may not be provided in some localities due to local resource constraints. Across the service, a great deal of informal rationing goes on.

The greater involvement of the public and patients in NHS decision making proposed in the NHS Plan is to be welcomed, but the agenda may prove difficult to sustain. Expectations have been raised. Patients and the public paying increased taxation for healthcare will need to see the results of their involvement, and although those of us who have been in the decision-making arena for some time can see some results, there is often a very long delay between participation and any resultant action. The NHS will need to focus far more on the patient and public and develop more 'member services' to reflect their needs and demands independently, and with real powers of sanction. As things stand, much of the consultation and involvement is advisory only, and the service has neither the obligation nor the incentive to heed that advice.

ALTERNATIVES FOR A MORE RESPONSIVE NHS

To address this agenda, other European states such as Germany and France have adopted a social insurance model to fund healthcare provision within principles of universal, equitable access for all citizens. This parallels the Medicare programme in the United States. Much debate has followed as to the effectiveness and efficiency of these systems. This is reviewed in Chapter 3 of the NHS Plan and rather too readily dismissed on grounds of cost and equity of access. As we move forward the NHS will become more expensive and the jury is still out on equity of access, as confirmed by the current wide variations in service availability and quality so eloquently described in the Plan. However, the insurance model deserves a more considered hearing in the wider context of the power that it provides to healthcare consumers and the control that it would give to people in decision making over their own service needs – such as the right to opt for complementary therapies without a GP sanction. Following the consumer-led principles of the managed care model would grant more power to NHS users to govern the choice between forms of treatment, medical staff and other providers. Such a development would certainly inject new energy into reform and patient focus. Providers would then become truly responsive to the needs of the consumer, expanding genuine choice. Geographic variations in the provision of, and access to, NHS services would also be ironed out, since services would need to gravitate to patients as conduits for funding.

Much has been made of the NHS Plan's proposals for increasing patient choice and yet the current system, constrained in a political, professional and bureaucratic framework, inhibits that freedom of choice. Where many services have long waiting times, and patients are offered access to only one provider, what real choice is there? Empowering patients and the public in a virtual monopoly healthcare system is problematic. The development of greater participation in healthcare decision making is to be welcomed and promoted, provided it results in real and effective control being vested in the hands of the consumer. This is clearly the lesson of the managed care model in the US. In contrast, the mechanisms for participation which have evolved in the UK over the years lack any real sanction for consumers. Not surprisingly, as the NHS Plan reports, they have yet to deliver the NHS that patients want and have a right to expect.

NOTES AND REFERENCES

1 P. Kongstvedt (1996) Member services and consumer affairs, in P. Kongstvedt, *The Managed Care Handbook*, pp. 479–80. Gaithersburg, MD: Aspen.
2 W. Hutton (2000) *New Life for Health: The Commission on the NHS*. London: Vintage Original.
3 Department of Health (1989) *Working for Patients*, Cmnd 555. London: HMSO.
4 Department of Health (1991) *The Patient's Charter*. London: HMSO; Department of Health (1995) *The Patient's Charter*. London: HMSO.
5 Department of Health (1996) Executive Letter (EL) (96) 87. London: DoH.
6 Department of Health (1997) *The New NHS: Modern, Dependable*, Cmnd 3807. London: HMSO.
7 Department of Health (1998) *A First Class Service: Quality in the New NHS*. London: HMSO.
8 Hutton, op. cit.
9 Department of Health (2000) *The NHS Plan: A Plan for Investment: A Plan for Reform*. London: HMSO.

INDEX